Start your child on the way to success *right after birth!*

Imagine a twenty-one-month-old child with a reading vocabulary of 160 words . . . a boy of four who enjoys teaching himself major number principles . . . a girl not yet four who reads at the third-grade level.

Not one of these children was born a genius. Yet, through the early learning concepts described in this remarkable book, they are being helped to develop above-average intelligence and a joyous love of learning.

Give your preschooler the same happy advantages. They'll last throughout life!

JOAN BECK—adviser to thousands of families through her syndicated column on child care—tells you about the important, new scientific findings on early learning, and shows you how to apply them to your child's particular personality and needs.

HOW TO RAISE A BRIGHTER CHILD
was originally published by Trident Press.

How To Raise A Brighter Child

The Case for Early Learning

REVISED EDITION

JOAN BECK

PUBLISHED BY POCKET BOOKS NEW YORK

HOW TO RAISE A BRIGHTER CHILD

Trident Press edition published 1967

Revised and updated POCKET BOOK edition
published August, 1975

L

This POCKET BOOK edition is printed from brand-new
plates made from completely reset, clear, easy-to-read type.
POCKET BOOK editions are published by POCKET
BOOKS, a division of Simon & Schuster, Inc., 630 Fifth
Avenue, New York, N.Y. 10020. Trademarks registered in
the United States and other countries.

Standard Book Number: 671-80038-8.
Library of Congress Catalog Card Number: 67-26451.
This POCKET BOOK edition is published by arrangement
with Trident Press. Copyright, ©, 1967, 1975, by Joan Beck.
Front cover photograph by Fred Samperi.

Printed in the U.S.A.

Acknowledgments

Permission to quote from published materials has been obtained from these sources:

The Ronald Press Company for J. McV. Hunt, *Intelligence and Experience*. Copyright © 1961, The Ronald Press Company, New York.

Holt, Rinehart and Winston, Inc. for Benjamin S. Bloom, Allison Davis, and Robert Hess, *Compensatory Education for Cultural Deprivation*. New York, Holt, Rinehart and Winston, Inc., 1965.

National Education Association of the United States for Educational Policies Commission, *Universal Opportunity for Early Childhood Education*. Washington, D.C., National Education Association of the United States.

John Wiley & Sons, Inc. for Benjamin S. Bloom, *Stability and Change in Human Characteristics*. New York, John Wiley & Sons, Inc., 1964.

The Atlantic Monthly and Wilder Penfield for "The Uncommitted Cortex," *The Atlantic Monthly*, Vol. 214, No. 1

(July, 1964). Copyright © 1964, by The Atlantic Monthly Company, Boston, Mass. 02116. Reprinted with permission.

American Montessori Society for George Stevens, "Reading for Young Children," *Building the Foundations for Creative Learning.* New York, American Montessori Society, 1964.

Princeton University Press for Wilder Penfield and Lamar Roberts, *Speech and Brain-Mechanisms.* Reprinted by permission of the Princeton University Press. Copyright © 1959, by Princeton University Press, Princeton, N.J., 1959.

Teachers College Press for Kenneth D. Wann, Miriam Selchen Dorn, and Elizabeth Ann Liddle, *Fostering Intellectual Development in Young Children.* New York: Teachers College Press, 1962, © 1962 by Teachers College, Columbia University. Reprinted with permission from the publisher.

American Academy of Pediatrics for Leon Eisenberg, "Reading Retardation: Psychiatric and Sociologic Aspects." *Pediatrics,* Vol. 37, No. 2 (February, 1966).

Modern Medicine, for "Tests Show Day-Old Infants Can Learn, Early Handling Can Influence Behavior," Vol. 34, No. 2 (January 17, 1966).

Random House, Inc. for Joseph Church, *Three Babies: Biographies of Cognitive Development.* New York, Random House, Inc., 1966.

American Academy of Pediatrics for The Committee on Accident Prevention, "Responsibility Means Safety for Your Child," 1964.

G. P. Putnam's Sons for "Naughty Soap Song," and "About Candy," from Dorothy Aldis, *All Together.* Reprinted by permission of G. P. Putnam's Sons. Copyright 1925–1928, 1934, 1939, 1952 by Dorothy Aldis.

Aileen Fischer for "A Bug," from Aileen Fischer, *Up the Windy Hill.* New York, Abelard-Schuman Limited, 1953. Reprinted with permission of Aileen Fischer.

Systems for Education, Inc. for Jack E. Forbes, "Mathematical Skills Development for Pre-school Children." Chicago, Systems for Education, Inc., 1965.

Vintage Books for Jerome S. Bruner, *The Process of Education.* New York, Vintage Books, 1960. Copyright © 1960, by the president and Fellows of Harvard College.

The National Council of Teachers of English and Arthur I. Gates for "Unsolved Problems in Reading: A Symposium," *Elementary English,* Vol. 31, No. 6 (October, 1954).

McGraw-Hill Book Company, Inc., for Calvin W. Taylor, *Creativity: Progress and Potential.* McGraw-Hill Book Company, Inc., 1964. Used by permission.

Prentice-Hall, Inc. for E. Paul Torrance, *Guiding Creative Talent,* © 1962. Englewood Cliffs, N.J., Prentice-Hall, Inc., Reprinted by permission.

American Medical Association for "Mental Retardation: A Handbook for the Primary Physician," *The Journal of the American Medical Association,* Vol. 191, No. 3 (January 18, 1965), pp. 193 and 195.

The National Foundation and J. B. Lippincott Company for Louis K. Diamond, "Erythroblastosis," in *Birth Defects,* The National Foundation, Philadelphia, J. B. Lippincott Company, 1963.

American Academy of Pediatrics for A. W. Liley, "Amniocentesis and Fetal Transfusion in Erythroblastosis," *Pediatrics,* Vol. 35, No. 5 (May, 1965).

Teachers College Record for Robert J. Havighurst, "Conditions Productive to Superior Children," *Teachers College Record,* Vol. 62 (April, 1961).

The *Chicago Tribune* for permission to use material from my column, "You and Your Child," distributed by the Chicago Tribune-New York News Syndicate, Inc.

To Ernie, who shares the adventure

Contents

Preface

This is a child-care book about your youngster's mind, not his body. It won't tell you how to feed, burp, diaper, and put your baby back to sleep—but what you can do to stimulate his mind to learn and grow. It concerns the nourishment you should be giving his brain, not his stomach. It is devoted to thinking, not thumb-sucking. It holds that parents should spend more time —and can have far more fun—sharing a youngster's delight in learning than fretting about toilet training.

For we now know that parents can raise a child's useful level of intelligence substantially by the ways in which they care for him during the first six years of his life, long before he begins his formal education. Even the most skilled and loving parents, in the best homes, have probably been stunting their children's mental development to a degree because they have not known what fast-growing young brains need so urgently.

The purpose of this book is to report to parents

about new research on the growth of children's intelligence during the first six years of life and to translate this research from scientific journals, learned symposiums, and experimental laboratories into a form that will be useful to those who live and work with small children daily. It aims to do for your child's mind what other books do for his physical and emotional growth.

This is a controversial book in many ways. For much of this research goes contrary to previous assumptions about raising children. Parents used to be told that a child would develop according to a timetable of inner "readiness" which the environment could not speed up or slow down. Now we know that this is not entirely so, that some changes in the environment can make a lifelong difference. We also know that parents—instead of being too emotionally involved to teach their own offspring—are the first and most influential teachers a child ever has. Just witness the way in which parents help a youngster master the complexities of his native language.

You won't be able to follow all of the suggestions in this book with one individual boy or girl. Children differ too much, one from another. So do homes, parents, circumstances. No child is ever developed, like a recipe, by adding precisely so much of each ingredient. Every youngster comes with different inborn characteristics and temperament and potentialities which a parent must take into consideration in rearing him. But this book will give you broad guidelines to follow; it will help you see your child in a new light, give you a fresh perspective on what his growing mind needs, and suggest hundreds of specific ways in which you can help to provide for these needs. Once you begin to think of him as an eager, growing, exploring, budding intelligence as well as a small human being with urgent physical and emotional needs, your whole relationship with him will be different—richer, happier, and more satisfying.

In reporting the research in this book, I am grateful to many physicians, educators, and behavioral scientists who shared their knowledge and explained their work to me, in particular Dr. Urban Fleege, Dr. O. K. Moore, Dr. Paul Dunn, Dr. Burton White, Dr. J. McV. Hunt, Dr. William Fowler, Dr. and Mrs. Frederic Gibbs, and Dr. Sylvia Richardson. Dr. Virginia Apgar made helpful suggestions and comments on Chapters 10 and 11. I wish to thank James Ertel for his advice and help.

I am deeply appreciative of the encouragement I received from Thomas Furlong and Walter Simmons of the *Chicago Tribune* and for permission to include some material from my column, "You and Your Child," published by the Chicago Tribune-New York News Syndicate, Inc.

I am grateful, too, to my own children, Christopher and Mindy, who first taught me unmistakably the eager insistence with which babies seek to learn.

The names of parents and children and identifying details used in illustrative examples in this book have been changed, although all of the incidents are factual. For convenience in writing, the pronoun "he" is always used to refer to the child, although both girls and boys are obviously intended. And although the book is addressed primarily to mothers, the suggestions also apply to fathers, who should, of course, share the adventure and the joy of helping their children's minds to grow.

1. Your Child's First and Best Teacher: You

How much is your child capable of learning before he's six years old and ready for first grade? What happens to his brain during these preschool years when his body is growing and changing so rapidly?

Is your youngster's intelligence level actually fixed for life by the genes he inherits from his parents? Or, can it be raised by the way you rear him at home, long before he ever meets a teacher in the classroom?

As a parent, what specifically can you do to give your child ample opportunity to grow in intelligence during these irreplaceable early years of life?

New research about learning and brain development in preschool youngsters has reached the stage where exciting and promising answers to these questions are available to parents. These answers are adding up to a larger, happier, and most important role for parents in fostering the mental development of their children before school age.

In the past, child-care books have concentrated on helping parents learn how to raise children who are physically healthy and emotionally well adjusted. They have detailed directions about how to become a competent diaper-changer, formula-mixer, tantrum-stopper, rash-identifier, bathroom attendant, and referee between rival siblings. But parents have received almost no help or information or credit for their role as teacher and nurturer of their offspring's developing intelligence. Much more has been written about what should go into a baby's stomach than what should go into his growing mind. More emphasis has been put on teaching a child to use the bathroom than to use his brain.

Today, knowledge about the development of intelligence in small children is increasing rapidly. Neurophysiologists and psychologists are beginning to learn more about the biology of the mind, to understand what happens to the brain of a child as he grows. There is now major evidence that the optimum time for many kinds of learning and for the stimulation of basic learning abilities in a child is already largely past before he reaches age six and enters first grade. Given some understanding and information about early learning, a parent can substantially increase his youngster's intelligence and joy in learning for the rest of his life.

You, as a parent, are of necessity the first and most important teacher your child ever has. You have the unique opportunity to mold your youngster's intelligence when it is most subject to change, to teach him individually, at his own rate and when and by what means he is most likely to learn. It's time you got more help in this vital role. That is the purpose of this book.

Parents who have tried using early-learning techniques with their preschool children often report delightedly about the results. Four cases in point:

In a small town in Indiana, Jeanne Jenkins was giving a birthday party for her four-year-old daughter and six small friends. Toward the end of the party there came the crucial five minutes when Mrs. Jenkins had to leave the four-year-old guests alone in the living room while she went into the kitchen to dip up the ice cream and light the candles on the birthday cake.

From the kitchen, Mrs. Jenkins could hear nothing but a worrisome quiet. Anxiously, she peeked into the living room and saw that one of the guests had pulled a "Smokey the Bear" book from the shelf and was reading with great delight to the other children, who were fascinated by the story.

After the party, Mrs. Jenkins telephoned the small guest's mother. "Oh, yes, Martha learned to read last summer," replied the four-year-old's parent. "No, she'd never read a 'Smokey the Bear' book before. But she does read everything she can get her hands on."

In a nursery school in a Manhattan skyscraper, Danny, four, happily strode over to a supply cupboard and pulled out a big box of beads and numbered cards. Sprawling on a little rug on the floor, he began to work. First, he arranged a set of the numbers in order from 0 to 9. Beside each he placed a little glass dish, and into each dish he dropped the corresponding number of beads.

Next, Danny put another set of numbers in "tens place," making his figures read 11 to 99. With ready-made chains of 10 beads each, he laid out matching rows of 10 to 90 beads beside the tiny dishes. Then he added a third set of numbers in "hundreds place," and the right number of 100-bead units. When he had finished, he had correctly created and labeled rows of 111, 222, 333, 444, 555, 666, 777, 888, and 999 beads —and happily taught himself a major lesson in number concepts.

In a Chicago apartment, a young father held up cards with printed words for his son, Jonathan, age twenty-one months, to read. By acting out what the words said, Jon demonstrated that he had a reading vocabulary of 160 words—larger than his speaking vocabulary.

In Florida, a fragile, dark-haired girl of forty-five months was reading a third-grade book to her father, a surgeon. Severely brain-damaged from birth and still unable to sit up or walk, Debbie had been repeatedly diagnosed as mentally retarded. At two well-known medical centers, her father had been advised to place her in an institution as a "human vegetable." Yet now, although she was not yet four, Debbie had a reading vocabulary that exceeded 1,000 words.[1]

None of these children was born a genius. But because someone who loved each youngster knew about new theories of early learning and brain development, each had the opportunity to learn more than most children usually do at the age when their fast-growing brain could absorb knowledge readily. All of them, including Debbie, are developing above-average intelligence and a joyous love of learning as a result.

Martha's mother taught her to read for fun, using a series of phonetic games and cartoons published by a Chicago newspaper. "We had no idea a four-year-old could learn so fast or enjoy reading so much," she wrote to the newspaper's editor.

Danny attends a Montessori school where he can choose freely from a wealth of early-learning materials. Jonathan's father has been casually exposing him to printed words as a game they both enjoy since the boy was sixteen months old. Debbie learned to read as part of a program of intensive brain stimulation used in an experimental type of treatment for brain injury.

Interest in early learning and research about it are coming from many different scientific fields. Neurologists, neurophysiologists, and pediatricians are trying to determine precisely what happens to the brain during its fastest growing stages. Psychologists are learning more about the biological and biochemical basis of behavior and are including in their research about the mind a consideration of the brain, which is the organ of the mind. Biologists are seeking links between such animal behavior as imprinting and the mental development of human beings and conducting thousands of experiments probing the effects of early stimulation on the brains of young animals.

Sociologists and teachers are urgently searching for ways to help culturally-deprived youngsters, many of whom reach first grade with learning abilities already stunted for lack of adequate stimulation during the first six years of life. Educators are turning to research about the preschool years as the most likely way to raise intelligence levels. Many intelligent, well-educated parents are discovering upon thoughtful observation of their own small children that they are ready and eager for learning previously assigned only to first grade level or beyond.

Research about early learning emerging from all of these sources, from the fields of neurology, physiology, psychology, biology and education, from specialists working from many divergent points of view, can be summed up like this:

(1) We have greatly underestimated what children under age six can and should be learning.

(2) It is possible, by changing our methods of child-rearing, to raise the level of intelligence of all children, and to have happier, more enthusiastic youngsters as a result.

"We are missing the boat in our educational systems, for they largely ignore the most sensitive and receptive period of development," said Dr. George W. Beadle, Nobel prize-winning geneticist when he was president of the University of Chicago. "We have been seriously underestimating a child's ability to learn. The trouble is we have not listened. I regard it as of the greatest importance that we do so—and soon." [2]

Early learning doesn't mean that you should try to teach your three-year-old to read to make him a status symbol, or because your neighbor's four-year-old can read, or because you want to be sure he gets into Harvard fifteen years from now. You aren't trying to make a six-year-old out of a four-year-old, or turn a nursery school into a first grade, or deprive your moppet of the chance to be a child.

Early learning does mean that you try to understand your youngster's innate drive to learn, to explore, to fill his developing brain's urgent needs for sensory stimuli and satisfying learning experiences, just as you try to understand and fill the needs of his body for nourishing foods. You aren't stuffing his brain with facts so he'll make Phi Beta Kappa, any more than you give him vitamins to force his growth so he'll make the Chicago Bears' backfield.

Early learning simply means using new knowledge about what your youngster's brain needs during the crucial first years of life so that his mental development will come nearer to reaching its potential and your child will be brighter and happier for it.

Research is showing that parents who rear their small children by currently-accepted practices may inadvertently be restricting their mental development in some ways. They may leave an infant alone and crying with boredom in his crib or playpen, in an attempt to train him to be "good" and undemanding. Yet the baby's needs for sensory stimuli and motor activity—to look at a variety of things, to listen to myriad sounds and voices, to move and be moved about, to touch, to hold—are as great as his hunger for food and for love.

Parents may spank the hands of a toddler who is not trying to be destructive, but merely trying to satisfy some of his insatiable desire to explore, to climb, to push, to pull, to take apart, to taste, to experiment.

"Curtailing the explorations of toddlers between nine and eighteen months old may hamper the children's rate of development and even lower the final level of intelligence they can achieve," writes Dr. Joseph McVicker Hunt, professor of psychology at the University of Illinois.[3]

Researchers have discovered that even well-read, educated, and intelligent parents have probably handicapped their children in the past because of child-rearing practices which ignored the needs of the developing brain. These are the parents who were most aware of prevailing childcare theories, who heeded the warnings about not "over-stimulating" a child, and who read the books which said a youngster would develop "readiness" for learning on his own inner timetable regardless of the amount of stimuli in his environment. Many of these parents feared to stimulate their children intellectually for fear of "pushing" or "pressuring" them and because they had heard that fathers and mothers are "too emotionally involved" with their youngsters to do an adequate job of teaching.

Much new research now shows that the idea of "readiness" has been overrated, and that a child's ability to acquire many skills depends on the stimulation and opportunity in his environment as well as his inner schedule of development. Only one of the new research programs about early learning has involved any kind of pressure or pushing. Some, like the experiments of Dr. Omar Khayyam Moore, professor of sociology at the University of Pittsburgh, with the "talking typewriter" (described in Chapter 7) are designed so that a young child participates only if he wishes and stops whenever he chooses and is never praised or criticized for what he does or does not do. Yet even under these circumstances, children of three and four eagerly teach themselves to read and type.

Observers in almost all early-learning research projects comment on the joy and happiness and enthusiasm of the children involved. And the most careful follow-up studies do not detect any ill effects on these youngsters' personality, emotional well-being, behavior, eyesight, or general health.

When Dr. Dolores Durkin, professor of education at the University of Illinois, made studies of children who learned to read before they entered first grade, she was surprised to find that few of them came from professional or upper middle-class families. In fact, more than half of the early readers in her California study had parents she classified as being "lower" class. One-fourth more she identified as "lower-middle class."

Studies of the home backgrounds of these early readers —and of a control group with similar I.Q. who could not read before first grade—pointed up an important difference. The better-educated parents in higher socio-economic groups knew the theories that reading should be taught only by trained teachers, and that parents should keep hands off the whole process.

Families less informed about these traditional concepts had happily and enthusiastically welcomed their children's questions about words, answered them, helped them, and accepted their preschoolers' ability to read. None of these parents felt guilty about their youngster's reading skill, as did two or three of the parents with professional backgrounds.

Dr. Durkin's research showed that the early readers consistently out-scored the control group with equal I.Q. in the elementary grades. (But part of the careful, scientific design of the research—which intended to keep each early reader matched with a non-reader of equal I.Q. as they advanced through several grades—was upset because many of the early readers were double-promoted.)[4]

The widely-accepted idea that a preschooler's only occupation should be "play" and the attitude that play is the direct opposite of learning have also tended to deprive youngsters of desirable mental stimulation. Small children love to learn. They are born with an innate hunger for learning. And they keep on having an insatiable desire to learn—unless we bore, spank, train, or discourage it out of them.

If you think carefully about what most interests your baby or your toddler, you'll observe that it is seldom "play," as adults use the word. It's much more apt to be learning. In fact, sometimes you can't seem to stop your baby from working hard at learning in order to persuade him to play or eat or rest, no matter how hard you try.

A four-month-old baby, for example, who is just learning to roll from his stomach onto his back works harder at pushing himself up and over than a runner trying to break a four-minute mile. Once he manages to flop over, he usually screams until you put him back on his stomach so he can try again. If you offer him a rattle or a cuddly animal so he will quiet down to play and you can get back to making the beds, he usually bats it away in his eagerness to resume his difficult learning activity. No one is forcing him or pressuring him or hurrying him or grading him or making him compete or threatening not to love him unless he learns to roll over. He wants to learn, urgently, on his own.

You can see the same phenomenon clearly when your baby is trying to pull himself up on his feet. He grunts and grimaces and struggles and works harder than a weight lifter. At first, when he finally does pull himself up on his feet, he doesn't know how to let go and sit down. So he screams. You lower him gently to the floor and give him a toy to play with. But he doesn't want to play. He wants to stand up. He wants to learn.

How long does a baby practice vowel sounds and consonant noises, stringing them together in delightful nonsense before he hits on a single word that brings recognition from his mother? No one pressures him into that concentrated practice which typically goes unrewarded for months. Yet this is what babies and toddlers do endlessly, of their own free choice.

How many questions do two- and three-year-olds ask in a single day? They're trying to find out all they can about the world around them, about cause and effect, and all the fascinations of existence. This is not what an adult considers play. Yet a busy, impatient, tired mother can't turn off the torrent of "Why's" even for an hour.

Three- and four-year-olds love what preschool educators call "imitative play"—pretending to be grown-up. But they seldom copy grown-ups at play. They imitate adults at work: washing dishes, caring for babies, mowing the lawn, driving a truck, as doctor, nurse, soldier, mother, grocer, fireman, policeman, teacher.

You can think more objectively about this entire question of preschoolers' play if you keep track of your child's activities for just one day. What makes him happiest? What stimulates him to the greatest concentration? What holds his interest longest? Almost always, it's an activity in which he is learning something which increases his competency, or satisfies his curiosity—especially if his mother or his father is right beside him sharing his excitement about learning.

It's an insult to a preschooler to write off his urgent and intense learning efforts as play, unless you want to define any absorbing adult occupation as play. And it's an injury to his developing intellect to deprive him of profitable learning experiences on the assumption that all he should be doing before age six is playing.

This play-oriented attitude toward preschool children in the past has had many unfortunate results. The most important: It has put a damper on research about ways in which youngsters under six can learn best. And it has influenced parents—with the best intentions in the world —to dull the learning instincts which are an innate part of all small children.

"Just keep your child clean, teach him to blow his nose and sit still, and get him to school on time; I'll do all the teaching," a kindergarten teacher told a mother. Many school systems still issue booklets to parents of incoming kindergarteners, warning them not to try to teach their offspring anything even remotely academic. But such attitudes are changing rapidly with the impact of new knowledge about how and when small children learn.

One great impetus for new research about preschool learning has come because numerous studies show that five- and six-year-olds from culturally-deprived areas typically have trouble learning in kindergarten and first grade. Many such children limp along academically all through school, then drop out as soon as they can, severely handicapped by inadequate education and unable to succeed in most jobs.

The more educators, psychologists, and sociologists study these culturally-deprived youngsters, the more they appreciate the value of a good home and mentally stimulating parents, especially during the preschool years.

If you've ever doubted your importance as a teacher during the first five or six years of your child's life, you should read some of the research reports about culturally-deprived youngsters. You'll see your job as a parent much more clearly and excitingly.

One such report is *Compensatory Education for Cultural Deprivation,* based on research papers presented at a University of Chicago conference.[5] This report points out that unless a youngster has had adequate mental stimulation during the preschool years, the work of the school for the next ten years will be largely wasted.

"All later learning is likely to be influenced by the very basic learning which has taken place by the age of five or six," emphasizes this report. "Ideally, the early intellectual development of the child should take place in the home."

If you love your child and spend considerable time with him, you do many things to foster his intellectual development almost by instinct and without realizing precisely why. But parents of youngsters in culturally-deprived homes are often too busy or too burdened with economic problems or too uninformed about child care to make the effort to stimulate a youngster's mental growth. The results show up markedly in kindergarten and first grade.

Just what does a good, caring, loving, stimulating parent give his preschool child which a culturally-deprived youngsters does not receive?

Opportunity for perceptual development, for one thing. Very early in a youngster's life, the University of Chicago report explains, he begins to learn about the world via his five senses: vision, hearing, touch, taste, and smell. An environment rich in games, toys and other objects a baby can handle helps stimulate this perceptual growth. So does a wide range of experiences and contacts with adults at meals, playtimes, and throughout the day.

Perceptual development is related to success in school during the primary years. And there are large, measurable differences in perceptual development between youngsters from culturally-deprived homes and those children who have had great opportunity to explore, to touch, to handle, to try, to play, to learn, and to be with interested adults.

Language skills is another area where loving, concerned parents stimulate their children, and neglectful parents hold their offspring back. A child's language development depends to a great extent on the adults about him in his earliest years of life. Parents who are aware of a child's learning needs encourage him to say words. They surround him with talk, used freely and naturally. They cheer on his efforts to say the correct words, respond to him when he tries and when he succeeds, read to him and provide him with what experts call "corrective feed-back."

In this kind of rich, verbal environment a child's vocabulary grows, and his ability to use sentences develops. As he becomes more skilled with words, he learns to put his emotions and intentions into language. He begins to compare and to differentiate and to express abstract ideas. He uses words as tools of thought.

But the culturally-deprived child is likely to be answered with a monosyllable, or to be ignored completely by an inadequate or overburdened parent. He isn't encouraged to think and talk about what he experiences.

According to the University of Chicago report:

> The child in many middle-class homes is given a great deal of instruction about the world in which he lives, to use language to fix aspects of this world in his memory, and to think about similarities, differences and relationships in this very complex environment. Such instruction is individual and is timed in relation to the experiences, actions, and questions of the child.
>
> Parents make great efforts to motivate the child, to reward him, and to reinforce desired responses. The child is read to, spoken to, and is constantly subjected to a stimulating set of experiences in a very complex environment. In short, he "learns to learn" very early. He comes to view the world as something he can master through a relatively enjoyable type of activity, a sort of game, which is learning. In fact, much of the approval he gets is because of his rapid and accurate response to his informal instruction in the home.
>
> Learning to learn includes motivating the child to find pleasure in learning. It involves developing the child's ability to attend to others and to engage in purposive action. It includes training the child to delay

the gratification of his desires and wishes and to work for rewards and goals which are more distant. It includes developing the child's view of adults as sources of information and ideas and also as sources of approval and reward.

If the home does not and cannot provide these basic developments, the child is likely to be handicapped in much of his later learning and the prognosis for his educational development is very poor.

Unfortunately, millions of good, loving parents who care deeply about their children's intellectual development have been given almost no help in the vital job of stimulating intelligence in their offspring and therefore miss many opportunities to do so. It's like trying to feed a baby without any knowledge of proteins and calories and vitamins.

It is not only youngsters growing up in slum areas who are deprived of necessary intellectual stimuli during the preschool years, of course. To a degree, this deprivation can be found in homes of every economic level where the urgent needs of a child's growing brain are not appreciated, and the proper mental nourishment is not provided.

Billy, six months old, is trained to stay quietly in his crib or playpen with little to do but suck his thumb and stare into space. Jimmy, two, is often denied the chance to explore because he creates too much chaos in his carefully-cared-for house. Jane, four, is constantly forced in the name of social adjustment into activities that hold back her intellectual growth. All of these youngsters are being culturally deprived to a degree, regardless of the income level of their fathers or the mortgage value of their big suburban homes. So is Laura, whose parents are wealthy, but often leave her in the care of uneducated, indifferent household help. Brad is too; his home contains an average amount of stimuli, but not enough to help him come near to reaching his superior potential.

We have already discovered how tremendously and expensively difficult it is to try to overcome the lack of stimulating environment during the early years of life.

Many massive and costly programs are now underway—at local, state, and federal levels, sponsored by public and private agencies and staffed by experts in many related fields—to help stimulate the mental development of culturally-deprived children before they reach first grade.

Many of the thousands of nursery-school type programs for preschoolers set up in the late 1960s and 1970s have not been very successful in producing measurable and lasting boosts in intelligence among disadvantaged youngsters. Typically, children who participate in Head Start or other early-learning programs for the disadvantaged in nursery school settings do make substantial gains in I.Q. But some or all of these measurable mental gains seem to level off as the youngsters progress through first grade and beyond.

There seem to be several reasons for this. A large percentage of the programs, particularly those under Head Start funding, have actually paid little attention to using new theories about how to foster intelligence. Most have been modeled on traditional social-adjustment nursery schools. And many have had to be so concerned about the youngsters' physical health and nutrition, and about helping their families find essential social and community services, that they cannot concentrate on encouraging mental development. Then, too, the children usually attend such nursery schools at the age of three or four for only two to three hours a day—this is too little and too late to compensate for an unstimulating home environment. The proportionately great influence of the home plus a lack of special followup programs in elementary school probably account for the leveling off of gains that often occurs later on. When programs of continuing mental stimulation, such as the federally-funded Follow-Through plans, are added in the early elementary grades, children are much more likely to keep their earlier gains in intelligence.

To help overcome these difficulties, Head Start and several other agencies and organizations are moving into experimental types of Home Start programs that usually aim to reach disadvantaged youngsters earlier than age three or four and to give parents new ideas about how to help their offspring learn. In some of these experimental plans, a visiting teacher—much like a visiting nurse—makes regular calls at a home to show the mother how to play learning games with a baby or toddler, and often to give or lend a learning toy or two. Often, a parent-child center operates in connection with such a home-visiting program, giving mothers a place where they can go with their offspring to learn more about child care and to find out about community services. Hundreds of such projects are now underway for poverty-area families and results to date have been encouraging.

Young children included in experimental early-learning programs based in the home do make substantial gains in I.Q. that last for many years, new research shows. Boosts in intelligence tend to be only temporary, however—unless the child's mother becomes involved in helping her youngster learn. The greatest and most lasting gains in mental ability by the child occur when mother and child become intently interested in working on and talking about a common activity, notes Dr. Urie Bronfenbrenner, professor of psychology and of child development at Cornell University, in summing up the results of experimental early-learning programs.[6]

Parents can be effective in fostering a child's mental development at any age, says Dr. Bronfenbrenner. But the earlier in life such stimulating activities are started, the more effective they will be. The first three years of life are the most crucial for fostering intelligence and the greatest gains occur with two-year-olds.

The family is the most effective and economical setting for fostering the mental ability of a child, emphasizes Dr. Bronfenbrenner, who bases this statement on several careful, long-term research projects. Without the continuing involvement of parents—particularly the youngster's mother—even visiting teacher programs are likely to produce only temporary gains in I.Q.

Because the needs of disadvantaged children are so obvious and so acute, most of the attention, expertise, and available money has been concentrated on poverty areas. But a few experimental programs—such as a large scale effort by Harvard University educators—offer *all* the parents of young children in a community the access to a community early-learning center, classes for parents, learning toys, and the expertise of early childhood educators with a special interest in fostering intelligence— regardless of income. Some day, such facilities may become a tax-supported extension of public schooling, so that all parents can have expert, personal guidance in providing an optimum environment for their children's mental development.

It is now clear that there are no practical alternatives to involving parents in providing the kind of home life and stimulating experiences that encourage a child's mind to grow. Most youngsters aren't ready to leave home without mother, even for the best of nursery schools, until they are fully three years old, sometimes four. Even then, nursery schools—kindergartens, too—usually account for only ten to fifteen hours a week. Home and parents are so pervasive, so encompassing, that without their participation in an early-learning program, it can accomplish little—as increasing research is making abundantly clear.

We now know that informed, caring parents—using many loving, happy, and easy ways—can do much to raise the level of intellectual functioning in their children and to help them realize to a greater extent their true intellectual potential. In fact, such stimulation may be necessary for the development of a "bright" or "gifted" young person, regardless of his innate potential.

"In *no* instance (where documentation exists) have I found any individual of high ability who did *not* experience intensive early stimulation as a central component of his development," points out Dr. William Fowler, professor of applied psychology at the Ontario Institute for Studies in Education and a former director of the Laboratory Nursery School at the University of Chicago. "The unvarying coincidence of extensive early stimulation with cognitive precocity and *subsequent* superior competence in adulthood suggests that stimulation is a necessary if

not sufficient condition for
abilities." [7]

You may never need to worry about you
being culturally deprived, in the sense that slum-a
youngsters often are. But, stresses Dr. Fowler, "deprivation is a relative concept which should be measured relative to ultimate potential. Deprivation may be just as extreme for the potentially bright who must endure average
conditions as for the potentially average to live through
conditions below the stimulation 'norms' of the affluent
half of our society."

Large numbers of potentially superior, as well as
average, achievers are probably lost to our society because of a lack of sufficient early stimulation, says Dr.
Fowler.

If you fill your child's life full of stimulation all of his
early years, if you make your home what scientists call
an enriched, "culturally-abundant environment," if you
use early-learning techniques we now know, you can do
much to raise your youngster's intelligence (as it is currently measured). In such a home, a child who would
have grown up to be "average," will almost certainly become an "above-average" individual. And a youngster
who would have been "above-average" in normal circumstances will probably grow up to be "bright" or "gifted."

But you, as a parent, will have to give your child these
opportunities, provide this enriched environment. Even a
good nursery school, at age four or even three, is too little
and too late.

This doesn't mean that you must set up a school in
your family room and proceed to hold formal lessons for
your three-year-old. It doesn't mean substituting the
alphabet song for your baby's evening lullaby. It doesn't
mean drilling a four-year-old in number facts, or teaching
him to recite for your dinner guests.

Using early-learning techniques with a young child can
be just as simple and easy as this incident that occurred
in a restaurant. A young couple brought their baby girl,
about nine months old, with them and plopped her into
a high chair at the table to wait for her dinner.

...aby reached
...e cube from the
...Her mother glanced
...baby's father, but kept
...tray to catch the goblet if

...ated minutes, the baby was seri-
...experimenting with the ice cube. She
... out of the goblet. She slid it around the
...ted it, rubbed her nose with it, passed it from
hand ...hand. As it melted, she repeated the activity with
the ice water.

Until her dinner came, the baby continued to fill her
brain with information and stimuli. And because this
filled a basic—although often unrecognized—need, she
was happy and absorbed. As a fringe benefit, the baby's
father and mother were free to talk together at an adult
level, without constantly saying "No," and fussing at the
youngster to "be good." It was far easier for them to use
the early-learning techniques of letting the baby explore
a tiny portion of her environment, using every possible
sensory organ, than it would have been had they acted as
most parents, taking the goblet away and then having to
cope with the crying of a bored and frustrated moppet.

Until recently, the fostering of a child's mental development could be done only haphazardly during the early
years, by parents who had instinctive feelings about their
child's innate curiosity and intellectual needs. But now,
research is showing all parents how they can help their offspring develop to a greater degree and why it is urgently
important that they do.

The future holds little promise today for men and
women who are not independent and interested in learning. Muscle-power jobs are rapidly decreasing in our
increasingly automated society. Mankind's vast total body
of knowledge is growing at a fantastic rate, and today it
is at least double what it was in 1940. No high school
student today can choose an occupation, train for it, and
be assured that he will not have to relearn it or take on
another completely different vocation before he's old

not sufficient condition for the development of high abilities." [7]

You may never need to worry about your own child being culturally deprived, in the sense that slum-area youngsters often are. But, stresses Dr. Fowler, "deprivation is a relative concept which should be measured relative to ultimate potential. Deprivation may be just as extreme for the potentially bright who must endure average conditions as for the potentially average to live through conditions below the stimulation 'norms' of the affluent half of our society."

Large numbers of potentially superior, as well as average, achievers are probably lost to our society because of a lack of sufficient early stimulation, says Dr. Fowler.

If you fill your child's life full of stimulation all of his early years, if you make your home what scientists call an enriched, "culturally-abundant environment," if you use early-learning techniques we now know, you can do much to raise your youngster's intelligence (as it is currently measured). In such a home, a child who would have grown up to be "average," will almost certainly become an "above-average" individual. And a youngster who would have been "above-average" in normal circumstances will probably grow up to be "bright" or "gifted."

But you, as a parent, will have to give your child these opportunities, provide this enriched environment. Even a good nursery school, at age four or even three, is too little and too late.

This doesn't mean that you must set up a school in your family room and proceed to hold formal lessons for your three-year-old. It doesn't mean substituting the alphabet song for your baby's evening lullaby. It doesn't mean drilling a four-year-old in number facts, or teaching him to recite for your dinner guests.

Using early-learning techniques with a young child can be just as simple and easy as this incident that occurred in a restaurant. A young couple brought their baby girl, about nine months old, with them and plopped her into a high chair at the table to wait for her dinner.

Looking around for something to do, the baby reached out and grasped a goblet with a single ice cube from the table and put it on the high chair tray. Her mother glanced at her, then resumed talking to the baby's father, but kept her hand near enough to the tray to catch the goblet if necessary.

For ten, quiet, fascinated minutes, the baby was seriously absorbed in experimenting with the ice cube. She slipped it in and out of the goblet. She slid it around the tray. She tasted it, rubbed her nose with it, passed it from hand to hand. As it melted, she repeated the activity with the ice water.

Until her dinner came, the baby continued to fill her brain with information and stimuli. And because this filled a basic—although often unrecognized—need, she was happy and absorbed. As a fringe benefit, the baby's father and mother were free to talk together at an adult level, without constantly saying "No," and fussing at the youngster to "be good." It was far easier for them to use the early-learning techniques of letting the baby explore a tiny portion of her environment, using every possible sensory organ, than it would have been had they acted as most parents, taking the goblet away and then having to cope with the crying of a bored and frustrated moppet.

Until recently, the fostering of a child's mental development could be done only haphazardly during the early years, by parents who had instinctive feelings about their child's innate curiosity and intellectual needs. But now, research is showing all parents how they can help their offspring develop to a greater degree and why it is urgently important that they do.

The future holds little promise today for men and women who are not independent and interested in learning. Muscle-power jobs are rapidly decreasing in our increasingly automated society. Mankind's vast total body of knowledge is growing at a fantastic rate, and today it is at least double what it was in 1940. No high school student today can choose an occupation, train for it, and be assured that he will not have to relearn it or take on another completely different vocation before he's old enough to collect his Social Security. Today's child will need every bit of intellectual power, every *soupçon* of learning ability we can give him to live happily and productively in tomorrow's world.

Fathers and mothers who have tried using early-learning principles with their offspring are delighted not only with the intellectual progress of their children, but also with the new and happy relationship that follows.

"I had no idea my daughter would be so interesting to me," commented a mother who had been teaching her four-year-old to read. "It's just like the way I felt the day she took her first steps toward me, only better." And because her four-year-old is seldom bored, she is seldom fussy, unhappy, angry, or defiant, like many four-year-olds.

You can help your child to become brighter, more intelligent, happier. There is no doubt about it. And in the process, your offspring will have a more satisfying childhood, and you will enjoy him more. You won't need to pressure or push your child, and your efforts to help him learn will not hurt him in any way, unless you make your love for him contingent on what he learns.

This is not just another job you have to do. It is a whole, new, exciting, wonderful way of looking at your child and your relationship with him during the first six years of his life.

Chapter 2 will explain the new psychological, neurological, and physiological concepts and research behind early learning. Succeeding chapters will give you more precise information about how and what you can do with your youngster.

2. Why You Can Raise a Brighter Child

The excitement about early learning—with its promise that children of every level of ability, from every kind of background, can learn more and become more intelligent—is based on several important theories, emerging from a convergence of research in the fields of education, medicine, and the behavioral sciences.

These concepts provide the "why" for the suggestions made in later chapters of this book, showing specific ways in which you can help raise the level of intellectual and creative abilities of your own youngster. By adding another dimension to the standard child-care books about physical and emotional development, they will also help you understand your child better.

Not all of these important theories have as yet been completely proven in statistically sound, controlled research. (For that matter, very few of the traditional ideas about how children should be raised are validated by this kind of scientific data, either.) Some of these theories still must be more thoroughly tested by research involving children from every type of social, economic, and educational background, with every level of genetic endowment and over long periods of their lives.

But thousands of scientific studies do back up these concepts, and together they add up to a new philosophy of child-rearing which is rapidly being put into practice.

A knowledge of these new theories will help you in thinking about and planning for and living with your child. And these concepts will give you a better understanding of the changes in child care which are occurring in this country as a result of research.

The major theories behind the emphasis on early learning include these:

1. *Your child does not have a fixed intelligence, or a predetermined rate of intellectual growth, contrary to much widespread opinion in the past. His level of intelligence can be changed—for better or worse—by his environment and especially during the earliest years of his life.*[1]

It used to be assumed that every child had a specific level of intelligence which remained the same all of his life and which grew and unfolded automatically at various stages of his development. This intelligence supposedly could be measured with reasonable accuracy by an I.Q. test. Such an I.Q. level was thought to remain stable during an individual's lifetime, regardless of how much education he received or what kind of environment he lived in. If your child tested in the 80 to 90 I.Q. range, for example, it was thought that he would always function at a somewhat lower than average intellectual level all of his life.

It's no wonder that psychologists and teachers worried about pushing children!

It is true that for large groups of school-age children, I.Q.s seem to stay relatively constant—if for no other reason than that I.Q. tests are constructed to yield such scores with large groups. But we now know that scores for some individuals can vary tremendously, particularly during the preschool years.

In one research project, in which the I.Q.s of 152 children were tested repeatedly between the ages of twenty-one months and eighteen years, two youngsters showed increases of 70 and 79 points.[2] This is enough difference to move a youngster from the general classification of "educable mentally retarded" to "gifted." The scores of two other youngsters in this long-term study group decreased about the same amount.

Even the school-age boys and girls in this study showed widely varying I.Q.s One changed as much as 50 points and several as much as 30 points between the ages of six and eight. In fact, only 15 percent of the group maintained I.Q.s with less than 10 points in variation, even during the supposedly stable school years.

Similar changes in children's I.Q.s have been noted in many other research studies, particularly when youngsters under age six are involved. Most research shows only a small relationship between a toddler's I.Q. at age two and the same child's score at age five. There is almost no relationship at all between the scores a child makes as a preschooler and again as a teen-ager.[3]

Why does the I.Q. change? And why does it sometimes change so greatly? Some researchers attribute it to inadequacies in I.Q. tests themselves. (It is true that such examinations measure only a few of the many factors that are part of what we usually call "intelligence" and fail to take into consideration such qualities as creativity, imagination, and motivation.) Others point out that the I.Q. tests for infants and toddlers rely heavily on motor abilities which may or may not be directly related to later intelligence. Emotional factors have also been suggested as triggering I.Q. ups and downs.

But it is now also considered likely that the I.Q. changes—simply because a child's actual intelligence also changes. And these increases or decreases are caused by stimulation, or lack of stimulation, in the environment.

If you put a normal, healthy youngster of average intelligence into an institution—hospital or orphanage, for example—where he gets adequate physical care but little mental stimulation, he will become mentally duller in as short a time as three months. The longer he stays in a deprived environment, the greater will be the decline in his intelligence. Some of this loss is reversible; much is not. This concept has long been accepted in the United States and is a chief reason why foster-home care has been substituted for orphanages in most communities.

Usually this retardation is blamed on a lack of a mother's love and is termed "maternal deprivation." But new research—both with infants and animals—indicates that a contributing factor is also a lack of all sorts of sensory stimulation.[4]

One of the most vivid examples of what can happen to institutionalized children is described by Dr. Wayne Dennis, emeritus professor of psychology at Brooklyn College of the City University of New York, in his study of three orphanages in Tehran.[5]

In the first institution, where most of the youngsters were admitted before the age of one month, the infants were kept almost continually in individual cribs. They lay on their backs on soft mattresses and were never propped up or even turned over until they learned how to do so by themselves. Their milk was given them in propped-up bottles, although they were occasionally fed semisolid food by an attendant. These babies had no toys. They were changed when necessary and bathed every other day. Four poorly-paid attendants cared for a room of thirty-two infants, and Dr. Dennis notes that the supervisors cared more about the neatness of the room than the development of the babies.

When a baby did manage to learn to sit up by himself and was in danger of tumbling out of his shallow crib, he was placed on a strip of linoleum on the floor during his waking hours. Dr. Dennis also describes seeing rows of children, who were able to sit up, seated on a bench with a bar across the front to prevent them from falling. They had nothing to do.

When these youngsters were about three years old, they were transferred to a second orphanage, where the same type of care and conditions, or worse, prevailed. In studying these children, Dr. Dennis found that of those between the ages of one and two, fewer than half could sit up, and none could walk—although almost all normal, noninstitutionalized American children sit alone by the age of nine months. Only one in every six could creep or scoot on the floor. Of the two-year-olds in this institution, fewer than half could stand, holding on to a hand or a chair. Fewer than 10 percent could walk alone.

Dr. Dennis reports that most of the three-year-olds in the second orphanage could sit up by themselves, but only 15 percent had learned to walk alone.

Children in the third Tehran orphanage provided a dramatic contrast. Most of them had originally been assigned to the first institution, but were transferred because they seemed to be more retarded than the other youngsters. But in the third orphanage they began to flourish. They had more contact with attendants, who were encouraged to mother them whenever possible. They were held during feedings, occasionally propped up in a sitting position and given toys to play with. As a result, most of these supposedly retarded children between the ages of one and two had progressed more than the supposedly normal babies. Most of the one-year-olds could sit alone, and a few could walk by themselves. All of the two-year-olds could sit up, creep, and walk, holding on to a hand or chair.

In a later study in an orphanage in Beirut, Lebanon, Dr. Dennis demonstrated how even a little added sensory stimulation could produce great gains in the development of babies.[6] An experimental group of foundlings between the ages of seven months and one year, none of whom could sit up, were taken from their cribs into an adjoining room for an hour a day. Here they were propped up in low chairs or on a foam-rubber pad and given a variety of objects to look at and handle: fresh flowers, paper bags, pieces of colored sponge, plastic flyswatters, metal box tops, bright jelly molds, multicolored plastic dishes, small plastic medicine bottles, metal ash trays. No adults worked with the youngsters or helped them play with the objects.

All of the babies quickly learned to sit up independently and, after considerable hesitation by some, all delighted in playing with the objects. Dr. Dennis reports that during the experiment, these infants made four times their average gain in development, just as a result of the daily hour of stimulation.

Once you accept the theory that a child's intelligence can change, and that it can be lowered by lack of stimulation during the earliest years of life, the next obvious question is: What happens if you deliberately enrich a youngster's environment with intriguing, loving stimulation from birth on?

Some behavioral scientists and many delighted parents and happy children have already demonstrated the answer: The child becomes brighter. It's even quite likely that we may eventually be able to raise the level of intelligence of our whole population as we understand better how to stimulate the learning abilities of small children.

Dr. Hunt comments, "In the light of the evidence now available, it is not unreasonable to entertain the hypothesis that, with a sound scientific educational psychology of early experience, it might become feasible to raise the average level of intelligence as now measured by a substantial degree. In order to be explicit, it is conceivable that this 'substantial degree' might be of the order of 30 points of I.Q. In a technological culture which is requiring more and more people with a high level of intelligence, this is an important challenge." [7]

Because behavioral scientists assumed in the past that intelligence was a fixed quality, they were not searching for ways to increase the intellectual abilities of children, Dr. Hunt notes. But now that the nature and development of intelligence is better understood, we are finding many ways of increasing learning abilities. More such intelligence-boosting techniques of rearing and educating youngsters will undoubtedly be developed in the coming years.

2. *Early stimulation can actually produce changes in the size and chemical functioning of the brain.*

Thousands of experiments with dogs, cats, rats, mice, monkeys, guinea pigs—and even with chickens and fish—show that when these animals are given stimulation in infancy, they develop at a more rapid rate and become more intelligent than others which are not stimulated. A rat, for example, which comes from a strain known to be dull, will outperform a rat of similar age from a bright strain, if he is given extra stimulation as a baby while the supposedly born-bright rat is not. It even makes a demonstrable difference whether the early stimulation comes before or after weaning. The more stimulation and the earlier the rats receive it, the brighter they become.

Very young laboratory animals which are handled and stimulated as babies develop at a more rapid rate than those which are not. They open their eyes at an earlier age and show better motor coordination. They gain weight faster than other animals in the same litter which are not stimulated—not because they eat more food, but apparently because their bodies make more efficient use of what they do consume. They also seem more resistant to disease.

An enriched environment actually produces changes in the anatomy and chemical characteristics of rats' brains, according to Dr. Mark R. Rosenzweig of the University of California's psychology department.[8] Dr. Rosenzweig and his colleagues divided litters of baby rats into two groups. One group received early stimulation; the other did not. Tests showed that the rats which received the early stimulation were more intelligent and could solve problems better than the nonstimulated litter mates.

Then, the rats' brains were studied closely. The brains of the early-stimulated rats were found to have a heavier cortex, with an increased number of a certain type of brain cells and more branching between cells than the brains of the unstimulated rats. Greater amounts of two important chemicals were also found in the brains of the stimulated rats than in their unstimulated brothers and sisters.

These same types of differences in brain weight and brain chemistry were also found when the scientists compared the brains of rats from bright and dull strains.

We can't assume, of course, that the results of experiments with animals apply *in toto* to human infants, too. And of course it's impossible to make the same type of controlled laboratory experiments with human babies. But because so many animal tests have been made with approximately the same results and because the more intelligent the animal the more difference early stimulation makes in its adult intelligence, researchers are increasingly sure the same answers hold for human beings, too.

3. *Heredity does put an upper limit on your child's intellectual capacity. But this ceiling is so high that many scientists believe no human has as yet even approached it.*

You will never be able to separate completely the effects of heredity and the influence of environment on your child. Countless research projects have been undertaken to answer this age-old question of nature versus nurture. But no one can even come close to controlling all of the complex factors involved in human intelligence. No accurate measurements of environment exist, for example. And so many complicated and interrelated factors are involved in heredity that it is virtually impossible to isolate even a few of them and separate them from environmental influences for study.

Is Mark doing well in school because he inherited his father's intelligence? Or because his father's interest in books rubbed off on him as a small child? Was Mozart born to be great? Or did his genius flower because his father began giving him lessons at the age of three and because his childhood was spent in a world of music and musicians who stimulated and encouraged each other?

Various researchers have estimated the proportionate influence of heredity in the development of a child at these figures: 60 percent; 65 to 80 percent; 66 percent; 78 percent; 77 to 88 percent. Newer studies suggest these percentages may be too high.

But the more scientists study the question, the more complex and subtle the relationship between heredity and environment is shown to be. For example, there is evidence that heredity can play a role in human emotions, which was not suspected before. And we are finding many ways in which environment can alter constitutional factors, which we had believed were fixed for life.

The genes that your youngster inherits certainly lay the groundwork for his intelligence. They determine the basic quality of his brain. Clusters of genes probably give rise to special talents, particularly those like musical and mathematical abilities, which can be traced through families for generations. And genes help determine your offspring's basic bodily constitution.

But it is your child's environment which determines how much of his genetic potential will be realized. Even an Einstein, born with the intellectual capacity for genius, might have been classified as mentally retarded all of his life if he had been reared in an atmosphere like that of the Tehran orphanage.

You can't do anything to change your child's heredity, of course. His brain has basic qualities, not yet understood by scientists, which help determine how much and how quickly he learns from his environment and by means of which sensory organs he learns most easily. He may have been born with a good quality brain, or a poor one— just as he may have been born with a strong bodily constitution or a relatively weak one.

But you can alter your offspring's environment in many ways, which will affect the development of his inherited potentialities—just as you can help your child develop the physique he inherits.

"It is highly unlikely that any society has developed a system of child-rearing and education that maximizes the potential of the individuals which compose it," Dr. Hunt emphasizes. "Probably no individual has ever lived whose full potential for happy intellectual interest and growth has been achieved." [9]

4. *Changes in mental capacity are greatest during the*

period when the brain is growing most rapidly. And the brain grows at a decelerating rate from birth on.[10]

The younger your child is, the greater the influence his environment has on him and the more his characteristics —including his level of intelligence—can be changed. So the stimuli you add to your youngster's environment will have the greatest results in raising his intelligence during the earliest years of his life. The same amount of change and stimulus during his elementary years or high school years won't result in nearly such large gains.

More than one thousand research studies carried out during the last half-century support this concept and its far-reaching implications. These findings were summed up in a scholarly volume, *Stability and Change in Human Characteristics,* by Dr. Benjamin S. Bloom, professor of education at the University of Chicago and a former president of the American Educational Research Association. The book has had tremendous influence on educators, pediatricians, administrators of anti-poverty programs, and other professionals concerned with child care. Because parents have the chief responsibility for managing the lives of children under age six—the years when their intelligence is changing most rapidly—it is important that you be informed about these findings, too.

We've tended to overlook the importance of intellectual development during the preschool years for many reasons, says Dr. Bloom. One reason is that education in our society lasts so long. Young people stay in school for a minimum of ten or eleven years. Many take for granted seventeen years of schooling, including college. An increasing number are seeking graduate training, upping their school years to twenty or more. What difference could a more or less wasted year at age three or five matter?

We now know that intellectual development doesn't proceed at a uniform rate, but at a decreasing rate. What is missed in the preschool years can be difficult or impossible to make up later on—as experience with deprived-area children has demonstrated.

Future learning, inevitably, rests on the basis of past

learning, Dr. Bloom points out. If your child has learned to learn and to enjoy the process, if he has sharpened his intellectual curiosity and found pleasure in using it, he will be a far different type of student in school than the youngster whose learning drives have been thwarted and dulled by his environment.

Six-year-old Todd, son of a lawyer-father and a college graduate-mother who spends much time with him in stimulating activities, learns far more in first grade than Carl. Carl's home is a dark, crowded apartment, containing no books, no records, few toys, and a weary mother who is too preoccupied to answer Carl with more than a shake of her head. Yet both Todd and Carl are exposed to precisely the same teacher and the same teaching every day.

Four-year-old Kathy, who can read at second grade level, learns far more from her everyday environment than does Barbara, who lives next door in a home of the same size with parents of similar educational and social background.

What a child learns early in life has a powerful, persistent quality that makes unlearning difficult, notes Dr. Bloom. We don't know enough yet about the neurophysiology of the learning process to understand precisely why this is so. But we do know that early learning differs from later learning in its effectiveness. This is another reason why parents urgently need more information and help in guiding their children through these vital years.

During the years of rapid learning, an environment extremely lacking or abundant in intellectual stimuli can change a child's I.Q. as much as 20 points, Dr. Bloom estimates. (Other researchers put this figure somewhat higher.)

"This could mean the difference between a life in an institution for the feebleminded or a productive life in society," Dr. Bloom says. "It could mean the difference between a professional career and an occupation which is at the semiskilled or unskilled level."

Dr. Bloom, too, holds out the hope that through a better understanding of early-learning processes and by changes in child-care practices "we can drastically reduce the incidence of low levels of intelligence and increase the proportion of individuals reaching high levels of measured intelligence," and that a general gain in intelligence in our country can be achieved.

5. *Your child has already developed half of his total adult intellectual capacity by the time he is four years old and 80 percent of it by age eight. After age eight, regardless of what type of schooling and environment your child has, his mental abilities can only be altered by about 20 percent.*[11]

An individual's I.Q. seems to stabilize at its adult level by about age seventeen, most research indicates, although some studies show slight increases or decreases during the college-age years and afterwards. But adult intelligence is generally considered to be a stable characteristic, just as adult height is.

Your youngster will continue to learn, of course, after age seventeen. He will be able to use his intellectual abilities in many different ways. But the opportunity of increasing his basic intelligence will be almost completely gone by the time he is old enough to be graduated from high school.

These findings, also from Dr. Bloom's important book, do not mean that your child accumulates half of all the facts he'll ever know by age four, or that by age seventeen he has filled his brain with all the knowledge he's ever going to have. They do mean that his level of intelligence is fixed by about age seventeen—whether he is brilliant or above average, whether he is trainable or educable, average or dull-normal, whether his I.Q. is 120 or 150, 50 or 70. He may use his mental capacity to a high degree in obtaining further knowledge and in productive work. Or, he may waste it. But after age seventeen, he can't change it to any significant degree.

As much of your child's intelligence develops in the first four years of his life as in the next thirteen years. This really isn't surprising, in view of the rapid growth of your youngster's brain these early years. You can see clear evidence of this same, fast growth in other areas of his development. Your baby increases in height, for example, as much in the nine-month period from conception to birth, as he does in the nine-year period from ages three to twelve. And if he kept on gaining weight all during his childhood at the same rate as in the first year of his life, he'd be too big to fit into your house by the time he became a teen-ager.

These findings about intellectual growth put enormous responsibility upon parents. "Although there must be some genetic potential for learning, the direction the learning takes is most powerfully determined by the environment," Dr. Bloom points out. "Home environment is very significant not only because of the large amount of educational growth which has already taken place before the child enters the first grade, but also because of the influence of the home during the elementary school period."

6. *The cortex of your child's brain can be roughly compared to a computer, which must be "programmed" before it can operate effectively. Your child "programs" his brain by means of sensory stimuli he sends to it along the nerve pathways from his eyes, ears, nose, mouth, and tactile and kinesthetic senses. The more sensory stimuli with which he activates his brain, the greater will be the capacity of his brain to function intelligently.*

The cortex is the thick layer of gray matter that forms the outer surface of the brain. It contains millions of nerve cells which can receive and send electrical impulses. Human brains contain much more cortex than do the brains of animals. Parts of the human cortex, like other portions of the brain, have a fixed function, even at birth. But parts of it do not. They are "uncommitted," explains Dr. Wilder Penfield, a neurosurgeon and for twenty-five years the director of the Montreal Neurological Institute of McGill University.[12]

"This uncommitted cortex is the part of the human brain that makes man teachable and thus lifts him above all other species," says Dr. Penfield, who has mapped out different areas of brain function during the course of many long neurosurgical operations. Electrical impulses generated by the sensory organs and transmitted by the nerve cells pass through this cortex, making pathways and activating cells which process and store information, in ways which are not yet completely clear to scientists.

These uncommitted areas of the brain are used chiefly for the memory and use of words and for the memory and interpretation of experience, Dr. Penfield explains. The dominant area concerned with speech and with written language usually develops in the hemisphere of the brain opposite from your child's dominant hand: in the left half of the brain if your child is right-handed, and in the right half if he is left-handed.

Part of the information an individual stores in his cortex isn't available for his conscious recall. But neurosurgeons are able to demonstrate that these "forgotten" experiences and feelings and learnings are still filed away in the brain. For example, during the course of an operation on the brain of a patient who is conscious (but free of pain), when the surgeon touches various areas of the cortex with a mild electrical stimulus, the patient suddenly remembers long-forgotten scenes and emotions.

The information stored in the cortex is used by the brain—perhaps much as a computer utilizes programmed material—in the process of thought. The precise kind of electrical activity which takes place when the brain "thinks" is not yet known. But there is little doubt that the quantity and quality of information cached in an individual's cortex determines to a great extent the level of his intelligence.

"What the brain is allowed to record, how and when it is conditioned, these things prepare it for great achievement, or limit it to mediocrity," comments Dr. Penfield.

7. *But there is a time limit to when these brain cells can be activated easily.*

"The human brain is a living, growing organ," explains Dr. Penfield. "But it is bound by the inexorable evolution of its functional aptitudes, and no one can alter this, not even an educator or a psychiatrist. One can draw up a functional timetable for the brain of a child. One might well say there is a built-in biological clock that tells the passing time of educational opportunity."

We know, for example, that when a small child injures the area of his brain used in speech and cannot talk, he is eventually able, after many months, to create a new speech center in another part of his brain, using cells which were "uncommitted" previously. But an adult, in whom this vital area of brain is hurt, has enormous difficulty building a new speech area. His cortex is already "committed." His brain no longer possesses its earlier plasticity.

Because of this changing plasticity of the brain, learning acquired early in life—even if it can't be recalled consciously—is almost impossible to erase. It is doubly important because it also influences future learning and behavior.

A simple case in point: A mother was driving a car pool home from school one day. Betsy, age nine, announced to the group, "My speech teacher said I would have to work on saying 's' better this whole semester."

"That's nothing" replied an eleven-year-old. "I worked on 's' for two years."

Yet parents take it for granted that their youngster will learn "s" and all the other sounds of the English language correctly, without undue effort and without formal teaching before they are three or four years old. Every speech teacher knows how difficult it is to change even one of these sounds at third or fourth or fifth grade level if it is learned incorrectly at the preschool age.

8. *Sensitive periods exist in the life of every child for specific types of learning. These sensitive periods are the stages in development when the physiological state of the growing brain makes certain kinds of learning most easy to acquire. After these sensitive periods, it is difficult, or sometimes even impossible, to acquire these kinds of learning.*

Occasionally, on a college campus, you can encounter a coed walking about followed by a half-grown duck or chicken which has been conditioned to think that the student is its mother. This phenomenon is called "imprinting," and it is the subject of much study in university psychology departments.

Experiments with geese, ducks, fish, sheep, deer, buffalo, monkeys, dogs, cats, guinea pigs, mice, and chickens have repeatedly shown that for an extremely short time after birth, these animals can be conditioned, or imprinted, by special types of learning situations—and this learning is almost impossible to change or erase afterwards. In the most common experiments of this kind, a baby duckling is encouraged to follow a moving wooden decoy for a short period after hatching. The duckling thereafter regards the decoy as its mother and remains attached to it, ignoring other female ducks and ducklings.[13]

Imprinting with a duckling can be done most successfully when it is between thirteen and sixteen hours old and rarely succeeds after twenty-four hours. The physiological condition of the duckling's brain that makes this particular type of learning possible at this specific age has changed beyond recall. Some research suggests that in the brains of children as well as animals there may be mechanisms which can be activated only during a certain period of life. If these are not triggered at the right time by stimuli in the environment, they cannot be activated later, even by the same stimuli. Such animals or children may suffer from lifelong disabilities as a result.

A baby lamb, separated from its mother after birth for a few days, never learns to follow the flock, no matter how many years it is kept with other sheep. Some birds which are isolated from bird song during the early weeks of life never sing well, regardless of how much they are exposed to singing birds the rest of their lives.

"Like the duck, we, too, begin to learn very early in life, maybe in part by imprinting, but certainly in many other ways as well," commented geneticist and educator

Dr. Beadle.[14] "It has recently become increasingly clear that early learning is much more significant than we have previously thought."

One special sensitive period in the life of a human baby has been identified by Dr. Ronald Illingworth and Dr. James Lister: learning how to chew solid foods. If a baby isn't given solid food to chew at the time he is first able to do so, he will later refuse to try to chew; he will push the food out of his mouth and/or vomit, these physicians explain.[15]

In normal babies, this particular sensitive period occurs at about the age of six months, according to Drs. Illingworth and Lister. But it can vary from one infant to another. Two good clues can help you determine just when the sensitive time comes to introduce your baby to solids, they say. He will learn most easily just after he loses the infantile tongue-thrust reflex—when he no longer pushes food placed on the front of his tongue out of his mouth—and about one month after he has started to reach out and grasp objects with his hands.

What other sensitive periods exist in the life of very young children? Much research is now underway to map out these periods more precisely and to help parents learn how to take advantage of these special learning opportunities.

The sensitive period for learning to read and to understand numbers is between the ages of four and five, according to Dr. Maria Montessori, the first woman ever to be graduated from a medical school in Italy and the founder of the Montessori method of teaching. (Chapter 9 describes Montessori ideas about preschool learning.) Dr. Montessori discovered that four- and five-year-olds learn to read with great enthusiasm, ease, and joy when given the opportunity.[16]

A child between the ages of three and one-half and four and one-half can learn to write more easily than he can at six or seven, Dr. Montessori also concluded. Her culturally-deprived, slum-area children in Italy wrote beautiful script before they were five years old. Today, many four- and five-year-olds in Montessori schools learn both reading and writing as a free-choice activity, with great enthusiasm.

The muscular control in hand and fingers needed to produce written symbols is far less difficult to acquire than the complicated coordination of lips, tongue, throat, and breathing apparatus necessary to produce spoken symbols, Dr. Montessori explained. Furthermore, it's much easier to help a child learn to control his hand and fingers than it is his speech mechanism.

You may see evidence of interest and readiness for reading and writing in your own three- or four-year-old. He may identify labels on cereal boxes in the supermarket because he has seen them on television. He may read gasoline station signs while you're driving, again because he's heard and seen the words on TV. Even a two-year-old can often tell one of his phonograph records from another, although the labels look identical except for the lettering. Your child may pester you to teach him how to write his name, your name, the names of his favorite toy animals. He may memorize the books you read him before you've gone through them three times and be able to recite them word for word to you.

In the past, parents have been told to ignore such signs, and advised to tell a youngster who asks questions about words that "You will learn all about that when you get to first grade." They have been warned not to teach a child alphabetical letters because they will probably do it all wrong, or because home learning will confuse the child when he gets to first grade, or because the youngster will be ahead of the group.

But new research shows these important signs of special sensitivity to learning should not be ignored, but observed and encouraged. The child who is eager and interested in reading and writing at four may already be almost past his optimum period for developing these skills by the time the school is ready to teach him at age six or six and one-half.

The sensitive period for helping a child develop a sense of order is when he is between the ages of two and one-half and three and one-half, Dr. Montessori concluded. This is the age when your toddler insists on routine. He wants his teddy bear put precisely in place before he's willing to go to bed and only then provided the door is open just so many degrees, the usual lullaby has been sung and the blankets adjusted just right. He insists on having the red boat, the blue submarine, the yellow bar of soap, and the white wash-cloth in his bathtub, or he refuses to get in. He demands his milk be served only in his special glass (and he can tell one glass from another, even if you can't). Barry fumes at dinner if his string beans aren't all the same length. Ann fusses until her mother finds the "fuzzy" corner of her baby blanket to put nearest her face, although her mother can't tell the difference. Colin gets upset if his mother tries to put on his left sock before the right one, when he's accustomed to right before left.

Most parents consider this stage a dreadful nuisance and talk about the "terrible twos." But some of the researchers interested in early learning see this typical two and one-half behavior as evidence of a special period of sensitivity. This is the age when the growing brain of the child is trying to form generalizations from observations, to draw conclusions, to formulate concepts from perceptions. That's why children of this age are so insistent upon routine and ritual. It gives them a sense of order and continuity from which they can draw valid and workable conclusions.

You can use this special period to teach your child orderliness and good working habits, according to Dr. Montessori. Children in Montessori schools are taught to put away every item of equipment they use before starting a new activity. They are encouraged to see every task or game as having a beginning, a middle, and an end, and to finish each cycle before starting another. These youngsters take great pleasure in being able to control their environment by ordering it precisely and show great satisfaction in completing self-chosen projects before beginning new ones.

More research needs to be done about sensitive periods in children so that parents can learn how to recognize these stages in their offspring and provide optimum learning opportunities. If you watch your child closely, you can probably see clear indications of some of these sensitive periods when he is eager for particular kinds of learning.

9. *In appraising the intellectual development of small children, we have failed to take into consideration the evidence of intelligence provided by the development of speech. Learning to speak the English language is probably the most complex intellectual task any individual of any age ever undertakes in this country—and our children master it as a matter of course before age five.*

"Grandma is coming to visit; Mommy telled me so," shouts Brian, three, to his father. Daddy smiles indulgently at Mommy over his son's head and then explains to Brian that he should say "told." It is just another charming, childish mistake, his parents assume, and think no more about it.

But "telled" is probably better proof of Brian's developing mental powers than "told" would have been. Brian didn't say "telled" because he was parroting an adult. What Brian did—although he was probably not aware of it—was to observe that the way in which we usually make a past tense in English is to add "ed" to a verb, and then, he applied this general rule to the word "tell." In this case, the English language makes an exception, of which Brian was not yet aware.

Your child may say "mouses" instead of "mice"—not because he is slow or stupid, but because he is highly intelligent. He has observed for himself that we usually form plurals by adding "s" to root words, and he has applied this conclusion to a word which doesn't follow this general rule. "Mice" he could have learned by imitation or repetition. "Mouses" is evidence of important conceptual learning.

It is this complex ability to observe abstract language forms, draw conclusions from countless observations, and apply them to the construction of new sentences that makes it possible for small children to speak sentences they have never heard before. It also makes it possible for youngsters to use correctly all the complicated parts of speech in the English language before they are old enough to go to school—without the help of teachers or textbooks and without the pressures of report cards or homework assignments or fear of punishment or failure.

David, in seventh grade, is having enormous difficulty with homework in grammar. He can't seem to remember the rules about complex-compound sentences, past perfect participles, gerunds, and adverbial clauses. Yet he can use all of these forms correctly in sentences, and he can tell what is correct and incorrect "by the way it sounds." All this he learned for himself, without any help, at the age of three or four. Yet now, at twelve, he can't understand the rules in school.

David's parents try to help him with the homework. But they have the same difficulty. They can use all the grammar rules correctly—because they learned to do so as preschoolers. But they can't remember the rules, either—which they were taught in junior high.

"In ignoring the implications of the mastery of language in the child, we are missing a fundamental aspect of human development," comments reading expert George L. Stevens.[18] "If we regard the preschool period as essentially one of physical and emotional development, how are we to explain the miracle of speech? It has been this failure to recognize the implications of language development in the young child and an overemphasis on emotional adjustment that has dominated the educational theory of the past forty years.

"Between the ages of three and six, a period during which all normal children are completing their mastery of a complex system of symbols and completing it with little apparent effort and no formal assistance, our educational theorists consider the child capable of only finger painting and playing musical chairs. By failing to understand the intellectual aspects of child development, the educational theorists have unwittingly retarded our progress in learning theory and educational practice. By not realizing that the very young child has the drive and the capacity for knowledge, educators have delayed the development of new and improved educational methods.

"The most damaging consequence of this educational philosophy has been the ruling idea that reading should not be taught to the very young child. This is the concept —taught in all schools of education—that reading instruction of any kind should be delayed until the age of six or over. This notion has been one of the most disastrous blunders in the history of education."

10. *Because of the brain's special physiological characteristics, a child has the ability to acquire a second or third language more easily during the first years of his life than he will ever have again.*

"A child's brain has a specialized capacity for learning languages—a capacity that decreases with the passage of years," emphasizes Dr. Penfield, who has studied the bilingual children of Canada extensively. "The brain of the child is plastic. The brain of the adult, however effective it may be in other directions, is usually inferior to that of the child as far as language is concerned." [19]

If you know any family with young children which has immigrated to the United States, you have probably seen examples of this early-language ability. Typically, the youngsters in such a family pick up English almost automatically, without formal lessons or obvious effort. But their parents, who may be highly intelligent, strongly motivated, and well instructed, learn English only with great difficulty and never speak it without at least a trace of foreign accent.

Dr. Penfield explains why. During the first few years of a child's life, his brain develops "language units," complex neuronal records of what he hears and repeats. These units interconnect with other nerve cells concerned with motor activity, thinking, and other intellectual functions. After about age six and increasingly after age nine, a child uses these language units in his brain as the basis for rapid expansion of his vocabulary. But these new words are built of the same basic units and sounds he has already recorded in his brain.

If, after the age of ten or twelve, the youngster begins studying a second language, he must use the same well-learned language units.

"Instead of imitating the sounds of the new language, he tries to employ his own verbal units—his mother-tongue units—and so speaks with an accent and even rearranges the new words into a construction that is wrong," notes Dr. Penfield. "This is a common enough experience. Even though they travel over the world, the Cockney and the Scot and the Irishman betray their origins all through life by a turn of the tongue learned in childhood, to say nothing of the Canadian and the American."

The teen-ager or the adult trying to learn a foreign language, using the units already fixed in his brain since childhood, must go through the mental process of translation, a neurophysiological process Dr. Penfield calls "indirect language-learning." Younger children who are taught by this same method—as, for example, by a teacher who uses English to explain French—must also use this translation process.

But children who learn a second or third language from a teacher who speaks to them in that language only—by what Dr. Penfield calls the direct, or "mother's method"—can actually establish language units for the second tongue in their brains.

"A child who is exposed to two or three languages during the ideal period for language beginning pronounces each with the accent of his teacher," explains Dr. Penfield. "If he hears one language at home, another at school, and a third perhaps with a governess in the nursery, he is not aware that he is learning three languages at all. He is aware of the fact that to get what he wants with the governess he must speak one way and with his teacher he must speak in another way.

"Although the cortico-thalamic speech mechanism serves all three languages, and there is no evidence of anatomical separation, nevertheless, there is a curiously effective switch that allows each individual to turn from one language to another," says Dr. Penfield. "What I have referred to as a 'switch' would be called, by experimental physiologists, a conditioned reflex. When a child or an adult turns to an individual who speaks only English, he speaks English, and turning to a man who speaks French and hearing a word of French, the conditioning signal turns the switch over, and only French words come to mind."

By the time a child is ten or twelve, it's too late for his brain to develop the switch mechanism, says Dr. Penfield. Unless he has acquired some language units of a foreign tongue by this age, he is forced to learn a second language by the difficult and relatively unsuccessful translation process.

It is often argued that it is useless to expose a small child to a second language if he lives in an English-speaking community and will not continually hear and use these foreign words all during the time he is growing up. Dr. Penfield disagrees. He says that it is true that such a youngster will forget the foreign words he has learned. But as a teen-ager or as an adult, if he studies that language or visits a country where it is spoken, he will discover an unsuspected gift of language-learning, because the basic units of that speech are still stored in his brain.

Dr. Penfield studied for a time in Madrid, during the period when his older son was five years old. For three months, the boy attended a Spanish school, where he played games, listened to other children speak, and was not taught Spanish in any formal way. It was assumed that if the boy had learned any Spanish, it was quickly forgotten when the Penfields left Spain.[20]

But twenty-five years later, it was necessary for Dr. Penfield's son to learn Spanish for business reasons. To his surprise, he discovered that he made very rapid progress, that forgotten pronunciations came flooding back, that he was able to speak excellent Spanish without the expected Canadian accent.

Dr. Penfield explains that units of understanding and

pronunciation were hidden away in his son's brain, but not completely lost.

Europeans seem to find it easier to learn foreign languages than do English-speaking Americans, notes Dr. Penfield. He attributes this special aptitude to the fact that European children are accustomed to hearing second and third languages routinely, during the first decade of their lives, while most youngsters growing up in the United States do not.

11. *A child has a built-in drive to explore, to investigate, to try, to seek excitement and novelty, to learn by using every one of his senses, to satisfy his boundless curiosity. And this drive is just as innate as hunger, thirst, the avoidance of pain, and other drives previously identified by psychologists as "primary."* [21]

Because of failure to recognize curiosity as a basic drive, much behavior among small children has been misinterpreted and labeled "naughtiness." Toddlers and preschoolers are frequently punished for "getting into everything" because their urgent need for mental stimulation isn't recognized, and they aren't helped to find outlets for this basic drive that are better than emptying dresser drawers or seeing what happens when a box of detergent is flushed down the toilet.

Bright youngsters with an abundance of curiosity are often considered troublemakers in schools which fail to understand their great need for learning stimulation.

"Most of us have the spirit of scientific inquiry spanked out of us by the time we are twelve years old," a research chemist comments.

Today, however, psychologists and biologists are finding ample evidence of curiosity as a basic drive—not only in children, but also in laboratory animals. Monkeys, for example, will work for long periods of time on mechanical puzzles, even when there is no reward involved—apparently just out of curiosity. Rats prefer to take a long but interesting route to reach their food rather than a short, quick one. Many laboratory animals can be motivated to perform tasks by the reward of a view out an open window, from which they can see activity outside their cage.

Even in newborn infants, behavior can be triggered by what psychologists are now calling "perceptual novelty." For example, when researchers show a two- or three-day-old baby in a hospital a simple, bright-colored object, such as a red ball or a red circle on a white card, his eyes can be seen to focus on it, and his whole body seems to become alert. The next time he sees the same object, the infant pays the same alert, interested attention. But the novelty begins to wear off. And the baby will give more attention to a second, different object or shape than he will to the first one.

Another research project demonstrated that infants who are between ten hours and five days old will pay more attention to a drawing of a face or a pattern, than they will to solid-color circles.

Much behavior which we have considered childish or immature may actually be a sign of this primary drive in operation. For example, we know that a small child has a very short attention span and have assumed it was because his brain was capable of learning only in small amounts. However, it is more likely, in view of new research, that a youngster can concentrate on one thing for only a brief span because of his brain's urgent need for more stimulation—because of his great drive to pay attention to many things.

When parents find better means of helping a youngster satisfy his urgent need to explore, to look, to experiment, to try, to experience a variety of sensory stimuli, he will not only learn, but he will be much happier and much more content. The baby who is dry, fed, neither too hot nor too cold and not being stuck by diaper pins, and who is still fussing in his crib or playpen, has an unsatisfied basic need—the need for new sensory stimuli.

12. *Your child has a built-in drive for competency, an inborn desire to do and to learn how to do. He manipulates, handles, tries, repeats, investigates, and*

seeks to master as much of his environment as he can, primarily for the pleasure of such activity.[22]

If you observe your baby's actions closely, as Swiss scientist Dr. Jean Piaget did his own youngsters, you can see this basic drive at work quite clearly. Dr. Piaget, for example, describes his own son Laurent, at the age of three months and ten days, lying in a bassinet. Over the baby, Dr. Piaget hung a rattle with a string attached. One end of the string he placed in Laurent's hand. Soon, by a chance movement, Laurent pulled the string to produce a noise. For the next fifteen minutes, the baby delighted in tugging the string and listening to the rattle, laughing with obvious joy.

Three days later, Laurent again by chance pulled the string and set off the rattle. This time he obviously experimented with the effects of pulling the string. He swung it gently, tugged at it, shook it, listening to the different sounds produced from the rattle and laughing exuberantly.[23]

Your baby may drop his rattle over the side of his playpen and howl for you to retrieve it. Then he drops it again. And again. And again, as long as you are willing to fetch it for him. If you see his actions as purposeless behavior, or as an attempt by your baby to control you, you'll probably become annoyed and cross with him. But if you understand that your youngster is trying to learn all he can about grasping and releasing, about falling objects and impact noises, you'll find it much easier to be patient and understanding and to help him with his enormous learning task. The perceptual observations your baby gains from this repeated experiment are nothing he can put into words. But they will be stored away in his brain, where they can help him later in forming concepts and in developing intelligent behavior.

This drive for competency is easier to see in somewhat older youngsters. A toddler will often delight in spending half an hour climbing up and down the same three front steps. A three-year-old discovering how to zip her jacket will insist on zipping it and unzipping it a dozen times before she is willing to hang it away in the closet. A five-year-old will draw the same picture of a ship over and over again for days.

Just how strong this drive is any parent knows who has tried to do something for a child that the youngster is determined to do all by himself. No matter how difficult the task or how frustrating the failure, a two- or three-year-old will often persist to the point of exhaustion in his efforts to master his self-selected task.

All of this seemingly random "play" has a great underlying purpose in human development, suggests psychologist Dr. Robert W. White. He says that all human beings have an innate, biological need for myriad perceptual and motor experiences to fill up the large, underdeveloped cortex area of the brain. A human infant is born so ill-equipped to function in the world and has so much to learn before he is able to care for himself, that this drive for learning—for competency—is essential to his survival. He has to spend the earliest years of his life filling his brain with information and perceptions, or he will not be able to act intelligently when he is older.[24]

The more we study the human infant, the more clear it becomes that infancy is not just a time when the nervous system matures and the muscles develop, says Dr. White. It is a time of active and continuous learning, which becomes the basis for all of the child's later thinking and activity. He observes that "Helpless as he may seem until he begins to toddle, he has by that time already made substantial gains in the achievement of competence."

Once a baby has had the opportunity to store up in his brain all of these many perceptions and experiences —to program his brain with information—then subsequent learning can be swift and complex, Dr. White points out. This conclusion, although it is based on psychological theory and research, is quite similar to that reached by Dr. Penfield, whose work is based on neurological findings.

This same need of a small child to develop competence was also observed by Dr. Montessori in her studies of preschool youngsters. She deliberately designed learning frames to help her tiny pupils develop competency in buttoning, buckling, tying, and lacing, for example. And she demonstrated how a young child can be helped to learn how to carry out many of the simple operations of a household if taught in very simple, logical, programmed ways. The great joy this feeling of competency, or control over the environment, gives to children is a basis of her teaching methods.

13. *Learning can be intrinsically enjoyable, and small children learn voluntarily when their efforts are not distorted by pressure, competition, extrinsic rewards, punishments, or fear.*

Long before a child is ready for first grade, he's well aware that you don't go to school for fun. He knows you have to go. He hears older boys and girls talking about the strict teacher or the hard assignments or the confining rules. His mother tells him that he has to do what the teacher tells him. He learns to stand in line, to keep quiet, to do what the group does, no matter how much it bores him.

By the time he's in high school, his interest in learning is so distorted by worry about grades, by competition, by the need to win the teacher's approval, by homework assignments, and by pressures that he has almost given up expecting learning to be a joy. Even if he is lucky enough to encounter a class or a textbook or a teacher he finds fascinating, he knows it isn't socially acceptable to admit it.

But in his beginning, it was not so. Because of his innate drive toward competency, because of his inborn curiosity, learning was originally a pleasure. He worked almost constantly at learning during his waking hours —by looking intently at everything around him, by touching, tasting, listening, practicing sounds, exploring, trying, falling down, trying again. He enjoyed the process of learning, and he enjoyed practicing again and again what he had learned.

Montessori schools and the preschools using Dr.

Moore's "talking typewriter" show clearly that when given free choice, three- and four- and five-year-olds will choose learning activities and enjoy them enormously. Dr. Moore has been particularly careful to eliminate extrinsic pressures and rewards from his experiments to prove this point, because the theory that learning is pleasurable in itself goes contrary to traditional views about motivation.

Until recently, learning was generally explained in terms of drives and reinforcements and was thought to occur when an activity produced a reduction in a primary drive, such as hunger or fear, or when it could be connected secondhand with such a reduction.

A parent who remembers that learning should be intrinsically pleasurable for a small child has a good guide in planning mentally-stimulating activities that aren't too immature or too advanced, too easy or too difficult. The purpose of these learning activities isn't to push the youngster or pressure him or make him compete with a neighbor's child or perform like a puppet to show off— but to make the youngster himself happy.

14. *The more new things your child has seen and heard, the more new things he wants to experience. The greater the variety of environmental stimuli with which your child has coped, the greater is his capacity for coping.*

Among the great mass of theories and observations by Dr. Piaget regarding intelligence in children, this concept is one of the most useful to parents.[25] By it, Dr. Piaget means, roughly, that stimulating changes in a youngster's environment trigger changes in the organization and functioning of his basic biological structures— in other words, they further the development of his brain. The more differentiated and flexible these structures become, the more capable the child is of reacting intelligently and appropriately to future stimuli from the environment.

At every stage in a youngster's life, moreover, his environment should supply him opportunity to use the range of mental abilities he has acquired. He also needs enough challenge and stimuli in his surroundings to trigger additional development of his potentialities.

If your youngster doesn't get enough stimuli to make effective use of what he can do, he suffers from boredom, and his development is curtailed because of lack of challenge and learning opportunity. This can happen, for example, when a kindergartener, who has already had two years of nursery school, is forced to sit through another year of group-singing games and coloring exercises, without any intellectual challenges. On the other hand, the child who isn't mature enough to cope with challenges in his environment suffers if he is pressured.

It is an art basic to both parenthood and education to match the stimuli and challenges in a child's environment with his growing abilities to learn. In the past we have greatly underestimated the learning capacities of our children. New research is now suggesting many practical ways in which you can help your child develop a high degree of his potential intelligence. These will be detailed for you in following chapters.

3. How the Atmosphere in Your Home Can Foster Intelligence

The emotional climate you create in your home can do much to stimulate your child to learn, to develop his growing mental abilities. Or, it can stunt his developing mind and dull his innate creative feelings. Your relationship to him as a parent, coupled with his inborn traits, will largely determine how he goes about learning for the rest of his life.

It's impossible to blueprint precisely the ideal home in which maximum learning can take place—and have it fit every individual youngster. Children differ too much. So do parents and family circumstances. But recent research suggests many important guidelines you can use to make your home a creative, stimulating environment for your child.

Many long-term research projects show that your youngster's intelligence will develop to a higher degree if the attitude in your home toward him is warm and democratic, rather than cold and authoritarian. In one study, for example, the I.Q. of small children living in homes where parents were neglectful or hostile or restrictive actually decreased slightly over a three-year period. But in homes where parents were warm and loving, where they took time to explain their actions, let children participate in decisions, tried to answer questions, and were concerned about excellence of performance, there was an average increase in I.Q. of about 8 points.

This doesn't mean that you should be completely permissive, or let your youngster run wild, or interfere with the rights and possessions of others. It doesn't mean giving him a vote equal to his father's in a council that makes all the family decisions. Nor does it mean that your home must be child-centered.

It does mean that you should love your child wholeheartedly and enthusiastically and be sure that he knows it. (If a youngster thinks his own parents don't love him or approve of him, how can he face his teacher or his friends with self-confidence enough to keep trying?)

Sometimes it even helps to point out to a three- or four- or five-year-old just how many different ways you do show your love for him, especially if you have a younger baby. Often an older child, who equates love only with hugging and cuddling, may think that the baby is getting the bigger share.

"I show my love of Libby by cuddling her and rocking her and changing her diapers," you can tell your firstborn. "But you certainly don't want diapers any more, and you only like to be rocked just once in a while, when you've hurt yourself or you are very tired. So I show my love for you in ways you enjoy better now—like inviting Michael over for lunch with you and making you sugar cookies and reading to you and fixing the pedal on your trike and taking you to the park to swing. I even show my love for you by not letting you play in the street, because I don't want you to get hurt."

A warm and democratic home also means that you plan your family's activities to take into consideration your child's needs to grow and develop as an individual, and that you give him as much voice in decisions involv-

ing him as he can handle. Your goal is to develop a thinking individual who can evaluate a situation and act appropriately—not a trained animal who obeys without
question.

Even a two-year-old can be given choices, when you
intend to abide by what he decides: "Do you want to
wear the blue shirt or the green one today?" "Would you
like to have your milk warm or cold this morning?" "Shall
we have peas or carrots for dinner this evening?" "It's
almost bedtime; shall we finish the puzzle or shall we stop
now so there will be time for a story?"

It helps, too, if you explain the why behind the rules
you set up and the decisions you enforce on your child—
not in tiresome detail, not as an apology, not at a level
above his understanding, but as a teaching device. Your
child will learn, gradually, to evaluate alternatives. He
will slowly begin to accumulate information upon which
he can make good decisions. And he will realize, increasingly, that the rules you set up and the discipline you
enforce are based on reason and love and wisdom—not
caprice or arbitrary or dictatorial power.

There's a happy by-product of this strategy, too. A two-
year-old who is permitted some choices of his own isn't
quite so negativistic and zealous of his independence as
a moppet who is struggling for some beginning recognition
of his developing self. An older child, who has learned
that his parents only set up rules and make decisions for
him when it is necessary, isn't nearly so apt to rebel as a
youngster whose mother or father expects him to obey
"because I say so."

"The intellectual tasks involved in the process of
socialization are formidable," stressed Dr. Kenneth Wann
and his associates at Teachers College, Columbia University.[1] "It is all too easy to come to see only the overtly
behavioral aspect of social development. When this happens, then the job of the child is seen as simply that of
conforming to the dos and don'ts of behavior codes. The
role of the adult, then, is viewed as primarily that of
restraining the changing, overt behavior. This, of course,
is not an adequate concept of the child's task or the

adult's role. Such activity is a part of the socialization process, but only a small part. The major task is intellectual. It consists of understanding and conceptualizing the demands of social living so that one can respond to the complex stimuli of continually varying situations with appropriate, adequate behavior. This is a giant of a task. And young children work hard at it."

Parents, said Dr. Wann, should do whatever they can to help children with this intellectual task of learning how to get along in the world. Within a warm and understanding home, you should see yourself not only as a parent, but also as your child's first, best, and most successful teacher.

"Teacher" doesn't imply that you help your child by means of structured, formal lessons. Your role is much more informal: to teach by example, by creating a stimulating environment, by talking to your youngster, by listening to him seriously, by loving him, by letting him teach himself with your guidance, by introducing him to the fascinations of the world you know, by taking advantage of every opportunity for learning in your life with him.

Just as you are not a formal teacher, so your preschooler is not a "pupil" in the sit-down-and-be-still-while-you-learn image of the word. Most youngsters can't sit quietly for very long before the age of six; that's one reason why it's often been assumed that they weren't ready to learn. Most preschool learning takes place on the go, along with much motor activity.

Many factors interlace to make most homes a good place to learn and most parents ideal teachers. At home, a youngster can learn at his own pace. He needn't wait in fidgety boredom for two dozen other pupils to catch up, or he needn't continually drag behind because he can't maintain the grade-level pace. He faces no competition. No academic pressures. No formal timetable for learning. No tests. No fear of humiliating public mistakes. At home, a youngster can receive immediate feedback of praise or correction, which is considered by many researchers to be important in the learning process and which is difficult for a teacher to provide for large groups of children.

At home, before age six, a youngster's growing brain makes him hungry for learning and uniquely easy to teach. During the preschool years, too, most children are eager to imitate and emulate their parents—to a degree seldom experienced by teachers or by parents themselves at other stages in their offspring's life.

These are positive strengths and great advantages which a parent possesses in his role as a teacher. Almost always they outweigh a parent's lack of special training and formal educational skills in dealing with his own youngster.

"But I have two other children and a house to take care of; I haven't time to be a teacher, too," some mothers object. Yet it takes no longer to think of your child in terms of helping him learn than it does to function chiefly as his caretaker, and it is certainly more pleasant for both of you.

A case in point: a trip to the shoe store. Often you see a mother with her fidgety preschooler waiting for a salesperson. The mother is bored, cross, impatient. The youngster is bored, restless, whining. He begins pulling shoes out of boxes off the shelves. The mother watches him idly for a few minutes, then scolds him to stop. He doesn't. She jerks him away. He pulls back. She hoists him back on his chair, scolding, "No, no, no." As soon as she lets go of his arm, he trots back to pulling shoes off the shelf. This time she yanks him away and spanks him. He cries. She slams him down on the seat in exasperation. He slides off defiantly and sits on the floor.

It's so easy to do it differently. The mother might have anticipated a wait in the store and brought along a book to read to her youngster. Then she'd have found ten bonus minutes the two of them could have enjoyed together. They could have played a beginning reading game, or a guessing game. The mother might have had a small, magic slate in her purse so she and her little boy could have drawn pictures for each other. They could have walked about the store together, talking quietly about the kinds of shoes they saw and guessing what kind of people would buy them. The mother might have shown the youngster how the salesman would go about fitting his shoes, or how laces go and how buckles work.

Almost anything the mother wanted to do to help the youngster learn or satisfy his curiosity, or direct his rest-less energy toward acquiring information or sensory ex-periences, would have kept him intrigued, interested—and better behaved—for the waiting period. The mother had to spend the time with the child anyway, and what-ever effort she put into reading or talking would have been less than the strain of scolding him or spanking him in public.

A child's attention span is usually short. You needn't hunt for big blocks of time in your day to help him learn. You can play word games with a moppet while you're doing almost every kind of housework, for ex-ample. You can count red cars or green trucks, or out-of-state license plates while you're driving. You can keep a mental file of ideas handy for all the times you wait with your child—for the doctor, the barber, the saleslady, the bus, or Daddy coming home for dinner. Even if you in-vest only the usual quota of scolding-whining-fussing time in learning, it will pay dividends for your child later on and make your relationship much more pleasant now.

As a parent, you have the time and the opportunity to study your child as an individual, not just as a member of a class or an age-stage group. Better than any teacher ever could, you know how he learns best, what en-courages him to try, when he needs a touch of humor and when a bit of firmness, how much challenge spurs him on and how much blunts his interest. You can observe his responses and understand his feelings and shape the learning environment in your home so it is uniquely right for your child.

Another way to foster your child's mental develop-ment is to make encouragement, love, and praise your chief methods of discipline. For these techniques work most effectively not only in helping your child grow socially and emotionally, but intellectually, too.

Five-year-old Christopher attended a four-family picnic one evening and was introduced to the architect-husband of one of his mother's friends. Although he had not yet been taught to do so, Christopher happened to stick out his hand for the man to shake at the introduction. Later that evening, the architect remarked to Christopher's mother what a fine impression the boy had created with this simple courtesy and how well the gesture reflected on the whole family

That night, when his mother tucked Christopher into bed, she repeated what the architect had said, and she thanked him for helping to make a new friend for all the family. Christopher glowed at her praise. Never once afterward has he failed to offer his hand promptly, courteously, confidently, and without a reminder, when he is introduced to an adult.

It isn't always so easy to reinforce a desirable response in a small child, of course. But it does help to be alert to opportunities to give your child legitimate praise. False compliments ring phony to even a small youngster. But no matter how dull or slow or troublesome a child, you can always find a few opportune moments to praise him justly for something he is doing right or well or thoughtfully. If you emphasize what he has done right, rather than scold him for what he has done wrong, you'll teach him to work from strength, not from weakness and discouragement.

Sometimes you can even create situations which will give your child small successes and you opportunities for praise. Some parents set their standards so high, in an attempt to keep their child striving toward major goals, that he never can satisfy them. But it's much more likely that the youngster will become discouraged, feel inadequate, and stop trying if you continually point out where he has fallen short.

It helps if you let your child know that you have confidence in his abilities so he will have enough self-confidence in himself to keep trying. Your youngster has enormous respect for your judgment. If you tell him he's "stupid," or "never will amount to anything," or he's the "naughtiest boy in the neighborhood," or he "won't get into college the way he's doing now," he's almost certain to believe you and quite likely to give up trying.

Because a child does believe almost any label a parent hangs on him, you can use this technique to foster a self-image that will enable the child to learn easily and without dragging self-doubts. You might tell him, for example. "This is hard, but you are the kind of boy who enjoys tackling difficult things. I can remember how hard you worked at learning to walk, how you never stopped trying, no matter how many times you fell down or how many black and blue bruises you got."

"I enjoy reading to you because you always listen so closely," you could tell a child. Or, "It makes me feel proud to take you to the supermarket with me because you behave so well, and you help me find the groceries I need." Or, "I know I can always count on you to be gentle with your baby sister; it's no wonder she loves you so."

Don't use fear—of failure, of scolding, of disappointing you, of physical punishment, of the withdrawal of your love, of ridicule, or of unmentioned consequences in the future—to motivate your child. Most parents do use fear of one kind or another as a handle to control a youngster, without intending to, or even being aware they are doing it. It may take time and practice to get out of the habit—but your child will learn more readily if you do, and your relationship with him will be more pleasant and comfortable.

Do encourage your child to feel that it's all right to try, that failure isn't a crime, and that a mistake can be one way of learning. Many youngsters spend so much energy worrying and trying to keep out of trouble and avoiding mistakes that their abilities to learn are stifled.

Your child will make mistakes, of course. Everyone does. It will encourage him to keep on learning if you teach him how to handle his mistakes. Spilled milk, for example, is just that, not a felony. All you need to do is show your youngster how to wipe it up and get himself another glass. If he accidentally breaks another child's toy, help him to apologize, work with him to make a plan for seeing that the toy is replaced, and then talk with him a bit about why some toys break and how they can be safeguarded.

This doesn't mean, of course, that you immediately absolve your child of responsibility when accidents or mistakes occur. You should help him try to understand what went wrong and how it can be prevented. But you can do it in an objective way that promotes learning, rather than discourages your youngster from trying.

Every child develops a "life style" or "learning style" that determines how he reacts to his environment, to people he encounters, to new experiences like school. This life style is shaped in part by constitutional factors with which he was born and to a larger extent by his experiences from infancy on. The older a child grows, the harder it is to change his life style.

Many parents, inadvertently, encourage a child to develop a life style that hampers learning. For example, Jeremy's parents seem to show their love for him only when he is quiet, clean, and undemanding. Their house is full of "no-no's" that Jeremy mustn't touch. His mother insists on feeding him, because "he makes such a mess of things if he holds the spoon." She runs to catch him every time he tries to take a step on his own, because he might fall. And she keeps him in the playpen most of the day so he won't be spoiled by too much attention and get into everything.

Sometimes the youngest child in a family finds it rewarding to develop a life style of being babyish and depending on others. Or a boy may discover he gets more of the attention he needs by clowning than by serious achievement. Or a little girl may be subtly encouraged to smile and wheedle, rather than to put forth learning effort.

One major way in which you shape your child's learning style is by your use of language with him, notes Dr. Robert D. Hess, former chairman of the Committee on Human Development, University of Chicago, and now professor of psychology and education at Stanford University. How you talk to your preschool child and the verbal method you use to control him have an enormous effect on encouraging—or discouraging—the growth of his intelligence, explains Dr. Hess.[2]

After studying groups of mothers and children from different social, economic, and occupational backgrounds, Dr. Hess and his associates conclude that a major difference between culturally-deprived youngsters and others is not basic intelligence or emotional relationships or pressures to achieve—but the way in which mothers use language with the youngsters.

Language largely determines what and how a child learns from his environment, and it sets limits within which future learning may take place, Dr. Hess points out. It can encourage, or discourage, thinking.

For example, a small child is playing noisily with pots and pans in the kitchen. The telephone rings. In one type of home, the mother says, "Be quiet," or "Shut up." In another, the mother tells the youngster, "Would you keep quiet a minute? I want to talk on the phone."

In the first instance, explains Dr. Hess, the child has only to obey a command. In the second, the youngster has to follow two or three ideas. He has to relate his behavior to a time dimension. He must think of the effect of his actions on another person. His mind receives more stimulation from the more elaborate and complex verbal communication.

The command, "Be quiet," cuts off thought and offers little opportunity for the child to relate information to the context in which behavior occurs, says Dr. Hess. The second type of communication helps the child to link his behavior to other factors in his environment and may encourage him to seek the whys in future situations.

If incidents like this continue to occur during the early years in the lives of the two children, and if they continue to receive quite different learning stimuli, their verbal and intellectual abilities will be significantly different by the time they are ready for school, Dr. Hess observes.

In studying "mother-child communication systems," Dr. Hess finds that middle-class mothers elaborate on what they say, use more complex and explanatory sentences, and give their child more information than do lower-class mothers. They use language to encourage a youngster to reflect, to anticipate the consequences of his actions, to avoid error, to weigh decisions, and to choose among alternatives.

Communication from mother to child that is stereotyped, limited, and lacking in specific information curtails a youngster's learning, emphasizes Dr. Hess. Such language patterns are characterized by short, simple, and often unfinished sentences, clichés and generalities, such as, "You must do this because I say so," and "Girls don't act like that."

But the mother who uses words to relate a child's behavior to his surroundings, to the future, and to possible consequences, is teaching her youngster problem-solving strategies which will be useful in other situations, suggests Dr. Hess. She is encouraging a wider and more complex range of thought. She is stimulating her child to learn, and she is laying the foundation for learning in the future.

In assessing how much your child is interested in learning and knowing about before he's old enough to start first grade, you're much more likely to err by underestimating than overestimating. Almost everyone does—including educators.

For example, three members of a research team from Teachers College, Columbia University, along with the staffs of five schools for three-, four-, and five-year-olds in the New York City area, made a detailed study of preschoolers' learning activities. The 319 youngsters observed came from a wide range of home backgrounds —deprived, immigrant, middle class, upper-income bracket, foreign-language speaking, city, suburban.[3]

At the beginning of the study, reported Dr. Wann and his associates, "No one would have denied that young children know and think. We had worked with children too long to be that naïve. We also had the benefit of the work of other people before us who have studied young children. None of us, not even the most sophisticated of our group, however, was prepared for what we found. The depth and extent of the information and understanding of three-, four- and five-year old children was much greater than we had anticipated."

For a brief time, the team kept anecdotal records of the children's activities and comments. In the first 600 such notes, the youngsters covered a total of 609 topics. Dr. Wann commented:

Impressive as was the extent of the knowledge of the young children, even more impressive were the ways in which they were using and testing their knowledge. Information became for these children the raw material for thinking and reasoning. . . . The children repeatedly sought more and more information, and they consciously tried to relate and test one bit of information against another. Their capacity for remembering a great range of information was remarkable. They employed all the essential elements of conceptualization in their efforts to make sense of the information they were collecting. They used and tested their information in many ways. They associated ideas. They sought to understand cause and effect relationships. They classified objects and phenomena they observed. And they attempted to make generalizations from their experiences.

Children are far more interested in questions of "how" and "why" than merely "what," observed Dr. Wann. He suggested that parents and preschool teachers should do more to make this type of information available to young children.

It was clear that the interests of these young children were global, even universal in scope. We found children attempting to understand people, places, and events remote in time and space from their own immediate surroundings. We found children struggling to understand phenomena in their environment. We found children developing confused and inaccurate concepts. We found children indulging in animism and the enjoyment of phantasy as they viewed their immediate world. More frequently, however, we found them seeking to understand the causes of the phenomena they observed and to test their own thinking about these phenomena. We also found children concerned about the demands of social living and struggling to understand the very complex symbol system of their social world.

Parents and teachers need to realize that children not only crave great amounts of knowledge, but they also enjoy having information and using it, said Dr. Wann. They often relay facts to another child, starting out, "Guess what!" And they frequently make a game out of testing their own or other moppets' information.

Adults—both parents and teachers—must find ways to encourage small children in their great efforts and desire to learn, emphasized Dr. Wann. "Probably the greatest resource for young children, in this respect, is adults who listen to children, who talk with them about their ideas, and who provide experiences for developing further understanding."

He suggested that adults should take preschoolers on more trips—to museums, zoos, and other places of interest, and to visit people working at interesting occupations. They can tactfully and encouragingly help children correct some of their misconceptions. They can not only furnish them with stimulating sensory material, but they can assist them in sorting it out and making sense out of their observations. One of the happiest and most successful ways to stimulate your child's mental development is to let him share your own interests and activities.

In studying the home backgrounds and child-rearing practices which produced famous twentieth-century men and women, Victor and Mildred Goertzel observe that parents who raise distinguished offspring themselves tend to be curious, experimental, restless, and seeking. The common ground for the highly-diverse types of families which produce outstanding sons and daughters—as well as many other highly-competent and successful children not quite so famous—is a driving need to be going, doing, learning, striving, involved in activities, or concerned about ideas.[4]

Family value systems have the strongest impact on these children, rather than schools or teachers, report the Goertzels. Parents help their children build on personal strengths, talents, and aims. They are usually so interested and interesting themselves that their youngsters eagerly tag along to share the excitement.

As you begin to understand and better satisfy your child's urgent need to learn, to experiment, to try, to explore, to handle, to touch, to see, to understand, you'll find he is much happier. He is easier to manage. He presents fewer discipline problems because his inner needs come closer to being fulfilled, and he has an outlet for his restless curiosity.

Much of the typical preschooler's time is now spent in activities which bore him and his parents and in matters of discipline. Parents who use early-learning principles with their youngsters report they cut down drastically on the frequency with which they say "Don't!" and "No!" and on the amount of "What-can-I-do-now?" whining.

Early learning also helps parents to enjoy a child more. They can't help enjoying their child's pleasure in learning, just as they shared great delight in beginning to walk and talk.

An emotional relationship between you and your child in which you act as guide and teacher and fellow-explorer in a fascinating world—rather than as judge, jury, examiner, therapist, or boss—is one that grows well with time. Your child will feel less need to rebel against you when he is an adolescent and less need to make a clean break for independence when he is a young adult.

4. How To Raise a Brighter Baby: Birth to Eighteen Months

When you bring a newborn baby home from the hospital, many of his needs are obvious. He must be fed, bubbled, changed, bathed, protected, loved. Dozens of pamphlets, scores of baby books, and millions of grandmothers can tell you precisely how. But because the needs of a baby's fast-growing brain are not so obvious, they have usually been overlooked or misinterpreted or left to chance. Many of the ways in which we usually go about caring for babies may actually be limiting the growth of their intelligence.

During the first few years of his life, your baby's brain will triple in size. Long before he is ready to be born, all of the 10 to 12 billion nerve cells he will ever possess have already been formed. But he has far fewer dendrites, nerve fibers, and synapses joining these nerve cells together than does an adult. These connecting links grow at a tremendous rate during early childhood, and their growth is apparently stimulated by the activity of the nerve pathways leading to the brain.

Thus, in a very real physical sense, your baby's early environment and the amount of sensory stimulus he receives can actually cause physical changes in his brain and foster the growth of his mental capacity.

During these first six years, your child will change from an organism that can do little more than cry, suck, sneeze, sleep, and grasp into a thinking, reasoning, creative, imaginative, remembering individual who has command of a difficult symbolic language and complex motor skills.

This "developmental explosion" does not happen by chance or by predetermined process, emphasizes Dr. Leon Eisenberg, chief of psychiatric service at Massachusetts General Hospital. "How fast it happens and how far it goes are, within limits, a direct function of the amount and variety of patterned stimulation supplied by the environment," he points out.[1]

You can understand this concept more clearly if you think of your baby's brain as a computer, just being built or programmed—an analogy researchers in early learning often use. The more circuits you activate in the computer and the more interconnecting links that are established, the more complicated and "intelligent" answers will come out of it. So it is, roughly, with a baby's brain. The more "input" that goes into his brain, in general, the better and greater will be the "output." The more opportunity a baby has to program his brain by means of sensory and motor input, the greater will be his intelligence.

Your infant's brain is being programmed from the very first day of his life, chiefly by motor activity and sensory stimulation. But because a baby has relatively little output, because he doesn't talk or walk and has only limited means of communication, the importance of early input has been largely overlooked.

But a vast amount of sensory stimulation is necessary to give the brain basic information to use in functioning and in forming concepts. It is during the earliest years of life that the brain is best able to record sensory experiences, researchers note. That's why parents should give a baby all possible opportunities, within the limits of safety and common sense, to learn through a wide variety of sensory stimuli. Your baby needs great experience in hearing, seeing, touching, moving—and to a lesser extent, in tasting and smelling.[2]

Yet many of our common baby-care practices drastically curtail an infant's chances to see and hear and touch. Typically, a baby is kept most of the time in a bassinet lined with solid-color material, where his view is limited to a white ceiling. Or, he's placed on his stomach, where he can see nothing but the sheet or the bassinet sides. Later on, he may be graduated to a crib, where his outlook is still blocked by padded crib bumpers. Even when he goes for a ride in his buggy, he's buried deep inside, and his view straight up is partially cut off by the hood. He is considered a "good" baby if he accepts these restrictions without too much complaint. If he protests, he may be ignored for fear he might become "spoiled."

It's only somewhat better when a baby is old enough to sit up by himself. Then he's often corralled in a playpen or strapped into a seat, both of which continue to restrict his motor activity. The amount of sensory and motor stimuli he can obtain for himself, and thereby his mental development, is curtailed.

This way of treating small babies seemed to make sense in the days when they were considered to be almost vegetables, whose primary need was to rest and grow undisturbed and unpressured. When mothers were told that their infants could see only vague, shadowy shapes and couldn't focus their eyes for weeks, there seemed to be little point in providing them with interesting things to look at. When mothers were taught that their babies could only act instinctively and were too young to learn or think, it seemed silly to even consider giving them a wealth of learning experiences. When mothers were taught that human development proceeded automatically in predictable stages, according to some sort

of unrushable, inner timetable, there seemed no reason
to increase the stimulation in a baby's environment.

Now new studies are changing these views.

Researchers have found that even newborn infants in
hospital nurseries can focus their eyes on shapes and
show obvious enjoyment in seeing them, provided they
are not crying or physically uncomfortable.[3] Babies pay
more attention to a second or third bright shape than
they do when the same design is shown to them repeatedly. Even newborns prefer complicated patterns, like
concentric circles or diagonal stripes to solid-color shapes.
Infants less than one month old are able to distinguish
stripes as narrow as one-eighth of an inch at a distance
of ten inches.[4] New research on the vision of babies
shows far less inability to focus and less drifting of the
eyes than previously thought.

Even in newborn infants during the first days of life,
learning is a "rapid and reliable" process, reports Dr.
Lewis P. Lipsitt, director of an eight-year study on the
subject, conducted by Brown University researchers at
Providence Lying-In Hospital, Providence, Rhode Island.
Babies just one day old can learn to distinguish between
odors, says Dr. Lipsitt, noting "it's not just a physical,
but a mental reaction; it demonstrates that the infant is
integrating information." [5]

Babies two and three days old learned to turn their
heads to get a sweetened liquid. They could discriminate
between tones. They could distinguish between round
nipples and rubber tubing placed between their lips. And
they showed that they were actually learning, by changing their responses to stimuli as a result of previous
experiences.

Our present ways of trying to describe how learning
occurs just aren't adequate to account for the marvelous
learning abilities and accomplishments of babies, concludes Dr. Joseph Church, professor of psychology at
Brooklyn College of the City University of New York.[6]
He has been collecting biographies of the learning experiences of children during the first two years of life,
as observed by their mothers. He notes that the babies

demonstrate "every sort of learning process yet conceived and perhaps even some without any precedent in our formal conceptual schemes."

Just how much difference the environment you create for your baby does make can be seen from the research of Dr. Burton White and his colleagues at Harvard University's Laboratory of Human Development.

Dr. White and his associates made intensive studies of babies between birth and the age of six months, trying to pinpoint how much of their development is an automatic result of age and growth, how much can be changed by the way in which they are handled, and how much they are influenced by their surroundings.

Because home environments vary so much and are difficult to measure precisely, Dr. White did his research in a Massachusetts hospital, where infants awaiting adoption lived in a special wing for several weeks or months. Here all the babies were exposed to the same environment, which was enriched in different, but measurable, ways.

First, researchers observed a control group of infants carefully, for long periods of time, charting what the babies did every minute they were awake. They developed complicated devices for measuring the infants' abilities to focus their eyes and to follow moving objects visually and for recording blink reactions to approaching objects.

All of the babies in Dr. White's studies were physically and mentally normal. Like many infants in private homes, those in the control group were kept in cribs lined with solid white bumpers. They lay on their backs; they were changed when necessary, picked up for feedings at four-hour intervals, and bathed daily by nurses who were devoted and kind—but very busy.

As newborns, these infants were visually alert—that is, paying obvious attention with their eyes—only about 3 percent of the daylight hours, Dr. White discovered. Gradually, during the first few weeks of life, they began to pay more attention to the world around them with their eyes. At an average of fifty days of age, they discovered their hands with their eyes. Fascinated by their fingers, they increased their visual attention sharply, to about 35 percent of daylight hours by the age of sixty days. For the next few weeks, these babies spent much of their waking time watching what their fists and fingers were doing.

Hand-watching tapered off a little between the ages of thirteen and fifteen weeks for the babies in Dr. White's control group. But another spurt in visual activity occurred at one hundred and five to one hundred and twenty days, when the infants were put into open-sided cribs where they had more chance to look out. About this time, their visual attention jumped to 50 percent of daytime hours.

Dr. White also studied the abilities of infants to follow an object with their eyes as it approached or receded. Until the babies were about thirty days old, Dr. White found, they could focus on and track a moving target only at one specific distance—usually about 7½ inches from their eyes. But by the age of one and one-half months, their visual accommodation had improved. At four months, babies had visual accommodation skills comparable to those of normal adults.

The precise steps by which an infant learns to co-ordinate the movements of his hands and eyes, so that he can reach out accurately and grasp what his eyes are seeing, were also studied.

Typically, at about the age of two months, the babies in Dr. White's control group began to swipe haphazardly at objects with their hands: By about seventy-eight days, they could raise one hand deliberately, and a few days later, both hands. Soon after they were three months old, they could bring both hands together in front of them to clasp an object offered to them.

At fifteen weeks of age, these babies learned to turn toward an object they could see. At eighteen weeks, they could grasp by moving one hand toward the object, glancing back and forth from the object to the approach-ing hand before making contact. What Dr. White calls "top level reach," or skilled one-handed grasping directed by the eyes, was achieved at about one hundred and fifty days of age.

Yet this normal pattern of eye-hand development, so enormously important between the ages of one and one-half and five months, is "remarkably plastic," according to Dr. White. It can be speeded up considerably by enriching the baby's environment.

For example, after he had recorded developmental data for babies as they were normally cared for in the hospital, Dr. White began to change and enrich their surroundings. First, he arranged for nurses to have time to give one group of babies twenty minutes of extra handling every day when they were between the ages of six and thirty-six days. After this period, these babies were more visually active than the control group—but their developmental timetable stayed about the same.

Next, Dr. White added more stimuli to the environment of another group of infants. The white padded bumpers on their cribs were replaced by bumpers and sheets with a multicolored, printed design, starting when the babies were thirty-seven days old. After each daytime feeding, the bumpers were removed from the cribs, and the babies were placed on their stomachs so they could see the activities of the hospital ward around them. A special stabile was erected over each crib to give the babies something colorful to look at.

The stabile, which Dr. White designed, contained a small mirror in which the baby could see his face, two rattles low enough for him to grasp, a rubber squeeze toy that made a noise, and a gaily colored paper decoration at the top. These objects were mounted on a red-and white-checkered pole at various distances from the infant's eyes, and the entire stabile was suspended above his head, where he could easily see it.

The babies in this enriched environment were a few days slower in beginning to observe the motions of their own hands and not quite so visually alert at the start of the experimental period. But soon, they became much more attentive and active than the control babies. In less than one month, they learned how to reach out and grasp accurately—a skill that took the control babies three months to develop. They reached the stage of top-level grasping at about ninety-eight days of age —about two months sooner than the infants in the normal environment.

For a third group of infants, Dr. White tried a modified environment. This time, instead of adding the bright stabile to the crib on the thirty-seventh day of each baby's life, he mounted a pacifier against a red- and white-patterned background on each side of the crib rails at an easy distance from the infant's eyes. Then, on the sixty-eighth day of life, he replaced these with the stabile.

These infants made the fastest gains of all, apparently because the stimuli in their environment were better matched to their basic needs. They were much more visually alert and active than the other groups of babies. They began swiping at objects several days earlier than control babies. They began guiding their hand visually toward an object at about the sixty-fifth day of life —twenty days earlier than babies in the normal environment. They reached top-level grasping at the eighty-ninth day of life, in contrast to one hundred and fifty days for the infants in the normal environment.

Dr. White's continuing experiments show to what a great extent "developmental landmarks" in early childhood can be speeded up by changes in the environment. And they demonstrate what major gains can be achieved by relatively small changes in an infant's surroundings.

Dr. White calls these changes "of striking magnitude." For when an infant is able to reach and grasp and learn from his sense of touch at the age of three months, he can learn more—and wants to learn more—from his environment than a baby who doesn't develop this skill until he is six months old. The infant who is paying attention visually 45 percent of the day learns more than the one who is attentive only 20 percent of the time.

You will see a great variety of learning activities occurring in your own infant, if you watch for them—and if you give him enough learning opportunities. Following are guidelines suggesting what you can expect as your baby grows and how you can foster his learning. But your best guide will be the reactions of your child. Watch him. Observe him carefully. Learn from him, even as he is learning from you.

(These age-level divisions aren't hard and fast stages. Some babies develop more quickly. Some go more slowly. Most grow and learn unevenly, by jumps and spurts, with plateaus and even some backtracking. If you begin providing your child with extra stimulation early in his life, you'll probably need to read ahead of these general age classifications to find ideas for him.)

BIRTH TO SIX MONTHS

You should begin filling your infant's life with sensory stimuli and motor activity the first week you bring him home from the hospital. Once you are aware of your baby's urgent and real need for this stimulation, you'll discover many delightful ways in which to provide it.

It isn't as difficult as it sounds. You can easily tell when a stimulus is effective, or when your infant is too sleepy or too hungry to care, or whether he's just not interested. Your baby will concentrate intently on sights and sounds and movements that interest him. And he'll fuss and cry when he's bored. When he's fed, changed, bubbled, and safely safety-pinned, but still crying, you can often quiet him by giving him something fascinating to look at, to feel or to hear, or by rhythmic motor activity.

As you come to know him better, you can also tell by his reactions the infrequent times when he's had enough stimulation—it's usually when he's been tickled or jiggled—and needs to be rocked or nursed or back-rubbed or soothed to sleep. But too much stimulation is comparatively rare, and almost all babies don't receive nearly enough.

From the first day of his life, your baby will enjoy having something interesting to look at. You can hang a bright shape or colorful mobile over his bed, make it move whenever you are in the room—and get him a new one every few days. (They are easy to construct yourself.) You can move your infant's crib about the room to vary his view. You can use bright colors in his room wherever possible, instead of hospital white or wishy-washy pink. You can tack or tape bright pictures on his wall. You can carry him from room to room with you and encourage him to look at objects in your house and outside of the window. You can put him in a safe, padded spot in the kitchen where he can watch you preparing meals and listen while you talk to him.

During the first few weeks of life, if your infant is crying and you pick him up and put him on your shoulder, he will usually stop crying and start looking around—at least for a short time. This visual alertness can be of major importance in your baby's very early learning, research at Stanford University School of Medicine suggests. This particular combination of a parent's soothing along with an opportunity to look about seems to be ideal for learning in very young infants, according to the Stanford study.[7]

As soon as your baby can hold his head up, buy a contemporary version of a cradle board—a canvas sling that holds him on your back or your hip, leaving your hands free. It's a convenient way to tote your baby along, and it gives him a wealth of sensory stimuli, even if you just pack him around the house with you occasionally.

A playpen and an inclined infant's seat make more sense during the first few months of your baby's life than they do later on. At this age, your aim should be to give your infant a wider view of his world, and both playpen and seat are better than bassinet, crib, or buggy for this purpose. It's when a playpen and seat are used to restrain a crawling baby from physically exploring his environment that they begin to limit development.

The foundation of language is laid during the earliest weeks of life, too. You should begin talking to your baby from the very first time you hold him. You should vary your tone of voice as you greet him in the morning, change him, feed him, put him to bed. Take his attempts to communicate with you seriously and respond—for even in the first weeks of life he'll learn how to tell you by his cry when he is hungry, hurt, colicky, or bored.

Soon, your baby will begin babbling, practicing vowels, consonants, syllables—sounds of every type. Linguists say that a baby makes all the basic units of sound in every language on earth during the first year of his life. But eventually, he will discard those which are not a part of the language he hears in his home. As an adult, he'll never again be able to make some of these sounds, even if he studies a language in which they are used.

Do listen interestedly when your baby babbles at you. When he stops, talk back to him. This will help him get the idea of what language is all about. When he makes the same sound consistently and deliberately, you can repeat it to him. But generally, you should avoid baby talk because your infant needs your example to learn correctly. Sing to your baby, too, and play records for him.

Dr. Fowler, for example, began an informal program of stimulation for his daughter Velia at birth.[8] As she was being changed and fed and bathed and played with, her parents would direct her attention to different objects and name them. Velia said her first clear words, "ball" and "dog," at the age of eight months. At fourteen months, she could say one hundred words and double that number by fifteen months. She began speaking in two- and three-word sentences by the age of fourteen months and in complete, simple sentences of four to eight words by eighteen months, with occasional compound sentences containing ten to fifteen words.

Velia's vocabulary at this point was unusually rich, including such words as "hippopotamus," "chrysanthemum," "spaghetti," and "theater," reports Dr. Fowler. Although she substituted a "v" sound for "th," her speech was exceptionally clear and her words complete.

In comparison, the average child can use only about three words by his first birthday, about nineteen by the age of fifteen months, twenty-two words by eighteen months, and about two hundred and seventy by his second birthday. Many of these words are pronounced so indistinctly and individualistically that only a mother can understand them—and sometimes even she can't. Most children don't string even two or three words together into a sentence until they have reached their second birthday.

At the age of two, Velia's I.Q. was tested to be 170, or higher, and her father then taught her to read, easily and happily, using play-based techniques, as a research project for which he received his doctorate. Dr. Fowler believes that Velia's high abilities would not have developed without the extensive intellectual stimulation she received, starting during the first weeks of life.

Physical movement is another major way in which your baby develops his intelligence. There is considerable evidence that the tactile-kinesthetic sense is the basic avenue of very early learning. Movements generate a great number and variety of sensory stimuli and sensory information, which is stored in the brain, accumulating and becoming interrelated until the baby has an organized body of information learned from movement exploration.

To this basic tactile-kinesthetic information, a baby then relates stimuli he gains through his eyes and his ears, his nose and his taste buds. A newborn probably learns to recognize his mother by the sensory stimulus of being cuddled close against her, and to anticipate feeding by the bodily position in which he is being held and the feeling of the nipple against his lips. But soon, he will associate the visual stimuli of seeing his mother and hearing her voice with the tactile-kinesthetic information he has already acquired.

Later on, as his brain accumulates more information gained from movement and touch and he has had a chance to receive much more visual stimuli, your baby will begin to rely more on seeing than on touching. Eventually, he will learn primarily by means of his eyes. But even as a two- or three-year-old, he will still feel a great need to touch new objects, to verify the visual stimuli, to learn through more than one sensory route.

Adults do the same thing when they finger a fabric they consider buying or handle a dish as they browse around a china shop.

To build up this basic body of sensory information obtained from movement, your baby needs great freedom and opportunity to touch, to move about, to manipulate objects, to reach, to grasp, to learn to release. He also should have as much freedom as possible—consistent with his safety and health—from constricting clothing and from a confining bassinet.

How a baby's environment can inadvertently retard development is illustrated by an observation Dr. Piaget relates regarding his three youngsters. Both Laurent and Lucienne reached the stage at which they could follow the movements of their hands with their eyes shortly after they were two months old. But Jacqueline didn't until the age of six months. The reason for the delay in development, suggests Dr. Piaget, was that she was born in the winter. So that she could be kept outside in the sun as much as possible, which her parents thought desirable at the time, her hands were usually mittened and her arms tucked under blankets.

During the first months of your baby's life, you can help him pour tactile-kinesthetic stimuli into his growing brain in many ways. You can give him opportunity during his waking hours to lie on a pad in the playroom or on the floor, where he can move his arms and legs freely without hitting the sides of the bassinet. You can put him on his stomach on a hard surface so he can eventually learn to roll himself over. You can hang a plastic ball or bell on the side of his crib for him to bat. You can suspend a simple toy from a piece of elastic so he can watch it move and learn to pull on it.

Most important, you can remember that your baby isn't an invalid who needs to live in bed and to be quiet almost all of the time, but a living, growing child who needs activity, exercise, and stimulation.

You can give your infant interesting textures to grasp: swatches of material like velvet, silk, wool, burlap, and satin; small blocks of foam rubber; a piece of sponge;

tissue paper that crinkles with a fascinating sound; simple wooden toys. (Do remember that he'll try to put almost everything in his mouth, so make sure that the materials are too big to swallow and watch him carefully.) You can touch his fingers gently with an ice cube and with a just-warm hot water bottle. You can play nursery rhyme games which involve counting fingers and toes, or touching eyelids, ears, nose, and mouth.

As your infant begins to coordinate his hands and eye muscles, you can encourage him to reach out for objects, and when he has grasped them, let him experiment freely in banging, testing, shaking, and using them in any exploratory way that is safe. Peek-a-boo, with a man's handkerchief laid across your baby's eyes, makes a delightful game as soon as you are sure that your baby can grasp the cloth and pull it away.

If you observe closely during the third, fourth, and fifth months of your baby's life, you'll probably notice that he likes repetition. He makes the same movements again and again. He may spend a surprising amount of time handling and looking at an object that intrigues him, or repeating motions of his hands. If you rock him or bounce him on your knee and then stop, he'll often try to imitate your motion to get you to repeat your activity. If you do, he'll smile and laugh delightedly.

This experimentation with familiar activity is based on preliminary months of absorbing a great variety of sensory stimulation, both Dr. Piaget and Dr. Hunt have noted. In turn, repetition of familiar patterns leads into the next stage—that of fascination and curiosity in exploring new objects and activities. Dr. Hunt says that "the more different visual and auditory changes the child encounters during the first stage, the more of these will he recognize with interest during the second stage. The more he recognizes during the second stage, the more of these will provide novel features to attract him during the third stage." [9]

These changes in your baby's basic motivation for learning, according to Dr. Hunt, explain what Dr. Piaget means by his statement that the more a child has seen and heard, the more he wants to see and hear.

SIX TO TWELVE MONTHS

By the time your baby can sit up by himself, he'll be enormously fascinated with looking at and handling objects of every kind, and he needs great opportunity to do so. By this age, too, he's ready to do more than just look and touch and record these sensory stimuli in his brain. He's beginning to make some primitive experiments with cause and effect. He'll pick up a small block and drop it out of his reach, cry until an adult returns it, then drop it again, testing repeatedly just what relationship there is between the movement of his fingers and the bang on the floor.

In fact, the force of gravity is the one constant point around which a baby systematizes all the spatial relationships he is working out for himself during his early sensory-motor stage of life, suggested Dr. Newell C. Kephart when he was director of the Achievement Center for Children, Purdue University.[10] (This *may* make you feel a little bit better about picking up your baby's toys for the eighty-seventh time in a morning.)

At this stage, you can stimulate your baby's mental development by providing him with a changing variety of objects to touch, taste, bang, throw, grasp, and shake. Toys with safe, moving parts that can be attached to playpen bars and plastic blocks with bells inside make stimulating toys. So does an unbreakable mirror with hard-rubber edging. Sponge toys, floating animals, boats, and pouring utensils encourage him to experiment with water in his bathtub. He'll want one or two cuddly, stuffed animals with interesting textures, especially for going to sleep.

But you needn't spend much money to buy toys for your baby. He can find great delight and learning stimuli in a block put into a small kettle, in a nest of lightweight plastic bowls, in a small cardboard box with a piece of tissue paper inside, and in scores of simple objects already in your home.

As soon as your baby is ready to begin moving forward with a crawling motion, he needs to be taken out of the playpen and put on a hard surface, where he can propel himself along. You can encourage him to start crawling by putting toys just out of his reach and by cheering him on.

There's increasing evidence that crawling is important to the development of a baby's intelligence and his visual development because of the complex and coordinated sensory stimuli this activity sends to the growing brain. This is a good reason for not putting your baby into a walker, for not trying to hurry him into walking, and for giving him all the opportunity you can safely arrange so he can get around on hands and knees by himself. One good way to promote crawling is to put your baby on his stomach on the floor frequently when he's five, six, and seven months old.

The best learning stimuli you can provide for a crawling baby is a big room with a clean floor, where he is free to move about safely and freely for a large part of his waking hours. The room should be kept warm enough for your baby to be barefoot, and he should be dressed in overalls, with padded knees, if possible. Everything that can be broken, toppled, swallowed, pulled over, or tripped on should be removed from the room and all exits and stairs gated and locked. Electrical outlets should be capped over, and electrical cords should be put well out of reach, where your baby can't pull or chew on them.

The point is that your baby should be free to explore and manipulate without discouraging and frustrating "Nos" and "Don'ts" from adults—although he does need your watchful, interested supervision. If you continually snatch objects out of his hands, slap his fingers, and scold him, he'll be apt to get the idea that it's wrong to be curious and naughty to investigate.

You will, of course, eventually need to teach your youngster not to touch objects which don't belong to

him and to have respect for the property of others. But
he is too young now for you to be sure he will heed
and remember your prohibitions, although he will sometimes. Your baby will learn more easily and obey with
less fuss in a few more months if he is getting ample
sensory stimuli and your "Nos" don't frustrate his learning attempts completely.

The room in which your baby does his crawling should
contain at least one low shelf of toys and objects your
baby can handle. A shallow box can also be used, but
the usual toy box is too deep to be effective and produces
only confusing clutter. A pot and pan cupboard offers
delightful sight, sound, and touch stimuli for a crawling
baby, if you can arrange your kitchen so he can explore
safely. But he shouldn't be permitted in the kitchen unsupervised, particularly after he is able to pull himself
up on his feet.

If the weather is suitable and you can supervise him
closely, you can let your baby crawl outdoors on the
grass. Opportunity to crawl on carpet, on wooden floors,
and on linoleum and vinyl flooring can also vary the
stimuli your baby's physical activity is sending to his
brain.

The first day your baby crawls an inch, you need to
safety-check every place in your house your baby can
possibly go. It's almost impossible to overestimate the
speed with which a crawling baby can pull a tablecloth
off a just-set table. Or reach a hand up to pat a hot
electric burner. Or locate a poisonous household cleaner
under your kitchen sink and swallow a dangerous dose.
Or pick up a pin or a button you had no idea had fallen
on the rug.

It's estimated that there are 250,000 household
products on the market today which could kill a baby
if swallowed. Some of these carry a poison warning.
Most do not. No cleaning agent of any kind, no detergent,
furniture polish or bleaches should be kept where a baby
could possibly get them. If you've been in the habit
of leaving medicine on a night table or on a kitchen
counter, change now. Many drugs can be lethal to a

baby. Aspirin is the greatest single cause of death by poison in small children, and even the pleasant-flavored baby aspirin can be fatal in large enough quantities. Babies can even die from drinking whiskey or other liquor stored where they can reach it.

You will, of course, have to put your baby in a playpen at times to keep him safe when you can't supervise him closely. But you shouldn't keep him there as a matter of course during most of his waking hours. A baby howling in a playpen from boredom has just as urgent a need for mental stimulation as a baby crying from hunger has a need to be fed. You aren't spoiling him or giving in to him or entertaining him when you help him learn, any more than you are when you feed him.

It will disrupt your household considerably to construct a home environment that gives a crawling baby optimum opportunity for learning, rather than one designed primarily for the convenience of adults and the protection of their possessions. But it is tremendously important for your baby during this early sensory-motor period.

During the second half of his first year of life, your baby will be making greater progress in matching up stimuli for all his senses. He can now anticipate your coming by the sound of your footsteps—and differentiate between those of his father and his mother. He may discover how to make the television louder by twisting a little knob. And he will start crawling toward the cookie box if you mention the word.

He'll also be learning more about space and time, about cause and effect, and about the sequence of activities. He'll scream now when you take him into the pediatrician's waiting room because he can remember that the last visit included an injection. He may cry when he sees a baby-sitter entering the house, not because he dislikes her, but because he knows that her presence means his parents will go away.

Your baby is now beginning to associate words with objects, although he won't be able to form most of the words himself for several months. You can encourage his development of language by naming an object he is looking at or holding: "cup," "bottle," "toast," "block." You can put his actions into words for him: "Now we're putting on your overalls" and "Sit on my lap and we'll rock." In addition to this simple labeling, you should continue to talk with him conversationally whenever you are with him and, in turn, listen seriously to his vocalizations.

When your baby makes a sound like "Mama" or "Dada" by accident, you can react with obvious delight; you'll want to, anyway, and it will help your baby understand that he can make noises which have meaning. At this age, it can be helpful if you recognize and use his first few approximations of words—perhaps "wawa" for water or "Nana" for grandmother.

When Diane, for example, began to make the sound "baba" rather consistently in her babbling her mother told her three-year-old that his little sister was trying to say "brother." Paul puffed up with pride and joy to discover that the baby's first word meant him. He responded eagerly and lovingly whenever Diane said "baba," and the baby quickly learned to associate the sound with him. The family used the syllables until Diane was able to say "Paul" properly.

Once your baby has grasped the idea that things and people have names, and that he can form the names himself, it's better to shift to correct pronunciations for every word. Your child's speech will progress more rapidly and efficiently if you do.

You should begin reading to your baby from children's books by the time he's ten months old. Find a quiet place and time, when your baby isn't engrossed in crawling or trying to pull himself up on his feet, and cuddle him close while you read. Picture books that show familiar objects are good. So are simple stories. Encourage your baby to look at the pictures and to attempt to turn the pages. A few excellent books for very young children also involve the sense of touch by including sandpaper whiskers on a daddy's face to rub, or a ring-shaped cut-out in the page to slip a finger through, or a cotton-soft bunny to feel.

Your baby won't understand every word that you read to him at this age, of course. But he will grasp more than most parents realize. And he will enjoy the cuddling and the sound of your voice and begin to associate books with pleasant feelings.

Your baby's experiments with banging, dropping, throwing, picking up and releasing, poking, pushing, and pulling will continue at this age. But if you observe closely, you'll see more purpose in what he is doing, more serious concentration on the results of his actions in contrast to the random behavior of a few months earlier. He now gets enormous delight from his increasing skill in coordinating thumb and forefinger to grasp and let go of small objects. He enjoys pursuing crumbs around the tray of his high chair and has great fun with small toys and objects of all kinds. (Do remember they'll still go into his mouth and must still be large enough to be safe.)

The amount of sensory stimuli and motor activity your baby has had during the first half of his first year of life will already be reflected in his learning behavior, as Dr. Piaget points out. For the more stimuli he has been able to store away in his brain and the more points of reference he now has for new objects in his environment, the more curious he will be and the more eagerly he will go about exploring his surroundings, instead of reacting with fear or indifference to new sights and new experiences.

ONE YEAR TO EIGHTEEN MONTHS

When your moppet discovers how to pull himself up into a standing position and to take a few staggering steps while hanging on to a low coffee table or chair and finally to walk independently, he'll begin to get a fresh perspective on old, familiar territory, and his intense interest in exploration will increase. His curiosity now seems insatiable. He can push, pull, climb, grab, pick up the tiniest objects, and move about with surprising speed. His attention span is short. His energy seems triple that of adults caring for him. And his ability to get into everything will exhaust his mother long before he is ready to stop and nap.

If it is tempting to keep an infant in his crib most of the day because it's easier, it's even more tempting to confine a year-old youngster to a playpen, despite his obvious and loud objections. Some parents do prefer penning up a toddler to putting away their breakable and dangerous possessions for the sake of his free exploration. They argue that a baby should be taught to conform to their way of life and be confined in a playpen or room until he can. This can be a costly mistake, in terms of the child's developing intelligence. For the opportunities for exploring, touching, manipulating, throwing, pushing, pulling, and experimenting are even more important during the second year of life than the first.

Babies growing up in crowded slum homes probably do not suffer greatly from lack of sensory stimuli during the first year of life, says Dr. Hunt.[13] They may even have the opportunity to hear more and see more than babies in middle-class families who are tucked away in clean, quiet, unstimulating cribs. The deprivation that leads to school failure and is apparently difficult or impossible to reverse completely by the age of five or six, probably begins when the youngster learns to walk. Now, he's a nuisance in his crowded home. His activities are apt to be sharply curbed. He has little chance for new experiences, new stimulations. And his opportunity to hear and use language in a rich, stimulating way is limited.

Further confirmation of the vital importance of a child's home environment starting at about age twelve months comes from the long-term Harvard Preschool Project. It is conducting ongoing research aimed at gaining basic, accurate knowledge about how young children develop ideally. The research group, headed by Dr. Burton White, has reached these conclusions: the most critical age in the development of superior, competent children is between one and three years. The most crucial requirements for competent growth are freedom to explore in a safe environment and encouragement and help in learning language. And the key to superior development is what a mother does—or doesn't do—during these two dozen months.

The Harvard Preschool Project started out to discover why there are such great differences in the abilities of six-year-olds. These differences have become a major national problem because of the difficulties they create in schooling, and because it seems to be almost impossible for the least competent youngsters to overcome their handicaps.

One of the first things the Harvard researchers did was define precisely what the results of ideal rearing during the first six years of life should be. What is a competent, successful six-year-old?

The Harvard researchers began by studying hundreds of preschool children with a great variety of educational, ethnic, and socio-economic backgrounds. They talked to teachers, parents, pediatricians. They gave tests. They observed youngsters carefully at home, at school, on playgrounds, in supermarkets. Then, they chose two groups of children. Half of these youngsters were rated high in overall competence, "able to cope in superior fashion with anything they met, day in and day out." The other half had no physical or mental abnormalities, but were "generally of very low competence."

Next, the researchers set out to analyze exactly what the differences between the competent and incompetent six-year-olds were. They observed the children carefully over an eight-month period, often recording their activities with minute-by-minute evaluations. The researchers didn't find much difference between the first graders in physical skills and abilities. But they did pinpoint several abilities that distinguished the competent six-year-olds from those who had poor ability to cope with their surroundings.

These are the characteristics that mark a competent six-year-old, according to the Harvard researchers:

- He is able to get and hold the attention of adults in socially acceptable ways, such as talking to them, showing them something, moving toward them, or touching them.

- He can use adults as resources when a task is clearly too difficult. He can get information or assistance in a variety of acceptable ways, without trying to get an adult to take over the task.

- He can express both affection and hostility to adults and to other youngsters his age.

- He can lead and also follow other children his age in a variety of activities. He can give suggestions, direct play, act as a model for others to imitate, and follow the suggestions of others.

- He is able to compete with other children his age.

- He can take pride in his own achievements, in something he has created, possesses, or is doing.

- He can play-act an adult role or adult activity, or talk about what he wants to do when he grows up.

- He can make good use of language and grammar and has a good vocabulary for his age.

- He is aware of discrepancies, inconsistencies, and other kinds of irregularities in the environment and can talk about them, and can occasionally act on these inconsistencies appropriately.

- He can anticipate consequences and act on them or talk about them.

- He can use abstract concepts and symbols, such as numbers, letters, and rules, in an organized way.

- He can put himself in someone else's place and can show an understanding of how things look to another person.

- He can make interesting associations, relating scenes, objects, or discussions to past experiences.

- He has the executive ability to plan and carry out activities that involve several steps.

- He can use resources effectively, choosing and organizing people and/or materials to solve problems.

- He can do two things at once, or concentrate on

one activity and still keep track of what is going on around him.

Once the Harvard researchers had a working definition of a competent six-year-old, their next step was to trace how children acquire these abilities and what factors in their home life favor the development of these traits. As a beginning, they analyzed their massive records, which covered the development of more than 100 preschool youngsters whom they had studied for more than two years, again sorting out the competent and the incompetent children. These studies turned up an unexpected finding: the competent three-year-olds had already developed most of the abilities that marked the competent six-year-olds. It was immediately obvious that the study needed to shift to an earlier age level.

Next, the Harvard researchers determined that there seemed to be very little difference at age one between those children who later turned out to be most competent and those who turned out to be least so. It was what had happened in the home when the youngsters were between the ages of one and three years that accounted for most of the crucial differences that were detectible by age three and almost impossible to change by age six, the Harvard researchers concluded.

In further studies, the Harvard group sought out families that had already produced highly competent or markedly incompetent children and that also had another child who was a year old or younger. With parents' permission, the Harvard researchers observed these babies and toddlers carefully for up to two years, correlating the degree of competence they developed with the child care practices in their homes.

Harvard researchers have now identified two areas of particular importance during the critical two years between ages one and three: freedom to move about in a stimulating environment, and the use of language.

In the first months after he learns to walk, about the time of his first birthday, a toddler's new-found ability to move around—combined with his innate curiosity—produces a great amount of work and stress for his mother or whoever is taking care of him. How his mother responds to this insatiable into-everything activity of her toddler helps determine whether he will be highly competent or incompetent by the time he is three yars old— and as a first grader.

Mothers who raise the least competent children use playpens and gates to restrict their children's freedom to explore and move around much more frequently than do the mothers whose youngsters are rated as highly competent, according to the Harvard findings. More effective mothers arranged their homes so that their children were protected from dangers in the house—and the houses were safe from damage by the youngsters. Then, they gave their toddlers free access to roam and explore. These mothers in particular made the kitchen safe and useful and provided kitchen cabinet space and safe utensils for their children's play, according to Dr. White.

Regardless of how successfully they are developing, one- and two-year-olds spend much more of their time interacting with objects than they do with people, according to the Harvard findings. One-year-olds average 88 percent of their time with objects and 12 percent with people; two-year-olds, 81 and 19 percent. Most, but not all, of the objects that hold the attention of toddlers are small and can be easily carried about.

Toddlers between the ages of twelve and fifteen months spend much of their time looking intently at objects (an activity the Harvard group labeled "gain information—visual") or simply exploring the qualities of these objects. But gradually, children begin to devote more time to mastering simple skills. The toddlers who turn out to be most competent later on put in more time mastering easy tasks during this age period than do the less competent youngsters. Poorly developing toddlers tend to spend far more time in idleness than other children; these statistics Dr. White calls "an index of emptiness."

The other major factor in how well a young child develops is the kind and amount of language his mother and the rest of his family give him, according to the Harvard studies. Talk between toddler and parent is often very brief, usually no more than a few words. Frequently the words come in direct response to what a youngster is doing or in answer to a short question from him, an interchange lasting no more than ten to thirty seconds. But because the language relates so directly to what the child is doing, because it comes when he is most open to learning, such talk is a powerful teaching device, the Harvard group reports.

"The mother's direct and indirect actions with regard to her one- to three-year-old children are, in my opinion, the most powerful formative factors in the development of the preschool child," says Dr. White. "I would expect that much of the basic quality of the entire life of an individual is determined by the mother's actions during these two years."

What makes an ideal mother for a one- to three-year-old? On the basis of the Harvard studies, Dr. White suggests: "Our most effective mothers do not devote the bulk of their day to rearing their children; most of them are far too busy to do so. Many of them, in fact, have part-time jobs.

"What they seem to do, often without knowing exactly why, is to perform excellently the functions of designer and consultant," notes Dr. White. "They design a physical world, mainly in the home, that is beautifully suited to nurturing the burgeoning curiosity of the one- to three-year-old." Such a home is full of "small, manipulable, visually detailed objects" and of opportunities to move about and climb, according to Dr. White.

The ideal mother he describes "is generally permissive and indulgent. The child is encouraged in the vast majority of his explorations. Although she is not usually involved directly in his activities, she is within earshot. When the child confronts an interesting or difficult situation, he goes to her and usually, but not always, is responded to by his mother with help or shared enthusiasm plus, occasionally, an interesting, naturally related idea.

"These effective mothers talk a great deal to their infants, and very often at a level the child can handle," according to Dr. White. In talking to their offspring, these women "consider the baby's purpose of the moment" and use language that is "at or slightly above his level of comprehension," and "do not prolong the exchange longer than the baby wants."

Dr. White also notes that "though loving and encouraging and free with praise, these mothers are firm. They set clear limits. They speak a disciplinary language the baby can understand. They don't over-intellectualize or expect the baby to do more than he is capable of."

Says Dr. White: "Effective mothers seem to be people with high levels of energy. The work of a young mother, without household help, is, in spite of modern appliances, very time- and energy-consuming. Yet we have families subsisting at a welfare level of income, with as many as three closely spaced children, that are doing as good a job in child rearing during the early years as the most advantaged families.

In the months after your toddler's first birthday, you can help increase his mental abilities by enlarging the environment in which he is permitted to play freely and safely. You can begin teaching him how to handle possible hazards—how to slide off an adult bed safely, feet first, and how to go up and down stairs sitting down, for example—so that he can be allowed wider freedom.

When it's warm and dry outside, you can fence off a sizable portion of your yard, make sure it contains no hazards, and let your toddler explore freely. Or tote him to the nearest park to let him roam. You will need to watch him closely, until he's over the habit of putting everything new and interesting into his mouth.

To help make this greater freedom possible, you will need to teach your toddler the meaning of "No." But it is important that you do not say "No" too often or too harshly, or your toddler may get the idea that you love him better when he isn't trying to explore and learn.

You need not resort to slapping a toddler's hands or spanking him to teach him to respect the rights and property of other people. Slapping hands to discourage active exploration usually teaches a moppet to slap back or to hit other, smaller children. Spanking carries a feeling of humiliation that isn't necessary in helping youngsters learn to behave properly. Spanking should be used rarely, only with toddlers too young to understand your words, and only when they are in immediate danger— reaching up to touch a hot stove burner, for example, or darting into the street.

For some adaptable, easy-going toddlers, it's enough to say "No," in a quiet, firm, disapproving voice, pointing out what is forbidden and offering a substitute object or activity. But most toddlers are more determined.

One good way to teach your toddler "No" without curtailing his exploratory drives or resorting to slapping or spanking is this: First, be quite clear in your own mind what objects you don't want your child to touch or what you don't want him to do. Keep this list as short as possible. Whenever your youngster reaches out to touch one of these objects or to do something you are forbidding, sit down in front of him and hold him securely by his forearms, so that his hands press against his cheeks and you can turn his head to face you squarely. Now he has to listen to you. Keep him facing you for about half a minute, saying firmly, "No" and "Don't touch."

When you let your toddler go, give him a hug. This method compels him to pay attention to you and lets him know that you mean what you are saying, but it avoids the idea of punishment. A toddler who is trying to fill his brain's urgent need for stimuli should not be punished; he merely needs to learn a lesson about the property rights of others and the dangers inherent in this fascinating world.

You'll probably have to repeat this strategem a few times. But after that, your child should understand the meaning of "No" and be convinced that you mean what you are saying. But you will have to be consistent. A little later, you can begin adding a short reason to the "Nos" you give your child: "No, that will burn you." "No, that is Daddy's," "No, that will break." This gives your child information he can apply in other situations (you are trying to raise a thinking, reasoning, independent adult—not obedience-train a puppy), and it will help convince him you aren't arbitrary and mean.

If you are giving your toddler plenty of opportunity to explore and fill his brain with sensory information, if you love him and he knows it, he'll accept your "Nos" in good grace—most of the time. If you begin this way, if you are warm and loving, if you understand your child's real needs, you'll find you almost never have any need to punish him, and discipline is just not a problem in your house.

Your toddler needs an increasing variety of toys and household objects he can manipulate and experiment with, without danger to himself or damage to your possessions. Look for toys that will give him practice with concepts like "in" and "out" and "inside" and "on top" and "larger" and "smaller." Nesting blocks or cups make good toys for year-old children. So do small boxes with lids. Stacking cones with wooden rings that fit around a central core intrigue toddlers. Other possibilities: wooden blocks he can line up to make a simple train or pile up into a tower; simple form boards containing a solid-color wooden triangle, square, and circle; a mailbox with geometric shapes to deposit and pull out below; simple dolls and cuddly animals.

He's ready now for push-and-pull toys of every variety. Bright balloons are inexpensive playthings that help a small child record basic information about air and gravity (but don't let him bite or suck on one). He'll have great fun with a large cardboard packing box, big enough for him to crawl inside, or with a sheet draped over a card table for a tent or cave. If your milk comes in rectangular paper containers, save them, wash and dry them thoroughly, and cover them with foil or bright contact paper for easy-to-handle blocks.

Stairs hold great fascination for a toddler. If you live in a ranch-type house where your moppet has no opportunity to practice, you'll find him fascinated with stairs you encounter on shopping trips or on visits to other homes. Some toy stores sell sturdy, three-step wooden stairs that intrigue one- and two-year-olds.

Water play (which must still be well supervised at this age) delights a toddler. Sponge toys to squeeze, sailboats, floating animals, and pouring utensils increase his pleasure in the bathtub—or outdoors in a clean, shallow, plastic pool.

Simple games of hide-and-seek played with familiar objects appeal to almost every toddler and help him form concepts about the permanence of objects not immediately in his sight. At least at first, you'll have to hide the objects while he's watching. But even then, he'll laugh with joy when he discovers them.

Another way to foster your toddler's intellectual development is to take him on many and varied short trips outside of your home. He'll enjoy visiting another moppet about his age, for example, even though he isn't nearly old enough to play with him at this point. Your child will be interested in just watching the other youngster and playing with different toys in the same room.

Outdoors, your toddler is better off in a stroller, where he can see more than in a buggy. But whenever you can, let him walk. You won't get very far, or make good time, but your youngster will have a better opportunity to pour a flood of sensory stimuli into his brain.

When you are outdoors with your toddler, encourage him to feel the rough bark of a tree, the prickliness of fresh-cut grass, the softness of a flower petal, the fur of the neighbor's friendly cat, the brittleness of an autumn leaf, the sting of snow, the gooiness of mud.

Use your trips to the supermarket to increase his opportunities for sensory stimuli. Buy a box of cookies and let him sample one. Let him try to drink from the cold arc bubbling out of the water fountain. Give him an orange to put in and out of a small paper bag. Let him feel the cold, frozen-food package, the heavy bag of sugar, the softness of a loaf of bread. None of this will take any longer than scolding him to sit still, or trying to prevent him from wriggling out of the shopping-cart seat in boredom.

In the six months after his first birthday, your baby will probably add only about two dozen words to his speaking vocabulary. But his understanding of what you are saying will increase enormously. You should talk to him whenever you are with him—when you change him, while he's eating, while you're doing housework and cooking, when you take him on an outing, when you rock him.

Asking a toddler to carry out a very simple direction can turn into a learning game in which he takes great delight, especially if you praise him and hug him when he's successful. He'll also enjoy games which involve his pointing to various parts of his body—nose, eyes, toes, knees, ears—or having you wash at his direction while he's in the bathtub.

You should continue to read to your toddler, of course —the same book again and again when he wants it, and new books, often, from the library, the book store or the supermarket. He'll enjoy looking through magazines with you, as you point out the babies, the toys, the chairs, an apple, a horse, a dog, a cat. Most toddlers like to have a stack of old magazines of their own, which they can look at by themselves.

The more language your toddler hears now, the larger and richer will be his vocabulary when he begins talking explosively, about the time of his second birthday.

Records and radio music can also provide your toddler with a considerable amount of auditory learning stimulation. There are many excellent records available for very young children—and many toddlers recognize and enjoy a few musical comedy songs and folk tunes. By eighteen months, a toddler who has had experience with handling and listening to children's records can usually tell one from another and has developed decided preferences about which record—and which side of the record—he wants to hear.

Research now indicates that this first eighteen months of your child's life, when his growth is most rapid, is one of the most important periods there will ever be in his life for increasing his mental abilities. This is contrary to earlier theories that an individual's intelligence is fixed and inherited, and mothers were advised to concentrate on the physical care of their infants and let the first grade teacher be the first to be concerned about intellectual development.

Many more studies are still needed to determine precisely how parents can best stimulate every type of baby to develop his intellectual potential to the greatest extent. But one thing is quite clear: Parents are the first and most influential teachers their child will ever have, and the environment they create for a youngster, from the day of his birth, will increase or decrease his mental abilities permanently.

5. The Insatiable Drive To Learn: Eighteen Months to Three Years

If you've ever doubted that small children have an urgent, insatiable drive to learn, just watch a moppet in the running-climbing-questioning-chattering-getting-into-everything months between the age of one and one-half and three. A two- or three-year-old can outexercise a professional athlete, outtalk a radio disk jockey, outrun most mothers in active training, and still have energy enough to fight going to bed. You're lucky if you can persuade your wiggler to sit still long enough to eat.

The months between one and one-half and three also include the four- to six-month stage called the "terrible twos." This is the frantic period—usually around two and one-half—when almost every moppet is in active rebellion against the restrictions placed on his free exploration by No-ing adults, and when he's most frustrated by his inability to become more independent and to "do it all by myself."

If you give your youngster more opportunity to learn

and to satisfy his curiosity and to become more competent, he'll be far easier to live with. If he has fascinating, challenging, learning materials to play with and ample opportunities to exercise his exploding interest in language, he'll not be as likely to empty the wastebasket into the goldfish bowl or throw food at the ceiling or flush socks down the toilet. And if you can help him learn to develop some degree of control over the everyday objects in his immediate environment, he won't experience nearly as much frustration.

During the one and one-half to three-year-old period, your child still needs great opportunity to learn through sensory-motor activity, just as he did in the earlier stages of his life. The more stimuli he can pour into his brain through looking, listening, tasting, smelling, touching, the more intelligent he will become.

But now, as he changes from a baby into a preschooler, he needs more than just a variety of sensory activities. These experiences must be integrated into patterns that help him understand relationships and form concepts. He is better able now to think, to reason, to draw conclusions, to use objects as symbols for ideas and activities. The great surge of language that comes between the ages of one and one-half and four not only helps him to express his thoughts, but also to formulate them.

During this period, too, your youngster's learning style begins to crystalize, and this will influence the way in which he goes about learning and his reactions to new experiences all the rest of his life. Your offspring's learning style is based partly on individual constitutional factors—whether he's quick or placid, impatient or relaxed, independent or clinging, happy-go-lucky or a born perfectionist. But it's determined to a greater degree by whether his attempts to learn at this age meet with enthusiasm and help from his parents, or whether the attempts are constantly frustrated, punished, or minimized.

How can you arrange a rich, stimulating, learning environment for a youngster between eighteen and thirty-six months of age—in view of today's expanding knowledge about how the brain develops? It isn't as big a job as it sounds.

Basically, you'll discover that your youngster gives you many useful clues to what his growing brain needs. You don't have to impose learning on him or try to teach him facts by rote. Your job, generally, is to see that he has opportunity and encouragement to teach himself.

Once your toddler has his walking well under control and can get where he wants to go without paying attention to his feet, his interest shifts to talking. He may only say fifteen to twenty-five words by the age of eighteen months. But by two, you won't be able to total up his vocabulary. By two and one-half, he'll hold up his end of a conversation quite effectively. And by three, you'll be wishing that he'd just stop talking for a few minutes so you can have some peace.

A great many parents do a superb job of helping their youngster acquire the mechanics of language—simply by filling the child's environment with good language models, by matter-of-factly correcting his mistakes, and by responding to and praising his efforts. The child delights in his increasing competence with words and in the power that words give him to function in his world. Parents usually enjoy his learning so much that they can't resist quoting him to any adult who will listen.

So receptive is a child of this age to the language he hears about him that he learns to speak it precisely as he hears it, whether it is French, Hebrew, Chinese, Bostonian English, Southern drawl, or slum patois. In homes where parents are too busy, too unschooled, too ignorant, or too uninterested to provide good models of language for their young children to absorb, the loss is almost impossible to make up later on without enormous effort. The lack of opportunity to learn correct language easily and naturally during the first few years of life is probably the major factor that depresses the learning abilities of culturally-deprived children.

The sooner your child learns to talk well enough to communicate his needs and feelings, the happier he will be and the easier he will be to live with. A considerable part of the frustrations and tantrums of the "terrible twos" is triggered by a moppet's inability to let his parents know what he wants. The whole area of discipline becomes simpler, too, when your child can understand language well enough so you can explain rules and safety regulations to him, instead of enforcing them physically.

You don't need to teach your child to talk by drilling him on syllables, of course. But you can help him absorb the words he needs most by talking to him casually whenever you are together. For example, you can name the part of his body he may not have learned yet as you bathe him—shoulders, heel, thigh, chest, chin. Then, when he knows them, let him tell you in what order he wants to be scrubbed. You can describe each article of clothing as you dress him—white undershirt, blue overalls, red sweater. Then, as he learns to say these words, let him have some choice about which clothes he'll wear. In the supermarket, you can ask him to bring you products he knows and to put them in your cart—crackers, paper napkins, bread, cake mix, salt.

You should not put words into your moppet's mouth before he has a chance to say them. (Sometimes when a two- or three-year-old is unusually slow to talk, it's discovered that his mother—or perhaps an older sister—is anticipating his needs so completely that the child feels no compelling urge to speak up himself and doesn't.) But there are tactful ways in which you can supply him with the words he needs but doesn't know.

For example, Stephen's ball is stuck so far under the sofa he can't reach it. He tries to explain the situation to his mother and asks her to get it out. But his vocabulary is so limited he can't make her understand, and he's getting so angry and frustrated he's about to cry.

Tactfully, his mother can hold out her hand and suggest, "Show me what you want me to do." When she sees the ball, she can remark in a friendly fashion, "Oh, your ball is stuck under the sofa. I'll pull it out for you." Or, she can say, "Let's get the yardstick to push it out." This sort of conversation supplies a small child with words he needs and helps him discover for himself how he can use language effectively.

Even at the age of eighteen months, when a youngster can say only a few words himself, it's not too soon to begin using language as a way of encouraging him to think, to see relationships, and to formulate concepts.

This doesn't mean that you should start lecturing him, or going into long explanations for everything you do. But in simple ways you can help him see cause and effect. ("If you turn the faucet just a little way, the water won't splash on you.") You can suggest time relationships. ("We're going to the grocery store now so we'll have hamburger to cook for lunch.") And you can supply facts that help him draw his own conclusions. ("This knife I am using is sharp, so I must be careful; scissors are sharp, too.")

As a parent, you should be teaching your child about the relationships between his actions and possible accidents by the time he's eighteen months old, according to the American Academy of Pediatrics.[1] "During this period, the child is learning the relationship between cause and effect," the pediatricians' organization points out. "In particular, he is learning that what happens may be the result of something he has done." Furthermore,

When minor accidents do occur—and they will— the child should be helped to understand the extent to which something he did caused the accident. In teaching the child the dangers of his environment and why he must avoid them, it is of little help to blame inanimate objects. If we say, "Oh, did the bad stove burn your hand?" we fail to show the youngster the true relationship between cause and effect, namely that the stove is hot, he placed his hand on it, and the hand was burned.

Compensating minor accidents with cookies, excitement, or gifts only convinces the child of his innocence. A careful, patient explanation, along with appropriate sympathy for the injury, will help teach the child about cause and effect and about his responsibility to be alert to dangers and obedient to parental rules.

At this age the child is learning obedience, which in some cases must be absolute. He should know and respond to the command, "No." But it should not be overused or it rapidly loses its effectiveness, or worse yet, stops the child from any investigation or experimentation. Its uses should be limited to situations that cannot be converted into learning situations.

As your two-year-old becomes able to use words himself, you can begin playing word games with him. An easy one to start with is: "I'm thinking of something in this room that is red; what is it?" You can play it with shapes and sizes and other variations—and while you're doing dishes, cleaning house, or even driving the car. As soon as your moppet can talk well enough, let him take his turn quizzing you.

By the time your moppet is two and one-half, you can change the games to: "I'm thinking of something that starts with the same sound as 'Timmy.'" Or, "I'm thinking of a word that has the same sound at the end as 'cat.'" Games of this type sharpen a child's ear for the sounds that make up our language and provide him with an excellent foundation for learning to read.

Variations of the "silence game" used in Montessori schools can delight two and one-half and three-year-olds and provide them excellent training in auditory perception. You play it, basically, by encouraging your child to remain just as quiet as he possibly can—for the purpose of hearing and identifying a sound. Perhaps it's a train or a plane or a siren in the distance, or water swishing through the dishwasher, or a key turning in a lock, or pudding just starting to bubble in a pot, or a bird outside the window.

Or, ask your child to play the silence game with his eyes shut and to guess what sound you make for him. Possibilities: a spoon striking a glass of water; keys jangling on a key ring; your hands clapping twice. Or, have him play the silence game and listen carefully until he hears you whisper a simple direction he is to follow or tell him about a small surprise.

When he becomes adept at these games, set a time limit of one or two minutes and see which one of you can hear and identify the most sounds during this interval.

These games make excellent antidotes for the mother who feels like she is screaming at her offspring half the time to attract his attention and for the youngster who has learned to tune his mother out so often he seldom hears her at all. They are also good ways to help a busy, active youngster make a tearless transition to bedtime, bathtime, or meals.

Between eighteen and thirty-six months, your child's pleasure in books and in reading will grow enormously with even the slightest encouragement from you. If you possibly can, begin the practice of reading to him regularly. If you make it just before bedtime, it helps him relax, gets him into bed happily in anticipation of the treat ahead, and establishes the habit of a quiet evening talking time you'll find invaluable at less communicative ages—like seven, eleven, and thirteen.

Let your two-year-old buy books of his own whenever you can afford it, even if they are just inexpensive paperbacks from the supermarket. Some PTA groups put on used-book sales as fund-raising projects, and here you can usually find stacks of hardcover children's books donated by parents whose youngsters have outgrown them; most are priced less than a dollar. By now, your moppet should be making some of his own choices in the library, too.

At this age, most youngsters prefer simple, factual stories about other small children, about animals, about what adults do, and about the world with which they are familiar. Their lives are already full of so much wonder and magic—at the world outdoors getting a shower bath when it rains, at the light switch that can chase away the night in a second, at water that gushes out of a faucet at a wrist's twist—that they don't appreciate fairy godmothers and magic lamps as much as six-, seven-, and eight-year-olds do. Two- and three-year-olds are still greatly intrigued with absorbing information about the world around them and forming concepts about it and their relationships to it. Some of the best-loved books of two- and three-year-olds tell what daddies do at work each day, about what they are like as small babies, about a child's pride in learning a new skill, or about a secret to surprise his family with.

Because two- and three-year-olds are so sensitive to language, most of them are fascinated by poetry. Even traditional nursery rhymes—the old English political satires which have no meaning for modern moppets—interest them because of their sound patterns.

But parents who make the effort to find meaningful poetry to read to their children find that they enjoy it far more than "Baa, Baa, Black Sheep" and "Mary, Mary, Quite Contrary."

Two- and three-year-olds find great delight in poems like Dorothy Aldis' "Naughty Soap Song:" [2]

> Just when I'm ready to
> Start on my ears,
> That is the time that my
> Soap disappears.
>
> It jumps from my fingers and
> Slithers and slides
> Down to the end of the
> Tub, where it hides.
>
> And acts in a most diso-
> Bedient way
> And that's why my soap's growing
> Thinner each day.

Or, her poem, "About Candy:"

> I say to lick a candy stick
> Until it's sharp enough to prick.
> If you have a lemon drop, then tuck it

Way inside your cheek and suck it.
To bite it would be very wrong
Because it would not last you long.

Better for today's two- and three-year-olds than Miss Muffet and her spider are poems like Aileen Fisher's "A Bug:" [3]

> *I saw a bug*
> *with twenty feet*
>
> *Go crawling up*
> *and down the street,*
>
> *And wondered if*
> *he stubbed ONE toe*
>
> *If he would ever*
> *really know.*

You can find collections of many such intriguing poems for very young children in almost every library—and a poetry anthology is a good Christmas or birthday gift for any child of two or over. There's nothing wrong with teaching your child nursery rhymes, of course, and most parents do simply because it's easy. There's nothing wrong with nonsense, either. But this is all that most preschool children get in the way of poetry. Your moppet will absorb more and enjoy rhymes more if they have meanings that fascinate him as much as the sounds do.

You will find your child wanting you to read the same poem or story seventeen times, even though both of you know it by heart. This is a characteristic need of children at this age level, and such repetition is important for them to gain mastery of the ideas and language patterns. It is not time wasted.

You can begin now to introduce your two-year-old to the idea that reading is just another form of language, that writing is just talk written down. You can show him what his name looks like in print. You can suggest that he dictate short notes to you to send to his grandparents or to his friends. You can point out the titles on books, the names on records, and the labels on grocery boxes. You can write memos to him, pin them on his bulletin board or tape them on his mirror, and read them to him the next day. You can answer any questions he asks about words. (If these steps make him eager to learn more, you may want to read ahead in Chapter 7 about teaching a pre-schooler to read, even before your child reaches his third birthday.)

Even though a moppet between eighteen and thirty-six months learns much verbally in an enriched home environment, he still does a great part of his learning via sensory-motor activities. He still needs great freedom and opportunity to touch, to manipulate, push, pull, put together, take apart, group, rearrange, throw, and explore. He still must learn by doing as well as by listening and looking.

This is not learning that you can impose upon him or lecture into him. It's learning he acquires on his own, by exploration and experimentation, by trying and sometimes failing. (Remember this, if you find yourself tempted to push him a little, or pressure him into learning.)

This need for constant, reliable perception from which a child can draw conclusions about the world around him is probably a major reason why youngsters at two and two and one half are so insistent upon routine and repetition. How can Johnny be sure just how far down a step is until he tries it over and over again? How can Sally learn that the same words written in her book always say the same thing unless she hears you read it in exactly the same way two dozen times? How can Tommy feel assured that the night will safely pass unless his frayed pink blanket and his teddy bear and his night light are all precisely in place?

A scientist's efforts to control conditions in his laboratory and to repeat experiments so he can test a theory are respected by his colleagues. Small children need the same respect and patience and understanding from adults in their absorbing efforts to control conditions and test out conclusions—even though they can't explain what they are trying to do, like the scientist.

Of course you can't let your pint-sized Galileo test the law of falling bodies by dropping eggs from the top of your kitchen counter. Nor can he experiment with the principles of aerodynamics by throwing rocks at the neighbor's windows. But understanding more about the needs of his growing brain may help you to be more patient when your moppet demands the same bedtime story thirteen nights in a row, or if he cries when you let the water out of the bathtub instead of waiting until he decides to do it.

Instead of being annoyed at your moppet's insistence on routine and repetition, you can take advantage of it to help him acquire habits of neatness and order and independence in personal care, as Dr. Montessori suggested decades ago.

A mother who uses Montessori techniques at home keeps her child's toys on low, open shelves where he can reach them easily and choose freely what he wishes to use. Each toy and learning material has its own specific location, and the youngster is encouraged to return it to this spot before he begins playing with something else. A small basket or box is used to keep parts of games together. She marks items which should be shelved together with bits of bright-colored tape. All the pieces of one wooden puzzle are identified with a smidgin of red tape on the back, for example; all the parts of another with green; all the equipment for a game is tagged with blue and kept in an open basket that is also marked with blue.

A low clothes rod and low pegs in his closet help make it possible for a small child to be orderly about his possessions. At this age, a youngster wants fiercely to become as independent as possible about his own dressing and undressing, as you know if you've ever seen a two and one-half-year-old on the verge of a tantrum because he can't button his shirt and won't give in and let his mother do it for him.

A small child who can manage his dressing and undressing—because of the tactful, behind-scenes planning of his parents—develops a great feeling of pride and competency. He has control of a particular feature of his environment, which gives him pleasure. And he has become independent of adult assistance in at least one area, at a stage in his life when he values this freedom enormously. If parents let a child grow past this sensitive period without helping him develop habits of orderliness, they often find themselves nagging at him for years about the state of his room and his belongings—with little observable results.

More than just neatness about possessions is involved in this sensitive period, according to Dr. Montessori. She felt that this stage of childhood could also be used profitably by parents to teach a youngster that tasks have a beginning and an end, that jobs begun should be finished, and that mental processes should be controlled and orderly, as well as physical surroundings.

A child's desire to be competent, to master as much of himself and his environment as possible, is particularly urgent when he is two, two and one-half, and three. If you take the time and effort to show a child how to perform many tasks, he will usually learn with great concentration, interest, and obvious satisfaction. In the long run, it will take less of your time and energy to help him learn than it will to cope with his negative behavior and to try to amuse him and keep him out of trouble.

But few parents bother to think through how and what they try to teach a small child—whether it's to wash hands, tie shoes, button a shirt, or set the table. Adults usually work too fast, too automatically, for a child to follow and imitate. Dr. Montessori urged that an adult seeking to help a child learn break down the activity into its component parts—the same technique modern educators call "programmed learning."

What precise steps are involved in buttoning a button? Adults do it so often without conscious thought that most of them can't describe the process without deliberately slowing down and thinking it through. But if you do break up the task of buttoning into its small, component steps and show your child clearly what these steps are, he will learn with delight and pride.

In her book about Montessori, *Learning How to Learn,* Nancy McCormick Rambusch describes seventeen steps by which a mother can successfully teach a small child how to wash his hands. This particular example has been criticized by some parents and nursery school teachers who feel that such a procedure is too ritualistic and unnecessary. They miss the point. By using these steps, a child can learn how to perform a necessary skill, successfully, by himself at an age when it gives him pleasure to do so. The alternatives are for the mother to continue to do it for him, which usually makes him impatient and rebellious. Or, he can do it inefficiently and unsuccessfully, which means his mother will nag, criticize, or send him away from the table to try again. The child need not continue to wash his hands in precisely the same way all the time, of course. The procedure will become automatic, and he will vary it as circumstances suggest. But he will be able to do it—at an age when he most wants to. Furthermore, the youngster learns a major lesson in how to go about learning. He discovers that there is a logical way to go about controlling his environment and accomplishing what he wants.

To help children isolate and practice the skills involved in dressing themselves, Dr. Montessori devised simple "dressing frames," which have since been updated for contemporary clothing design. Each square frame holds two pieces of cloth which can be fastened together in the center—by buttons, snappers, ties, buckles, laces, or a zipper. Three-year-olds in Montessori schools often spend thirty to forty-five concentrated minutes snapping and unsnapping, buckling and unbuckling—by their own free choice. These frames can now be purchased from several sources, or they can easily be made at home. (One point: In constructing a frame to teach tying, when your child is three or four years old, make the left-hand ties one color and the right-hand ties another. This makes it easier for a small child to follow the tying action.)

Using programmed learning techniques, you can help

your two- or three-year-old learn many household tasks that will give him immense satisfaction, such as polishing furniture, scrubbing a table top, shelling peas, washing plastic dishes, setting a low table.

It's important to remember that you are making it possible for your child to learn these skills because he wants to become more independent, and because it gives him satisfaction. When he scrubs or polishes, he will do it because the performance gives him pleasure. So discipline yourself to let him polish and repolish, scrub and rescrub as long as he wishes. Do respect his work; if you must redo something, never do it over in his presence.

To avoid putting undesirable pressure on a child to learn what he is not yet ready to learn, all of these activities should be completely free choice. Ask your youngster, "Would you like to have me show you how to button the button?" If he says "No," don't pressure or push or urge or coax or show any disappointment. Just change the subject and offer the suggestion again in two or three weeks. If your youngster is the kind who routinely says "No" to everything, you may change the question to a more positive, "Here, I'll show you how." But stop if he resists or isn't interested. And do it in a friendly manner.

Whenever your bairn begins to lose interest in a learning demonstration or wiggles away or says he's tired of it, stop. Put the material away and offer it again days later. This technique will not only protect your child from pressures, but it will help to avoid his developing a resistance to your teaching attempts.

Teach the very young with real things, as Rousseau urged long ago, is still a cardinal rule in helping children between eighteen and thirty-six months to learn. Your house is full of utensils and equipment your moppet can learn to use effectively with a little help. And most of it is easier for small hands to manipulate than the cheap, flimsy miniatures made as toys.

Toys are, of course, an obvious and delightful way to help feed your youngster's great need for varied sensory stimulation and motor activity during the years between one and one-half and three.

Toys serve many purposes in a small child's life. There are toys to love (the soft, cuddly, feels-good-to-touch stuffed animals and dolls that are always there when mother turns out the light and goes away, that always listen when things go wrong). There are toys to trigger the imagination (paints, paper, dolls, doll house, blocks, sand, puppets—the more simple and less structured, the more creatively they can be used). There are toys to help a child try out the idea of being a grown-up (realistic dolls and their pint-sized paraphernalia, housekeeping toys, garden tools, doctor kits, costumes, trucks, trains, farmyard sets). There are toys to help a child find the action (tricycle, scooter, wagon, anything with wheels; swing, glider, climbing bars, tire-on-a-rope-hung-from-a-tree, slide, sled, small trampoline, rocking horse, balls of every variety, any equipment which moves and encourages a child to run or chase or sway or swoop or bounce).

Even though some of these toys seem chiefly to foster the development of a child physically, socially, or emotionally, they also encourage his mental growth. For there is an intellectual component in all of these areas.

There are also toys which are primarily for intellectual learning, whether or not they are so labeled. These are often the toys with which you are most apt to get your money's worth in terms of hours-of-play-value-per-dollar.

In addition to the general categories of toys already listed, your youngster can learn much and have fun with playthings like these:

- Giant magnifying glass on legs.
- Kindergarten blocks, in as large an assortment as you can afford, made of smooth, accurately-cut, natural wood in squares, oblongs, diagonals, triangles, curves, half-circles, and pillars.
- Flashlight.
- Nesting blocks, bowls, barrels, or eggs.
- Inlaid puzzles of wood or hard rubber (some have pieces which can be removed and used as toys).
- Indoor wooden slide, with stepladder.

- Simple rhythm instruments—bells, triangle, tambourine, drum, wrist bells, finger cymbals, small xylophone.
- Take-apart trucks and toys.
- Collection of hats for playing different pretend roles.
- Inlaid form board containing simple geometric shapes.
- Giant magnet.
- Unstructured playhouse.
- Counting toys and number puzzles.
- Phonograph simple enough for a small child to operate himself.
- Fabric tunnel for crawling through and exploring.
- Sand machine, with wooden hopper and trapdoor from which sand can dribble to spin a wooden paddlewheel.
- Bean bags and baskets for targets.
- Farm layouts with animals.
- Large wooden beads to string or fasten together.
- Simple lotto games.

Art and craft materials and projects suitable for youngsters over two years old are described in Chapter 8. Some of the Montessori techniques and equipment listed in Chapter 9 can be effective with children younger than three.

Taking your two-year-old on a variety of very short trips is one of the happiest and most effective ways of increasing the amount of learning stimuli he receives. Even a walk around the block can be a good learning experience, if you take the time to let him watch the ants hurrying in and out of an anthill and poke his finger into a puddle and scuff in the leaves and go up and down every step that beckons.

A zoo and a farm and a pet store are all full of delightful learning possibilities for a two-year-old. If you can arrange it, let him have a chance to pat a horse, sit on its back, listen to it, and watch it eat—to learn about it through all of his senses. Then talk about the experience afterwards and encourage him to put his feelings into words. He'll learn more this way than if you plop him into a stroller and try to cover the whole zoo in one afternoon.

Here are some other good expeditions for two-year-olds: A short trip on a bus. A train ride between two or three commuter stations. A visit to a bakery, a fire station, a shoe-repair shop. A trip to the beach and to as many different neighborhood parks as possible. An expedition to a drive-in hamburger stand, a greenhouse, an apple orchard.

The transition from this stage into the preschool period of three to six isn't a definite line that children cross in a birthday month. By about thirty months, a few youngsters will be ready for some of the activities listed in the next chapter, particularly if their parents have been enriching their environment since the earliest months of life. So you will probably want to read ahead in the sections about language, science, math, and perception before your child is fully three years old.

6. How To Stimulate Intellectual Growth in Three- to Six-Year-Olds

Larry, just six, is entering first grade this fall, already able to read independently and with great delight, at about third grade level. He can count as far as he wants to, do simple addition, subtraction, and division, and he has a good grasp of what numerical symbols mean. His vocabulary is probably about 25,000 words, and he has developed many sound concepts about the natural and social sciences. He is eager, curious, fascinated by the world around him, responsive to adults, and happy. And because he is also self-confident, outgoing and energetic, he finds it easy to make friends with the other children.

But for Fred, also six, first grade is a threat. He can't talk well enough to make the teacher understand him. He has had no experience in interpreting even the pictures in his preprimer, let alone the more complicated symbolism of the obscure, black marks underneath the illustrations. It seems easier to Fred to withdraw, to look out the window, to keep quiet, rather than to try. Fred already feels that he is a failure, and he shows it in the classroom and on the playground.

Yet Larry and Fred started life—just a few miles apart in the same large city—with far less difference in innate mental ability than these first grade contrasts show. If they had been given an infant I.Q. test, they would both have scored in the same general range. They never will again. The differences between them now will almost certainly be self-perpetuating, and will probably increase.

Larry, obviously, will be classified as a "bright" or "gifted" child. He will go immediately into the top reading group in his class. His eagerness to learn and his quick successes will delight his teachers. He will bask in their approval and this, plus the joy he has already experienced from learning, will motivate him to keep trying and prevent him from being too discouraged if he draws a poor teacher or dull assignments. If he's lucky enough to be in an ungraded primary, he may even save a year of elementary school—time he can use to great advantage later for graduate study or for an earlier start in a profession.

It won't be long before Fred's teachers will stop expecting him to succeed. Even a patient, understanding teacher will find it hard not to become discouraged with Fred's obvious lack of effort and interest. Because of his lack of readiness and his deficiencies in language, Fred will be slow in learning to read, and thereby handicapped in all of his other school work. A sad, familiar cycle will probably begin. Because he can't keep up, Fred will begin to fail. Because he fails, he'll tend to stop trying. The less he tries, the less he will learn. Fred may spend an extra year in an ungraded primary. Or he, like about ten percent of first graders, may be kept back a year. Despite automatic promotions after that, he may be only a high school freshman or a sophomore before he is legally able to drop out of school and does.

The contrast between Larry and Fred is not an exaggeration. There are thousands of Larrys in our first grades today, the product of informed homes, of Montessori schools, of laboratory schools in university settings, of nursery schools where teachers practice early-learning principles. Happily, the Larrys are increasing rapidly.

Boys and girls like Fred, however, can be counted by the hundreds of thousands. Most come from the culturally-deprived homes of poverty, but some of the Freds also belong to affluent families where parents are too busy or too uninformed or too uninterested in seeing that their children get the mental nourishment they need.

In between the Larrys and the Freds are millions of other youngsters whose minds have not been stunted as much as Fred's nor stimulated as much as Larry's. What they bring to first grade they have learned chiefly by osmosis in homes where they are loved and cared for physically, but where their urgent need for mental stimulation has not been fully recognized.

What can you give your child between the ages of three and six to boost his mental abilities and start him off to first grade confident and destined for success?

No preset curriculum can be devised that will fit all preschoolers, all homes, and all parents with their varying talents, responsibilities, and available time. Even if such a curriculum could be devised by extensive research, it would not be desirable. The Educational Policies Commission points out that youngsters are so active physically and mentally, that no preplanned pattern of experience can take advantage of the opportunities for learning that constantly occur.[1]

A small child's mind works so fast and reaches out in so many unexpected directions that you'd miss great teaching opportunities if you tried to stick to a prescribed, formal lesson pattern. One of the great advantages of preschool learning at home is that you can adapt it to the needs and immediate interests of each individual child—an opportunity for personalized learning that rarely occurs throughout your youngster's years of formal school until graduate level.

Here are general guidelines for the major areas you'll want to cover during the years between three and six. Like any good teacher, you'll improvise and adapt the suggestions for your own child. How fast he will go in which areas will depend on how much time you spend with him, his own individual speed and way of learning, how much early stimulation he has had before age three, and whether he attends a nursery school which actively fosters intellectual development. That's why these guidelines are not grouped more specifically by age levels.

Do remember that your youngster will learn best if you set the stage for him to make his own discoveries, rather than impose rote memory drills on him, or formal lessons. If you keep in mind that the basic purpose of this early stimulation is to give your child the joy of learning, you won't be inclined to rush him or to push him.

LANGUAGE

Between the ages of three and six, your child's vocabulary will grow explosively and excitingly—and in imitation of yours. If you speak English correctly, so will your child by the end of this period. He will also pick up your swear words and pet expressions. One of the most important aids you can give your preschool child—and one which a culturally-deprived youngster is most apt to lack —is a good language model to copy.

This doesn't mean that you have to speak copybook English with completed sentences every time you talk. But it does mean that you should use a full range of tenses, subordinate clauses, pronouns, adjectives, and adverbs for your child to absorb. He'll discover—without apparent effort—how to form tenses, plurals, and clauses without overt assistance from you, if you provide the example. His ability to do so is greater when he's a preschooler than it will ever be again.

Don't be afraid to use words your child doesn't understand. He'll absorb them and gradually decipher their meaning. That's how he learned to talk originally. It's easy to underestimate a youngster's comprehension vocabulary because, like almost all adults, he understands a far larger number of words than he uses.

Sometimes, for the delight of it, you can deliberately

teach your moppet big words. Four- and five-year-olds often enjoy learning the precise names of various types of dinosaurs, automobile parts, or flowers, for example. Tyrannosaurus, brontosaurus, carburetor, and philodendron are far more fun to roll off a tongue than meaningless polysyllables, like polyunsaturated, that youngsters pick up from television commercials.

Although you don't need to make obvious, formal attempts to teach sentence structure or vocabulary to your preschooler, you should make frequent, uncritical use of corrective feedback. Your three-year-old may tell her father about her morning activities by saying "I help she make she beds." Father can respond with respect and interest, "You must be getting pretty big if you can help her make her beds." He doesn't point out the mistake in grammar, but simply provides the correct model without further comment. This helps the youngster learn without the criticism that could inhibit her flow of words.

Almost all preschoolers go through a stage in speech development when they seem to stutter. This may occur simply because their thinking outraces their vocabulary. "I don't have enough words for my thoughts," one three-year-old told his mother in a worried voice.

It's also been suggested that this stuttering stage comes just before the establishment of dominance by one hemisphere of the brain, where the control of speech normally becomes fixed during the early years of life. This speech area of the brain can be mapped out quite precisely in cases of brain surgery, or when a stroke deprives an individual of the ability to talk. Normally, in a right-handed person, the speech control center is located in the left side of the brain; in a left-handed individual, speech is usually controlled by the right half of the brain.

According to this theory, stuttering should disappear naturally about the time a clear-cut and natural handedness—either right or left—is established. It is known that stuttering often persists in a child who does not have a consistent preference for his right or left hand, or whose dominant eye and/or foot is not on the same side of his body as his dominant hand. It's also been observed frequently that stuttering may start in a child when a parent or a teacher attempts to force a natural leftie to switch to his right hand for most tasks.

Regardless of the cause, the type of normal stuttering that occurs in most children between the ages of two and one-half and four should be ignored. These "disfluencies," as speech experts call them, almost always disappear as a child's skill in using words increases (or perhaps as the speech center in his brain becomes better established).

But a parent who calls a child's attention to his hesitancies and disfluencies may, with the best of intentions, turn his youngster into a persistent stutterer, some speech experts warn. There is risk, they caution, not only in telling your child not to stutter, but also in even suggesting that he pause and think, or take a deep breath, before he talks. This tends to make the youngster so conscious of the mechanisms of speech that the hesitancies and disfluencies increase and turn into habit.

You can help in one way: Give your preschooler the courtesy of listening to him with as much respect and attention as you'd give an adult guest in your home. If your youngster feels that you are really listening to him, he won't try to rush through what he's saying, and there's less danger that he will stumble over sounds or skip syllables. This courtesy will also increase his feelings of self-confidence and personal worth and make him less inclined to whine for your attention.

Most youngsters continue to mispronounce one or two speech sounds, even until kindergarten or first grade, speech therapists say. Unless your child's speech is almost impossible for others to understand after about his fourth birthday, you needn't be concerned about a few mispronunciations until school age.

As your child begins to acquire a beginning command of the mechanics of language, you'll want to help him learn how to use this marvelous tool. Language is so closely related to thought that some theorists even consider them almost synonymous.

During your child's irreplaceable years between three and six, you can help him learn to use language to foster thinking. When you talk to your child, you can encourage him to plan ahead ("When you have helped me carry out the dishes, we can go to the park"). And to consider alternatives ("Should I make a cake for dinner, or would you rather go to the park this afternoon and have cookies for dessert?"). And to avoid mistakes ("If you move your glass of milk toward the center of the table, you won't knock it over with your elbow").

Helping your preschooler learn to put his feelings into words makes life easier for everyone in your family. If your youngster knows he can make you understand what he is feeling with words, he won't be so likely to whine or sulk or throw things or have a tantrum or pat the baby too hard.

You can also use words to help your preschooler understand the feelings of others and begin to act accordingly. "I know you are angry because the baby snatched your toy car away," you might say. "But you see, the baby admires you so, and she is trying to do everything you are doing. She wants to grow up and be just like you. Will you help me teach her how to become as fine a person as you are?"

You can make it become a fascinating game if you sometimes ask your preschooler to choose precisely the right words to describe a cloud, a feeling, the taste of a new food, the touch of a fabric, the beauty of a flower. He'll delight in these verbal treasure hunts if you let him know you enjoy the aptness of his choices and join in the game, too.

A parent who listens with respect and interest and without being condescending or all-knowing can have delightful conversations with a preschooler. If you make it a happy habit to converse with your child (not talking down to him or issuing orders or preaching at him) when you're driving in the car, riding the bus, tucking him into bed, doing the dishes, or whenever you can find time, you'll not only stimulate his mental development, but you'll keep open lines of communication with him which are invaluable later on in his life.

It will help your child's vocabulary to grow and his

skill in using language to flourish if you give him something interesting to talk about. A trip, a visit to a museum or zoo, a shopping expedition, or a kitchen-sink science experiment not only provides a child with new words to use, but spurs his desire to try them out. Another incentive: At the dinner table, see that each member of the family has a chance to tell the others what he did that day.

Television can be turned into a stimulus for your child's vocabulary development, too, especially if you encourage him to discuss programs he's seen with you. This gives you a good opportunity to help him sort out fact from fiction—often very difficult for preschool TV viewers— and to clear up misunderstandings he may have about what he has seen. Television can also whet a thirst for more information about a subject—outer space, rockets, airplanes, a foreign country, the ocean, the presidency— which you can help him find in a library, newspaper or encyclopedia. Hopefully, these conversations about television will aid your youngster in developing critical judgment about television, and he'll be less inclined to watch indiscriminately when he's older.

Good parent-child talk is often silly, funny, absurd talk, as any parent knows whose moppet has twisted Pooh Bear's "Help, help, a Heffalump, a Horrible Heffalump" around and around on his tongue with delight. A quick, happy sense of humor is one of the most common characteristics of gifted children, research shows. And the more your youngster enjoys the fun of jokes, riddles, verbal puzzles, puns, silly rhymes, and absurdities, the brighter he probably is. The more you join in his fun, the more he'll come to enjoy words and the more open he will be to learning through language.

Your four-year-old may sound to you like the village idiot as he murmurs to himself, "tooth-fairy, gooseberry, moose-perry, boose-narry." But he is learning to enjoy the sound of language and to learn how he can control it and make sounds work for him.

You can build on this interest by suggesting games to heighten your moppet's awareness of sounds and sound patterns—a fundamental step in learning to read.

You can help him recognize similarities and differences in beginning sounds by asking him to see how many words he can think of that begin with the same sound as "Margie" or "book." Or, you can take turns thinking of all the words you can that end the same way as "Sam" or "Dad" or "pop."

Skill with language involves listening and understanding, as well as talking, and there are many happy games you can play with your child to help him sharpen his listening ability. "Simon Says" is a good game for three-year-olds. "May I?" is fun for children old enough to count to ten. "I Packed My Sister's Suitcase" appeals to four- and five-year-olds.

Reading to your child should continue to be a shared pleasure, even after he is old enough to read easy books for himself and well into the early elementary school years. A child's level of comprehension is much higher than his reading level for many years, and he needs to have you read to him to sustain his interest in books and to provide him with mental nourishment until he can find enough for himself.

Regular trips to the children's room of the nearest library should be a routine part of your moppet's life, starting no later than the age of three. As a special treat, he should be permitted to choose books to own on gift occasions, or whenever you can afford it. Books, generally, cost less than many toys, especially when figured on a dollar-per-hour-of-pleasure basis. Providing your child with his own special bookshelf, or bookcase, or bookends—and with inexpensive bookplates that carry his name—also will increase his interest in books.

It is important to keep reading a pleasure, not a task or a lesson. For example, you can show your preschooler how much fun it is to spread out a blanket under a shady tree on a summer afternoon and read together. Or, let him cuddle up in bed with you on a stormy night while you read to him. Or, let him substitute a story session for a nap on a day it's too hot for sleep. You can suggest that he help you in the kitchen, then reward him with a story. You can encourage him to avoid boredom by reading a book when he must wait for the dentist or for the next motel with a "vacancy" sign on a vacation trip.

"When I was about four years old, I used to get these awful earaches," recalls a teen-age boy. "I'd wake up in the night crying because it hurt so much. My mom would get up and give me the medicine the doctor sent, and then she'd sit beside my bed and read to me all sorts of good stuff, until the hurt let up. She told me that reading couldn't kill the pain, but that it would fill up such a big part of my brain I wouldn't pay so much attention to the hurting. Sometimes reading still makes me feel good, like it did then."

You should make certain your child realizes that reading is also an adult activity you enjoy independently of him. You should let him see you read often for pleasure and for information. You should make your trips to the library a time for you to select adult books, too. You can request books as gifts for yourself (a paperback is one of the least expensive material gifts a child can choose). And you can comment often on what you do read. A youngster who grows up seeing his parents get most of their information and entertainment from television is quite likely to do likewise and may never become happily addicted to reading.

Your child's interests and responses will be your best guide to the type of books you choose to read to him. As they did at the age of two, many preschoolers still prefer factual books that explain the world around them and books about children much like themselves to fairy tales. A book about thunder and lightning can seem just as wondrous to a four-year-old as a story about fire-breathing dragons, yet it gives him information he craves about a familiar phenomenon. Given a choice, he'll usually take reality.

Often a book for small children that is considered cute or charming by an adult will have almost no appeal for a four- or five-year-old. Some books for preschoolers are condescending in tone and far too limited in vocabulary and content.

In helping your child select books, a guiding principle should be that it's better to challenge his mind than to bore him. Your youngster's response to books will be a clear guide to his level of comprehension—far more accurate than any prepared book list (although you might consult one as a starter). If a book matches your moppet's mental development, he'll probably ask you to read it to him again and again, and he'll listen quietly and carefully. If it's too easy or too difficult, he'll probably wiggle away and begin to play with something else.

Good poetry stirs great interest in three- to six-year-olds, and you should continue to read poems to him all during this preschool period. Encourage him to memorize those he especially enjoys—not so he can recite for your dinner guests, but so he will have them in his mind for his own pleasure.

Your reading to your child shouldn't be limited to books, of course. You can also stimulate his interest in printed symbols by reading to him traffic signs, labels, historic markers that you encounter on vacation, menus when you go out to dinner, directions that come with toys and games, words that flash on the TV screen, signs that help him tell the difference between the "men's room" and the "ladies' room," reminders that you chalk on your kitchen blackboard for yourself and for other family members—anything that helps him to understand that printed letters make words which have meanings.

READING

If you've been following the suggestions in this book, your youngster will probably be showing clear signs of readiness to learn to read sometime between his third and fourth birthdays. He'll be fascinated by books, questioning you about the meanings of signs and labels, wanting to learn to print his own name, interested in pictures, and adding to his speaking vocabulary faster than you can keep count of the words. Chapter 7 will tell you, in detail, about teaching him to read easily and happily yourself.

SECOND LANGUAGE

The years between three and six, when your child's ability to absorb language with great facility is at its peak, are the ideal time to introduce him to a second language, if you are lucky enough to have the opportunity.

At this age, your youngster can learn a second language almost as readily as he learns English and without any sort of formal lessons, provided it is taught in the same way he learned English. He merely needs to hear it spoken frequently, naturally, and well by someone who can speak it like a native. A grandparent, a parent, a nursery school teacher, a neighbor, or a household helper can be an effective teacher simply by speaking to the child only in the second language (or by speaking to him only in the second language in a special part of the house, or during certain hours at nursery school). Your goal should not be to help your preschooler build up a large vocabulary, but rather to establish the basic units of the second language in his growing brain. Then he can build on them later instead of having to learn the second language cold, using English sounds or speech units when he's a teen-ager or an adult.

It is important that whoever teaches your child the second language speaks it correctly. Bilingual children who come from culturally-deprived homes where neither English nor their parents' native tongue is spoken well, usually do poorly in school, research shows. And experiments in teaching a foreign language in elementary schools, using teachers who do not have a mastery of the language and who do not use a "direct" or "mother's method," usually seem to be a waste of time.

If you aren't fluent in a second language yourself and don't know anyone who could teach your child by the "mother's method," you will probably not be able to give your child this opportunity. There have been almost no successful experiments in which parents have helped to teach a second language that they did not know to preschoolers via phonograph records or coloring-workbooks or other techniques. Parents who try to learn a second language along with their child always find that he learns more quickly and easily than they, as immigrant families for generations have discovered.

PERCEPTION

Perception, as the word is increasingly being used by educators, physicians, and psychologists, means the ability to transmit stimuli to the brain and interpret them accurately. It involves recognizing a voice as being mommy's, a doll as being small enough to fit into a wagon, ice cream as being cold, a picture as representing reality.

Perception includes all of the senses—hearing, seeing, smelling, tasting, feeling. But because seeing is the key ability in learning, perception usually refers to the ability to see and to comprehend accurately in the mind.

Even though a child's eyes may function perfectly, visual stimuli may be modified as they are passed along the nerve fibers to his brain, or they may be misinterpreted or not recognized in the brain itself. These distortions can be so great in some children that they have great difficulty learning in school. They may not be able to separate background and foreground, or recognize left from right, or focus on one part of a scene or on one word on a page.

Children who have perceptual difficulties may number from five to fifteen percent of the average first grade class, researchers now estimate. Sometimes these learning disabilities appear to be caused by minor injury to the child's brain before, during, or after birth. Sometimes they seem to be related to a general lag in neurological development. Often there is no evident cause. Many youngsters with perceptual problems also have what doctors call "soft neurological signs." They may be clumsy, overly active, impulsive, irritable, explosive, and have a tendency to stutter, an unusually short attention span and/or poor powers of concentration.

Special training in perception does seem to help most of these youngsters, researchers are discovering, especially if it is begun before a child has tried and failed in first grade and before emotional problems are piled upon his neurological difficulties. In fact, every child can profit from training and practice in perception before he starts school, many educators and doctors now believe.

To help your child sharpen his perceptual abilities, try playing some of these games with him:

• Arrange two to four blocks in various patterns and let your moppet copy them with identical blocks.

• Conceal a small toy in a paper bag. Let your youngster put his hand in, without peeking, and identify the object by touch alone. Vary the game by hiding several toys in the bag and by calling out which one he is to find and remove.

• Invent matching games of all types with lotto cards, color swatches from the paint store, numbers, letters, and magazine pictures pasted on cardboard.

• Try the Montessori activity of giving your youngster a bowl containing a dozen each of four kinds of unshelled nuts which he is to sort by type into four small dishes. When he's adept at this, challenge him to try it blindfolded.

• Have your preschooler lie flat on the floor and ask him to identify different parts of his body as you point to them or call out their names. Vary the game by playing it while he is standing, sitting, and kneeling to help strengthen his perception of his body position in space.

• Set up an obstacle course for your moppet to follow through the house that will include crawling under a table, over the end of a sofa, around a chair, and jumping, hopping, rolling, climbing. For fun, cut out foot, hand, and knee outlines and make a trail for your child to follow.

• Make a walking beam for your youngster, using a 2- by 4-inch board at least 8 feet long and mounted on three supports that hold it about 2 inches off the floor. A youngster can have all the walk-the-railroad-rail delight with it, while he is developing visual-motor coordination and perception of his own body position in space.

• Help your child learn about right and left. Identify his right sock and shoe, and then his left sock and shoe as you dress him. Call out which arm he is to put into his sweater or coat first, and which mitten he is to slip on first. Teach him that his knife and spoon go on the right, his fork on the left. Point out that you are sitting on the left in the car when you drive and he, as a front-seat passenger, is on the right. And when you read to him, call his attention to the fact that words go from left to right along the lines of a page.

• With a small box and a block, have your youngster follow the directions you call out, putting the block into and out of the box, in front of and behind it, under it, to the left and to the right of it.

• Teach him about geometric shapes—circle, square, rectangle, oval—and make a game of his trying to recognize them elsewhere. A table top can be a circle or a rectangle, for example. A circle can be seen in a headlight of a car, a jar lid, a drop of water, or a slice of carrot.

• Invest in two small pegboards. Set up a simple design with colored pegs on one for him to copy on the other. Make the designs increasingly complicated as he progresses.

• Put several small objects on a table and let your youngster look closely at them for about one minute. Then ask him to close his eyes while you take one of the items away. Let him try to remember which object you've removed.

• Look at large pictures in a magazine with your child; encourage him to talk about what is going on in the foreground and what he can see in the background.

• Challenge your child to tell you, in order, all of the things he can see on a trip to the grocery store, or on a walk to the playground, or on some other familiar short trip.

• Play a game with adverbs. Ask your child if he can demonstrate how to walk sadly, slowly, loudly, softly, proudly, fearfully, bravely.

• See how many different types of roofs you and your child can find in your neighborhood, or on a car trip—hip, gable, flat, single and double pitch. Then play the game with varieties of fences.

If your child is unable to succeed with at least some activities like these by the time he is five, if he seems particularly clumsy, if he is unusually prone to temper tantrums, is overly active, and has more behavior problems than most children, he may have a perceptual handicap or learning disability. It's a good idea in that case to call these symptoms to the attention of your pediatrician. Good techniques are now available to help these youngsters considerably.

MATH

Even if you never were a whiz in math yourself, you can help your preschooler discover and absorb many basic mathematical concepts long before he's ready for first grade. Whether he is eventually taught in school by traditional or new-math methods, he'll profit greatly by these early-learning experiences.

The key to teaching a preschooler about math is to set the stage for him to make his own discoveries and to present ideas in the form of games which you both enjoy. You gain almost nothing by trying to stuff his head with number facts learned by rote.

"Too often, children have just learned to memorize names and to recite a few number facts without understanding what they mean," comments Dr. Jack E. Forbes, professor of mathematics at Purdue University and author of a modern math program designed for parents to use with preschoolers.[2] "Parents need to help children organize this spotty knowledge they have picked up and to acquire a basic knowledge of what mathematics is really about."

A preschooler should be helped to learn, suggests Dr. Forbes, that "(a) mathematics is something we think about in an orderly way and talk about in a careful, precise manner; and (b) learning is a game that we play with our minds; it should not be painful labor or memorization."

You need not worry about pressuring your child too much, reassures Dr. Forbes. He will simply close up his mind and refuse to learn anything for which he is not ready and in which he is not interested. Nor should you be concerned about teaching materials which the school might duplicate later on. He explains:

> In modern mathematics programs, the big ideas are introduced to children at a very young age. It's not like learning to read, where you learn a word and then know it forever afterward. In mathematics, you keep returning to the basic concepts, expanding them, building on them, learning more about how they relate to other aspects of life.
>
> We need to learn a great deal more about the marvelous ability of very young children to learn directly through the senses, without having to learn formal rules or patterns. For the present, we can try to help the child capitalize on this ability and to help him learn —at a time when this ability is strongest—much that will be useful to him in later years.

Because your preschooler will learn best by perceptual methods, mathematical ideas should be taught with interesting materials he will enjoy handling. For example, don't just teach him to count to ten by rote, or by pointing to his fingers one at a time. Encourage him to use anything he can move into groups—buttons, raisins, blocks, cookies, pennies—as he counts. Otherwise, he may get the idea that "four" means the fourth in a series, rather than all four in a set of objects.

You should also introduce your preschooler to the idea that "zero" is a number, too. The number of elephants in your kitchen is "zero," Dr. Forbes explains, not "none." "It is common practice to allow children to think of none, nothing, and zero or "0" as meaning the same thing. This practice leads to great difficulties later on. For example, consider 35 (meaning 3 tens and 5 ones) and 305 (meaning 3 hundreds and 0 tens and 5 ones). In the first, there is 'nothing' between the 3 and 5. In the second, there is a 0 between the 3 and 5. Certainly there is an important difference!"

Next, show your moppet how to write the numerals he is counting, from 0 to 9. Most youngsters learn more quickly if you make large-size numerals for them to trace with their index and middle fingers. In Montessori schools, big sandpaper letters are used for this purpose. These can now be purchased for use by parents at home, or you can cut out a set of numerals from sandpaper yourself and mount them on squares of cardboard. Wooden jigsaw puzzles that match numerals with the proper number of dots or pegs or small animals are also available.

Several Montessori techniques can easily be adapted to teach mathematical concepts to your preschooler at home. For example, after your child has learned to count and to identify numerals, give him a box divided into sections numbered from 0 to 9 (an egg carton with two compartments taped shut will work) and 45 beads, beans, or buttons he is to distribute correctly. The box will give him some degree of self-correction and make it possible for him to practice and learn independently.

For another game, write a single digit on several slips of paper and put them into a bag. Let your child draw them out one at a time and then get for you the corresponding number of items—blocks, leaves, buttons, books.

To teach your preschooler the concept of "odd" and "even," make a series of number cards, using index cards marked 1 to 9. Then let him place the corresponding number of buttons in pairs under each card so he can easily tell whether there is one left over or not.

Make a second set of cards and you can teach your

child the concept of "same" or "equal" by putting out two identical numerals and corresponding numbers of buttons and by having him pair them off. Then, using two different numerals, with the correct number of buttons, help him discover the meaning of "more" and "fewer."

These cards and buttons are useful, too, in introducing your child to the idea of addition. First, lay out two numerals, with matching buttons, the sum of which is less than 10. Have him combine the buttons into one pile, count them, and find the matching numeral from your stockpile. Then you can show him how to write down what he has done, using the appropriate plus sign. Subtraction can be introduced in this same way.

In Montessori schools, the concept of "tens" and "hundreds" and "thousands" is taught by means of golden beads. These beads are available for the children to use as single units, in strings of ten, in squares in which ten rows of ten beads are securely fastened together, and in cubes which are painted to resemble ten of the hundred-bead squares.

The child learns to match the printed numeral 10 with a 10-bead string, the numeral 100 with the 100-bead square, and the numeral 1000 with the cube. Then, with a printed card that says 1000, another marked 600, a 50, and a single numeral card 3, he can stack them together to form for himself the numeral 1653. By actually laying out one 1000-bead cube, six of the 100-bead squares, five of the 10-bead strings, and three single beads, he can gain a concrete idea of the numeral 1653.

Montessori-type golden beads can now be purchased by parents, although they are expensive for individual use. Mothers who have used Montessori methods at home have devised several ingenious substitutes. For example, instead of beads, you can fasten sticky-backed tape which has a small, unitary design—flower, Santa Claus, circle, bell—onto cardboard and cut it in the required sizes. You'll need single units, rows of 10, and squares which contain ten rows of 10 figures. For the 1000-unit cubes, you can tie ten 100-figure squares together.

You'll also need some filing cards. On one set of cards, with a marking pen, write large-sized numerals—1000, 2000, 3000, 4000, 5000, 6000, 7000, 8000, and 9000. Before marking the second set of cards, cut off about one-fourth from one end, so that they can cover only the last three digits of the thousands cards. Then number them in ink—100, 200, 300, 400, 500, 600, 700, 800, and 900.

The third set of cards is cut in half and numbered—10, 20, 30, 40, 50, 60, 70, 80, and 90. The fourth set is only one-fourth as wide as the full-size cards, and it is marked with single digits from 1 to 9. By stacking these cards in proper sequence, a child can construct any numeral from 1 to 9999.

One game you can play with your child is to put the cards in piles on a table. Then say to your youngster, "Please get me four thousands." When he has succeeded, instruct him to find a certain number of hundreds, tens, and units and have him stack the cards properly to make the correct numeral. Then challenge him to lay out the same number of whatever equivalent you are using for the golden beads.

When your child can handle this game easily and happily, you can progress to more complicated forms of addition. First, have him construct two different numerals —1433 and 6354, for example—and lay out the "beads" that illustrate both numbers. First, he counts the number of unit beads in both piles, combines them into one pile, and finds the numeral card that corresponds. In this case, of course, it is a 7. In a similar way, he counts the tens, the hundreds, and the thousands, until he has 7 units, 8 tens, 7 hundreds, and 7 thousands. He forms the corresponding numeral and has the sum of the two original numbers.

At first, you'll want to use numbers that can be added without involving carrying. But when your youngster has become adept at adding, you can show him graphically how to carry. When he has ten or more units, he can take ten of them back to the original stockpile, or bank, and exchange them for a strip of ten. Similarly, he can exchange ten 10-strips for one 100-square, or ten hundreds for one 1000-cube. It's easier for him to understand if he performs the operation first with the beads and then sets up the numerals to match his answer.

If you wish, you can teach your child to subtract by much the same method. The easiest way is to have him set up a number with both beads and cards. The subtrahend should be formed only with the cards. Beginning with the units, have your child take away the number of beads called for in the subtrahend. When he has finished the operation, he can construct the correct answer with the cards. Your first numbers should not involve the concept of borrowing. But after the basic process has been mastered, you can introduce borrowing by having your child actually exchange a 10-strip for ten units, or one 1000-cube for ten 100-squares, so that he can perform his subtraction operation.

You can also show him how to check his results by adding the difference and the subtrahend to form the original number.

Short division can also be taught to a preschooler, using these Montessori-type materials. First, give your child a four-place number (with each digit an even number) to set up, using both beads and cards. To show him how to divide by two, have your moppet take turns with you removing one 1000-cube at a time from the pile set up to illustrate the dividend. If the dividend is 8682, each of you would have four 1000-cubes. Do the same with the remaining digits, until each of you has four 1000-cubes, three 100-squares, four 10-strips, and one unit. Then you can set up the number cards to indicate your quotient. In Montessori schools, the directress may vary the divisor by asking additional children to participate. For fun, she may suggest that the youngsters march once around the table each time they take a unit or square or cube.

When this step has been mastered, you can vary the

dividends so that the digits cannot be divided equally by the number of individuals used as divisors. Then you can show the small fry how to change the leftover thousands or hundreds or tens into hundreds or tens or units which can be divided equally.

Another excellent tool for helping preschoolers understand mathematical concepts is a set of number rods. Both Montessori-type rods and Cuisenaire rods are now available for home use. Both will help your preschooler to acquire basic mathematical ideas by perceptual methods and to make many of his own discoveries about mathematical relationships But you will need to spend some time learning about the rods yourself before you set the stage for your child to make his own mathematical explorations.

Dice make an excellent device for helping preschoolers to learn about numbers in a games context and to reinforce learning already acquired. In one nursery school for four- and five-year-olds, for example, youngsters play long, concentrated games in which one moppet shakes the dice and calls off the numbers to other children who chalk them on a blackboard and then add them up.

Any board game that involves dice or a spinner and counting can be useful in helping a child grasp number concepts. Four-year-olds can do quite well at "Sorry" and "Parchesi" if one opponent is an adult or an older child who can help out, if necessary. A preschooler may shake a 3 and a 4 on the dice, for example, and count as he moves his marker, "one, two, three, one, two, three, four" to find the seventh space. But it isn't long before he announces "seven" after his shake, without the preliminary steps.

Playing bingo is a delightful, no-pressure way in which to help a child learn to identify and pronounce numbers between 10 and 75, especially if you call out the numbers as "fifty-seven, that's five, seven." In a game situation, a child often wants to play and win so badly that he absorbs basic mathematical concepts without even realizing it.

Rummy-type games that give practice in number concepts are available in most toy stores, but are generally intended for elementary school age groups. Four- and five-years-olds with a background in math can usually play the games, but lack the ability to hold enough cards in one hand. This difficulty can easily be overcome by giving each moppet a large-sized cardboard box, turned with its opening on the side facing the player, in which he can spread out his hand in secret.

Once your child has learned to read numerals, it's not difficult to teach him to tell time and to read a thermometer. Both of these skills are well worth the teaching effort. A preschooler finds it easier to accept the fact that it's bedtime, or that it's too-soon-before-dinner-to-have-another-cookie when the clock makes the ruling and not an arbitrary parent with whom the child can argue. Many a parent has sidestepped arguments about whether a child needs a heavy jacket or just a sweater by posting a code that goes approximately like this: above 70, no wraps; 65–70, sweater; 45–65, light jacket; below 45, heavy jacket and cap or scarf.

To teach your moppet about money, begin by helping him learn the names of a penny, nickel, dime, quarter, half-dollar, and dollar. Then, suggests Dr. Forbes, explain to him that we use money to trade for things we want, and that we have different kinds of money so we can pay different prices for these things. Then play matching games with him to show him that one nickel will buy as much as five pennies; that a quarter is equal to two dimes and one nickel, or five nickels or 25 pennies, or one dime and 15 pennies, and all of the other combinations. After several short sessions of practice with these coin equivalents, your child should be quite knowledgeable about money and ready for a small allowance.

SCIENCE

A preschooler comes equipped with a probing, poking, questioning, exploring, insatiable interest in science of all kinds. Or at least he does until a parent or a teacher has spanked or discouraged or ignored or scolded him out of it.

Even if you can't tell a pipette from a test tube, you can do much to encourage the scientist innate in your child. Your aim shouldn't be to pressure him to memorize scientific facts, but to absorb scientific attitudes—to question, to make sensitive observations, to look for cause and effect, to test conclusions, to wonder and to marvel.

(Your encouragement of scientific interests and attitudes is important for your daughter as well as for your son. Research shows that most girls start out with the same type and degree of scientific interest as boys, but are discouraged by lack of support from adults and shunted away into other areas of interest long before junior high school.)

With practice, you'll discover many ways in which to encourage your preschooler's natural scientific bent. For example: Find every way you can to help your child become more sensitive to his environment, to look beyond the obvious, to use all of his five senses to explore the world around him. In March, for example, help him hunt for the first signs of spring in the tender shoots of green under snow-soggy leaves. Encourage him to notice the differences in the shapes of leaves, the coloring of birds, the sounds of a city or a suburb.

You don't have to live on a seacoast or on a farm or even in a wooded suburb to find natural phenomena to delight your child. You can make a special expedition to a park to watch the stars or a rising, full moon on some crisp, clear October night. You can make the acquaintance of animal babies in a zoo or in a pet shop. You can collect leaves in a park. Find tiny fossils in crushed stone in a driveway. Watch a caterpillar hump along a sidewalk. Grow small plants in jam jars on a windowsill. Marvel at floating castles and gray dust-rolls of clouds. Take walks in the fog and in a warm rain. Learn the feel of the wind as it whips and whispers down apartment house canyons.

One of the most fascinating ways in which to make

nature intriguing to a city child—or any youngster—is to buy a good hand lens, or magnifying glass. Even the tendrils of ivy clinging to a building, an ant in a sidewalk crack, a stalk of geranium in a flower box, and a few grains of sand take on a magical aura when magnified.

Your job isn't to try to teach your child precisely about what he observes. You don't have to know exact scientific names or explanations or make lessons out of what you do together. All you really need to do is to be interested yourself and invite your offspring to share your wonder.

Often, just following your child's lead is enough. Four-year-old Jeanne, taken by her mother on a routine shopping trip, became intrigued with smelling the flowers in the raised concrete boxes decorating the shopping center's walkways. She tugged on her mother's hand to share her discovery. Mother and daughter spent almost half an hour smelling the various types of flowers, comparing their scents, their shapes and their coloring—happy and oblivious to other shoppers. This, too, can be called science.

"Now that Jeanne is ten and much too dignified to smell flowers in public, I remember that day with special delight," recalls her mother. "You need a small child for an excuse to take time to appreciate the small, daily wonders of living."

Do try to answer your child's questions—even when they come when you're frantically busy trying to feed the baby, keep the bacon from burning, and answer the doorbell. If you must postpone his queries, take the initiative in reopening the subject. If you're on a crowded bus when your moppet asks you why that lady sticks out in front, or what happend to the leg of the girl wearing a brace, or why that man has no hair, you'll have to whisper you'll tell him later. Then do. You want him to understand that it's always all right to question, but that sometimes questions should be saved for a more appropriate time. After you've done this several times, you can probably avoid embarrassing questions in a childish treble by a look that says "Later," in recognition of an unspoken "Why?" in your offspring's eyes.

Sometimes, you'll discover that your youngster is satisfied with just a short, quick answer. "Why is that cloudy stuff coming out of the teakettle?" "Because it is hot."

But more often than most parents realize, a child is seriously questioning a physical phenomenon and would be fascinated by a more complex explanation of steam. And his interest could lead to a number of learning experiments with boiling and freezing water.

When asked a what-is-steam-type of question, one mother replies to her child, "Do you want a long or a short answer?" Almost always the youngster answers, "Long!" and wiggles comfortably in anticipation of a fascinating learning session.

If you don't know an answer, tell your child, "I've wondered about that myself; let's find out together." Teaching your youngster how and where to find information to feed his boundless curiosity is one of the most valuable gifts you can give him during his early-learning years. If you're stumped about finding adequate source material, ask the nearest librarian. Invest in an elementary science encyclopedia and look up answers for your child. Other possible sources of knowledge: a science museum (many exhibits are not too old for preschoolers), a natural history museum, a TV science program, or a science-discovery kit from a toy store.

Sometimes when your child asks a what-would-happen-if type of question, you can answer, "Let's experiment and see." What happens if you bring a snowball into the house? If you keep it in the refrigerator? The freezer? Is it really pure, clear water, if you let it melt? Is snow always the same? Do snowballs pack better in some snowfalls than in others? Can you make snow again if you refreeze the water? Can you make ice again after it has melted?

There are many excellent books describing experiments in the physical sciences which are written, usually, for elementary school youngsters, but which are also suitable for preschoolers, with the help of parents. The library nearest you should have several of these books. The experiments are not only stimulating, learning activities, but also delightful rainy-day fun for you and your small fry.

In trying these experiments, you can begin to encourage your child to have a scientific attitude about them. Before you begin, talk over these questions: "What are we trying to find out?" "How can we set up an experiment to discover the answer?" "What do you think will happen?" "What materials will we need?" Whenever possible, let your youngster perform the experiment himself. He'll learn far more that way than he will watching you.

When the experiment has been completed, urge your child to review precisely what did occur. Then ask him, "Do you think it would happen again this same way if we did it again?" "What did this experiment teach us?"

Your child will do a better job with these experiments if you've given him opportunities previously to pour water, to wash plastic dishes, and to measure dry materials and liquids with measuring cups and spoons.

No more than a brief sampling of science experiments for preschoolers can be included here, but they will give you an idea of materials you can find in your library.

For example, to help your youngster sense the reality of air, suggest that he crumple some newspaper at the bottom of a glass or a glass jar, turn the glass upside down and submerge it, straight down, in a pan of water for several seconds. When he removes it, he will find that the newspaper is not wet because the glass was already filled with air, which kept the water away from the paper.

To see the air itself, have your moppet repeat the experiment, this time turning the glass on its side after it is submerged in the pan of water and watching the air bubble up.

For a third experiment, suggest to your child that he submerge an empty glass in the water and turn it on its side so it fills with water. Then, show him how to tuck the end of a piece of rubber tubing into the top of the glass, turn it upside down again in the water, and force the water out of the glass by replacing it with air blown through the tubing.

Demonstrate to your moppet how he must empty the air out of a medicine dropper before he can fill it with water. Let him blow up a balloon and watch it jet around the room when he releases it. (On a visit to the nearest big airport, you can point out the jet planes that fly on this same principle.) Help him make a pinwheel on a pencil to demonstrate the force of moving air. Let him watch firsthand how a gas station attendant puts air into tires and how basketballs and footballs are filled with air to make them more fun to play with.

You can even turn the pouring of fruit juice or a soft drink from a can into a science experiment. Punch one hole in one can and two holes in an identical can and encourage your small scientist to observe which empties faster. See if he can deduce why.

Experiments with water hold a special fascination for a small child, especially when he is permitted to perform them himself. For example, you can help him learn about evaporation by having him measure out a tablespoon of water in a shallow dish, set it in a warm place, and observe what happens to it. Add a drop of food coloring, if you wish, to make the experiment more interesting.

Next, suggest that he set out three shallow dishes, the first with one tablespoon of water, the second containing two tablespoons, and the third, three, and watch to see whether the amount of liquid in the dishes affects the rate of evaporation.

Here's another experiment you can try when your preschooler comes indoors from play with a pair of wet mittens. Suggest that he put one in a warm place and another in a cold spot and observe which one dries more quickly. If it isn't mitten weather, try the experiment using dishcloths or washcloths dipped in water and wrung out. On a windy day, your youngster can experiment to see whether a wet dishcloth hung on a line in the breeze dries faster than one hung in a bathroom.

To teach your child about another property of water, have him fill a small glass or wide-mouth jar to the brim with water. Gently and slowly have him stir in about two tablespoons of sugar or salt, using a thin wire, such as a straightened paper clip. He should notice that the water does not run over, because the sugar and the salt will dissolve. Then have him repeat the experiment using sand and see what happens.

If your child has begun to understand about evaporation, ask him what he thinks will happen if he lets the salty or sugary water evaporate. Suggest that he experiment to check his conclusions by spooning out some of his salt or sugar solution into a shallow dish and check later to see what has happened.

When your moppet has grasped the idea that the air picks up water, ask him if he thinks the water can ever be taken out of the air again and suggest that you try to see if it is possible.

One of the easiest experiments is to take a cold bottle of milk from your refrigerator (or a glass of ice water, if your milk comes in cartons) and let it stand a few minutes on your kitchen counter on a hot, humid, summer day, or at a time when your kitchen is warm and steamy. Your child can observe the drops of water collecting on the outside of the glass.

Other ways to demonstrate condensation: Let your moppet squiggle or letter on a steamy, bathroom mirror after a warm shower. Show him how you can boil water in a pan on the stove, and how the evaporated water will collect on the bottom of a second pan you have filled with ice and hold over the steam. Let him feel summer dew and autumn frost and make the connection between these phenomena and the idea of condensation. Let him run his finger over a car window that has fogged up in cold weather; talk about why it happens and how the car's defroster functions.

Your preschooler can have great fun experimenting —in the kitchen sink, bathtub, or plastic outdoor pool—

to see what kind of objects will float and which will sink. Help him to keep a record of his experiments as he tests such everyday materials as blocks, bottle caps, paper clips, pennies, paper, bobby pins, pencils, crayons, capped empty bottles, capped bottles full of liquid, various types of soap, cork, empty milk cartons, milk cartons full of water, and cloth. Encourage him to form conclusions about why some objects float and others do not.

For a fascinating variation, let your child experiment and demonstrate that if he puts a fresh or a hard-boiled egg into a small pan of water it will sink. But if he gradually adds salt to the water, the egg will float.

Experiments with sound usually delight preschoolers. For example, one of the simplest ways in which to demonstrate that vibrations produce sounds is to make a cigar-box guitar or a cereal-box banjo by stretching rubber bands of various thicknesses around the box. Your child can be helped to observe that the thinnest rubber band produces the highest notes when plucked and the thickest band the lowest. Tuck a thin block of wood or a strip of plywood under the rubber bands to act like a violin bridge. Have your child listen to the change in sound as you move the block to stretch the strings.

To help your child understand that the more vibrations per second, the higher the sound, tape a playing card to your child's up-ended tricycle so that the edge of the card is flipped by the spokes of a wheel as it revolves. Let your child spin the wheel by rotating the pedals and observe that the faster he turns, the higher the sound the card produces.

To demonstrate to your youngster that sound can travel through other media than air, suggest that he take two wooden blocks or two flat stones or two small pot lids and bang them together, listening carefully to the sound. Then, in the bathtub or in the backyard pool, have him put his head under water and repeat the banging. He'll discover that it's much louder, because of the sound-conducting property of the water.

One child discovered an interesting variation of this principle. Lisa found that if she put one side of her face tightly against her brother's, she could hear him scratch his opposite temple much more clearly than if his face were only an inch or two away from hers when he was scratching. Her father explained to her that bone is also a good conductor of sound.

For other sound-conduction experiments, put a watch on a bare, wooden table and have your child press his ear to the other end. He'll hear the ticking quite clearly. If you blow up a balloon and press it tightly between your child's ear and your ticking watch, he'll also be able to hear it distinctly.

Use a long garden hose as a telephone, with you on one end and your preschooler on the other. Or tap a signal to your child from one room to another or from one floor of your house to another, using a water pipe to conduct the code.

Make your moppet a tin-can telephone this way: Find two empty tin cans with no sharp edges where the lids have been removed. In the center of the bottom of each one, punch a small hole with a nail. Through each hole, thread one end of a long, stout, cotton string and tie it into a large knot or around a little stick to anchor it securely. Stretch the string tight and use as a telephone, with you speaking into one can while your child holds the other against his ear and listens.

For a variation in sound-conduction experiments, cut a piece of cotton cord about one yard long. Loop the center of the cord around a teaspoon and have your preschooler hold one end of the string in each of his ears, as he bends over slightly balancing the spoon. If you strike the spoon gently with another spoon or a nail, your child will hear a sound like church bells.

The world of growing things abounds with opportunities to help your young sprout gain a firm grounding in science, and you don't have to have a green thumb yourself to plant seeds of interest. Even if it isn't green-up time in the suburbs, there are dozens of experiments you and your budding botanist can try.

To demonstrate how a plant grows from a seed, buy a handful of large, dried beans. Let your child try to break one of the beans open. When he finds it too hard to split, remind him that seeds usually need rain to start growing and suggest that he see what happens if he soaks several of the beans overnight in water.

The next day, your child will be able to peel off the coating of a bean seed and open it to discover the tiny shoot and root inside. Tell him that the surrounding sections of the bean, called seed leaves, are food for the baby plant.

To show your preschooler how the baby plants grow, try this: Line a glass with a wet paper towel. Keep water in the bottom during the experiment. Tuck one of the soaked beans between the towel and glass, where your child can watch it grow.

Cut off one of the seed leaves from a second soaked bean, carefully leaving the embryo plant and add it to the glass. Do the same with a third, removing one entire seed leaf and half of the second. The difference in the growth of these three tiny plants demonstrates how much they need the food contained in the seed.

Radish seeds can be used to point up other essential needs of growing things. Fold two paper towels in the bottom of each of three glasses. Have your child put ten radish seeds in each glass and cover each glass with a third folded paper towel.

In one glass, have your child sprinkle only a few drops of water. Soak the paper thoroughly in the second glass. Have your child fill the third glass almost full with water. Label each one and check the results in about five days. Help your youngster to understand that the seeds in the first glass did not get enough water; those in the third didn't get enough air.

Plants need proper temperature to grow, too, as you can help your child to learn. In the bottom of each of two cups, have your bairn put a pad of wet, absorbent cotton. Sprinkle with bird seed. Cover the cups with saucers; place one cup in the refrigerator and keep the other at room temperature. Compare the results every day for a week.

Seeds can sprout in the dark, if they are wet, airy,

and warm enough. But they also need light to grow into leafy plants after they have used up the food within the seed. Demonstrate this to your child in this way: In each of two bowls, have your youngster place a wet sponge and sprinkle it with bird seed. Keep half an inch of water in the bowls during the experiment. Place one bowl on a sunny, warm windowsill; cover the other with a large pot, or keep it in a very dark spot. Have your child check them every day for two weeks, but be careful not to let the second bowl stay in the light longer than a minute.

You can show your child other ways in which to make new plants besides starting them from seeds. For example, put young pussy willow stems in water in your home and watch new roots grow from the bottom. After they are well rooted, you and he can plant them outdoors.

Here's another way. Let your moppet cut a long leaf from a snake plant into 2-inch pieces. Have him plant each piece about 1-inch deep in damp sand in a bowl. Keep the bowl covered with glass and in the light until new plants grow.

A favorite experiment to show how plants use water is this: Cut off the end of a white carnation stem under water, place the carnation in a glass of water colored with bright ink, preferably red, and let it stand in the sunlight. Within a few hours, the petals will turn the color of the ink. You can even split the bottom half of the stem carefully and put each section in ink of a different color to obtain a two-tone bloom.

If you can't get a carnation, the experiment works, too, with a leafy stalk of celery you have freshened in water for half an hour.

Encourage your preschooler to make collections—insects, leaves, rocks, shells, pressed flowers—for the beauty of the objects and the pleasure of having them. When he runs out of shelf room to keep his collections, suggest that he begin to compare and classify his treasures, to keep his prizes, and to discard his duplicates. Then help him follow where these interests lead.

For example, suggest that your child start a collection of seeds and keep a count of how many seeds and what kind he finds in apples, grapes, peaches, cherries, watermelons, peanuts. Let him study closely dandelion seeds, milkweed seeds, an acorn, a coconut, and a maple seed. Ask him to guess how seeds can travel from one place to another. Then give him an opportunity to plant some of his seeds and watch them grow. (You'll have to do some background research first to guide this experiment to a fruitful conclusion.)

If you can manage it where you live, give your preschooler a chance to learn about a pet firsthand. If you can't house a dog or a cat, try goldfish, tadpoles, turtles, a hamster, a gerbil, a parakeet, or an ant farm. In learning to care for another living thing, your child will gain much information about the needs of all creatures for food, rest, water, protection, and clean living quarters, and he will also learn about the inevitable cycle of birth and life and death.

Today, there is only a thin line between scientific learning materials and some types of toys—both help your child learn more about physical phenomena. For example, magnets make fascinating playthings, especially if they are extra large and your child has a collection of nails, paper clips, and metal buttons with which to experiment. Help your preschooler make a list of the household objects that can be moved about by a magnet and the ones that cannot. And you can put paper clips on slips of paper that have the letters of the alphabet or the numerals he is learning and let him go fishing for them with a magnet that is on a string attached to a stick. He can "read" you the ones he hooks and throw back into the pond those he misses.

Other materials that can help children absorb scientific ideas in the guise of play include: a large-size prism, field glasses, a see-through alarm clock that permits observation of gears in motion, a two- or four-egg incubator, a stethoscope (a real one isn't expensive and permits a child to hear actual heartbeats and chest sounds).

CONCEPT FORMATION

Whether you help him or not, your preschooler will constantly be sorting out and combining and reorganizing and shifting the great mass of sensory impressions he is receiving and the perceptions he is acquiring, as he tries to understand the world around him. Often he makes mistakes. Often he draws incorrect conclusions. But usually the fault is not in his way of thinking, or in his reasoning abilities. He just doesn't have enough of the right information to begin with.

Four-year-old Carolyn hears her mother tell her father that Mr. Simpson, next door, has gone to the hospital. "I wonder what they will name the baby," she comments, for her only knowledge about hospitals concerns mothers who have returned from hospital stays with infants.

Donna, also four, is listening when her mother remarks to her older brother that she only has a dollar in her purse. "Why don't we go to the toy store and get some more money," Donna suggests, helpfully. Her brother hoots and calls her a ninny. She cries, and through her tears says to her mother, "Well, every time you buy something in the toy store, you give the lady at the counter money, and she gives you back more money." Donna's observations have been correct; she simply has not had the opportunity to learn that money can come in different denominations.

The exposure of small children to television has compounded this problem of concept formation. Television gives youngsters great masses of information and impressions for which they don't have enough background knowledge. Why does the Indian lady who comes to see the President wear a long sort of dress, instead of moccasins and a feather? Did dinosaurs live back in the olden days when grandma was a little girl? Is that cowboy really dead like the robin we found in the backyard the other day?

Preschool children actually want to learn, can learn,

do learn enormous amounts about history, geography, and economics without overt adult help, educators and psychologists are now acknowledging. They formulate surprisingly complicated explanations for facts they can't comprehend—not so much because they enjoy fantasy and magic, but because they crave understanding. And they are capable of dealing with important and significant ideas about the physical and social world.

Today, some educators are beginning to pioneer the teaching of major concepts about social studies, economics, and the physical sciences to children in nursery schools and kindergartens. These programs generally take inspiration from the contention of Dr. Jerome Bruner, professor of psychology at Harvard University, that "any subject can be taught effectively in some intellectually honest form to any child at any stage of development." [3] They are backed by studies in which researchers and nursery school teachers have recorded and studied the conversations of small children who strive to understand major concepts about life and death, God, outer space, the community in which they live, the world of work, cause and effect, and natural phenomena.

"It is important to see and accept the fact that young children are not 'unready' for the many challenges involved in intellectual experience," explained Dr. Wann.[4] "Unreadiness is a concept as fruitless as it is difficult to determine. The notion of unreadiness arises from overgeneralization about a given period or age in the development of children. It is more helpful to think, rather, of individual children as being ready at all times for some kind of learning, ready perhaps for different kinds of experiences, a different approach, another level of concept development. This way of looking at the problem leads to action whereas dismissing children of a given age as 'not ready' leads to stagnating inactivity. The children, meanwhile, go on with their trial-and-error learning which involves much misinterpreting and misconceiving."

Designing new curricula for nursery schools and kindergartens to meet this new awareness of the intellectual needs of small children is still in the exploratory stages. A few nursery schools and kindergartens where these intellectual needs are officially recognized are developing new types of teaching methods and goals. And research is underway in many academic fields to try to determine more precisely what the "key concepts" are that small children should acquire as a basis for future learning. These key concepts are not to be taught by rote, researchers emphasize. But learning experiences should be designed to help small children discover and use these understandings for themselves.

Unless you are unusually fortunate, your preschooler will probably not have an opportunity to attend a preschool where his needs to form significant concepts about the world are appreciated and directed. Even if he does have, you, as his parent, still have the major role in guiding his development of accurate concepts.

What can you do to help your youngster? Although research is still in the preliminary stages, several guidelines are emerging: It's a help, first of all, just to appreciate your child's need to form concepts. Listen to what he says and try to understand the information or misinformation behind his remarks. Let this guide you into activities that provide him with more correct information. Carolyn's mother and father just laughed indulgently at her, for example. But her mother might have made it a point to read her a beginning book about where babies come from. She could have been taken to see the neighbor's new kittens and to the zoo to visit baby animals with their mothers. Some museums have exhibits depicting how babies grow inside of mothers, and they have displays in which baby chicks can be observed pecking their way out of their shells. Her mother could also have read her books about hospitals and what happens to people there and about the role of doctors and nurses.

For Donna, a complicated game of playing store might be useful. In some experiments with intellectual development in kindergartens, playing store has been successfully used to help youngsters understand not only the role of customers, food producers, manufacturers, and retailers, but also about profit and pricing.

Donna's mother might have helped her daughter set up a grocery store in one corner and used it as a way to teach her about money, about making change, about the problem of getting produce and products to sell, and about how prices are determined.

In the course of such activities, a parent can guide a child into formulating questions he does not have answers for and can suggest that he take his questions to people who can supply him with missing information. A grocery store manager, for example, would probably be willing to explain to a small child the answer to a question he has thought through ahead of time with your help.

In addition to helping your child gain experiences that supply him with information to correct his misconceptions, you can also guide him into new ways of thinking about the information he has.

A bus trip, for example, can be much more meaningful to a preschooler if you help him fit it into an over-all concept about transportation. Help him to think of all the kinds of transportation he can—boats, horses, cars, buses, trains, planes, rockets, bicycles, feet, helicopters—and talk about when he would use each one. Which methods would he use for hauling big packages? Which if he were in a hurry to go a long way? Which would probably cost the most money? This gives more meaning to short excursions on which you take your child and provides a foundation for future learning.

Children younger than first grade can absorb a surprising amount of learning about time, given some help, researchers have discovered. One good way to begin is to make a short, simple time line for your child. In a piece of string or rope, tie a knot about every foot to represent each of your child's birthdays to date. Then explain to him that the section of string in between the knots represents a year of his life. Talk with him about what events occurred during each of these periods—the time when he was so little he had to drink out of a bottle, and when he first learned to walk, and when you took that vacation trip to California.

Then make him a time line for yourself and point out

some of the major events—perhaps when you moved into your present home, or you started going to kindergarten yourself, or you were married, or he was born.

Then you can tell him that a time line back to when Abraham Lincoln was president would stretch around your living room and to the kitchen. And one back to the era of George Washington, when our country got started, would go to the end of Jeff's driveway. A time line reaching to the year Columbus came to America would extend to the corner of your block, and one showing the period of the first Christmas, when Jesus was born, would go all the way to his school. To make a time line that would represent the era when dinosaurs lived on this earth, it would probably have to stretch from your house to his grandmother's in the next state and back again thirty times.

It also helps your moppet gain some understanding about the changes that come with passing time if you can take him to a museum of history. Seeing the tools used by Indians or in ancient civilizations or even by pioneers in the United States a century ago gives him more observations upon which to base his developing concepts.

A preschool child won't be able to grasp completely the immeasurable periods of time that have swept over this earth, or even to sort out all the events that he has heard about according to chronology. But, Dr. Wann emphasized, "to assume that we should wait to encourage and help children to gain concepts of time and change until they can handle true chronology is to deprive children of one of the important learnings of early childhood. To defer help and encouragement in this area is to frustrate a basic intellectual need of today's young children."

Maps make a good tool to help you orient your preschooler in your community, in our country, and in the world. Researchers who have worked with four- and five-year-olds, especially the kindergarteners, find that they can grasp many major ideas associated with maps.

You might begin, for example, by helping your child draw a map of his room—locating chairs, bed, lamps, windows, door. He can learn that north is always at the top of the map and something about the concept of scale. Next, the two of you might construct a map of your block or your neighborhood, laying it out on the floor on a large sheet of white oilcloth or wrapping paper. You can crayon in streets and driveways, construct houses and buildings out of blocks, and use toy cars and trucks for traffic. From this point, it's relatively easy for your child to use and appreciate a map of your community, and eventually a map of the United States. He'll be able to follow your route on a trip and to locate places talked about on television news programs, with some assistance.

By age four, many youngsters are able to put together an inlaid puzzle map of the United States and by five, maps showing all of the continents and oceans. Many five-year-olds can be helped to use a globe to find foreign countries they have heard about.

Because of frequent television programs about rocket launchings, most preschoolers have acquired many small pieces of knowledge about outer space. You can help your child form this smattering of facts into useful concepts by showing him a model of the solar system and explaining how it functions. (You can buy solar systems in the form of mobiles for his room, or make one yourself with his help.) He's not too young to look for mountains on the moon with you, or to grasp the basic principles governing eclipses, should one be visible in your area.

Adult occupations is another subject about which most preschool children have garbled knowledge and misconceptions. Where Daddy goes in the morning and why can be the basis for much learning, both by conversation and by actual experience. If possible, it's a valuable learning experience for a small child to go to work with his father—perhaps on a Saturday or on his father's day off—riding the train or bus, sitting at his desk, and watching what he does for a few minutes. If you are employed outside the home, even part-time, you should plan ways to help your youngster understand as much about your job as possible.

You can point out to your moppet what other fathers do—policemen, barbers, pilots, doctors, firemen, salesmen, factory workers, gas station attendants, musicians, actors—and the relationship of this work to the community's welfare. You can encourage him to make some beginning discoveries about the division of labor (perhaps by comparing the amount of time it takes you to check out of a supermarket when the checker does the sacking, and when both a checker and a packer work on your purchases together). You can compare mothers' work with fathers' and help him discover why both are of importance to the family.

You should also be helping your child learn that an increasing number of women are taking on jobs traditionally held by men. A girl, in particular, needs to understand that there are policewomen as well as policemen, that women can be doctors as well as nurses, that her sex should not be a limiting factor in what she will eventually choose to become. This may not be difficult, if you are working outside your home yourself or if you have working women among the friends your youngster knows. But if the only women your child sees are fulltime homemakers or are working in such traditionally female jobs as supermarket checker or teacher, you may want to make a special effort to give your offspring opportunity to see women in other occupational roles—on television programs, in a few of the newest books for children, or actively at work, if you can.

A child's sense of sexual identity is established early in life and you don't want your daughter's ideas about being female to become limitations on the development of her ability. The changing role of women in society is something you should talk about with your child—boy or girl. And you should discuss with your offspring your own feelings about what you are doing: perhaps that you held a paying job before you had a baby but now you want to be a full-time mother, though some day you may take a job again. Or that you are working full- or parttime outside the home because you enjoy it or because you want to contribute to the family's income. The point is not to provide a role model yourself for a daughter so much as to help her become aware of the choices she will eventually have. You don't want to put limitations on her options for the future by letting her get the idea that full-time homemaker and mother is the only adult occupation available for most women.

Yet you should also help your child—boy or girl—to understand the enormous importance of mothers and how valuable their work is both to the family and to society as a whole. You should also talk about the special contributions a father makes to a family and see that each child has an opportunity to play an appreciated part in keeping the family functioning well.

A study of occupations can make a good, basic frame of reference for many of the short field trips you take with your moppet. For example, if your child is getting bored with helping you buy groceries, suggest that he try to count the number of different types of workers in the supermarket on your next trip. Help him to observe which jobs take the least training, and which call for experience. And encourage him to speculate on other types of jobs which might be done behind the scenes, or by other workers in other places.

Often you can take advantage of events in your neighborhood to help your youngster learn important concepts. For example, if there's a new house or apartment building being constructed in your neighborhood, you can use it to stimulate your child's formation of concepts. Why do you think a bulldozer is used to dig the foundation, instead of men with shovels, you can ask your child. (His reasoning should lead him to observe other situations in which machines are employed to spare men hard, physical labor.) Why does one group of men work only on putting in the pipes while another crew does nothing but lay the brick? Why is insulation placed between the inner and outer walls of the house? Why is a building inspector's permit tacked on that tree in front? What is the purpose of the blueprints the builder is reading?

You also should be aware that your child is constantly forming concepts in the area of social relationships. Often these concepts can be distorted, psychologists and doctors have discovered, by misinformation and incorrect assumptions garnered from television.

Melissa, age five, had been unusually weepy and upset, clinging to her father and unwilling to play with her friends, for the past two weeks. After much cuddling and questioning, she finally told her mother that she was afraid her parents were going to get a divorce. Melissa's mother could think of no reason why her daughter could have had such a mistaken idea, but finally the little girl whispered something about "that lady who had dinner with Daddy."

Then Mrs. Whitman remembered that she and her husband had invited a woman business associate of his to dinner about two weeks previously. Melissa had connected the woman with a family-situation drama she'd seen on television in which a divorce had been precipitated by a dinner-table incident involving another woman.

Mrs. Whitman assured Melissa that she and her husband intended to stay happily married and looked for experiences which would help the child understand more about family relationships. About this time, the entire family was invited to a wedding. Mrs. Whitman spent several days before the ceremony explaining to her daughter what would happen, what words would be said during the service, and how seriously she and her husband took the marriage vows they had made in the same way, long before Melissa's birth. Melissa listened spellbound to the marriage ceremony and for weeks afterward played "wedding" with her dolls.

If you observe carefully how your child plays with other children and relates to them, you can also help him form intellectual concepts that will guide his social behavior in the future. Why should you share your toys with your guest, you can ask your child. How would you feel if you were Billy visiting at our house? Why do you suppose good manners are important? Why does Jerry act like such a bully, and how can we help him to play in a nicer way with other children?

One reason television has such a powerful effect on

small children is that they usually can't separate reality from make-believe on the programs they watch. Often you can suggest play activities to your youngster that will aid him in making this distinction.

Monica's mother, for example, was concerned because her four-year-old seemed to believe everything she saw on television as being true and real. So she arranged for the child to visit an audience-participation show, see the cameras, and watch the show being produced. Then she encouraged Monica to play "television show" at home. Together they made a television "camera" by mounting a cardboard box on an old, doll carriage base. Then they talked about whether they would put on a real-life program, or a pretend story. For factual programs, Monica gave weather reports, neighborhood news, and helped her mother stage a cooking demonstration. For "made-up story" shows, she had her dolls act out cowboy-and-Indian plots, spy thrillers, and talking-animal dramas. And now she asks her parents to label programs she watches as being made-up or true whenever she isn't sure.

As your child begins to grasp new concepts based on his observations, you'll often notice that he plays them out, in variations, with his toys and with other small fry. If you listen to his conversations and watch his play, you'll usually discover how much he has actually grasped of the concepts you want to help him learn, and you'll have a good guide to the type of experiences to offer him next.

It will be years before your child can fully grasp and use most of the concepts you introduce him to as a pre-schooler. But they form a basic framework upon which he can build his future learning and make sense out of the great masses of information and detail his brain is recording.

Your child is going to be gathering information and forming concepts whether you help him or not. But with your assistance, he will form more useful concepts and fewer misconceptions, and his future learning will be more efficient.

TOYS

The years between three and six are the peak years for toys, the ages when your child most needs and most enjoys playthings. Many of the toys listed in Chapter 5 for eighteen- to thirty-six-month-old youngsters are still appropriate for three- to six-year-olds. Some of the learning toys for preschoolers have already been mentioned in this chapter. But here is a quick summary of basic-learning toys for this age group. Your child won't need them all, of course, and many he can use in the park or at a nursery school. But generally, he should have access to some playthings in each category:

• Blocks—well made and in as large an assortment as possible; simple, fit-together construction materials of wood or plastic, block cities, giant cardboard or hollow wooden blocks, if you can afford the money and the space.

• Toys to imitate grown-up activities—dolls, doll house, doll clothes, doll carriage, doll equipment, telephone, cash register, trains, trucks, planes, play money, unstructured playhouse that can serve a multitude of purposes, doctor and nurse kits, farm and zoo animals, housekeeping equipment, gardening tools, carpenter tools. (Whenever possible, give your child the real thing instead of a toy. It works better, lasts longer, gives a great sense of pride and accomplishment.)

• Materials to encourage creative arts—crayons, finger paints, colored pencils, chalk, blackboard, clay or the equivalent, poster paints, paper of all kinds from little colored pads to large sheets of wrapping paper for murals, weaving looms. Invest in a stand-up easel if you can.

• Musical equipment—record player, drum, tambourine, finger cymbals, triangle, bells, xylophone.

• Props for dramatic play—costumes, costume box full of discarded clothing and large pieces of cloth, masks, hand puppets, hats, wigs, materials for playing store and school.

• Games that teach numbers—dice, counting puzzles,

dominoes, simple board games that involve counting, measuring tools, number rods, telling-time games.

• Toys for loving—cuddly baby dolls, stuffed animals (which small boys need as much as little girls).

• Equipment for active, physical play—swing, glider, wheelbarrow, wagon, scooter, tricycle, balls, trampoline-type bouncing equipment, climbing apparatus, tree house, crawling tunnel, skates, merry-go-round, ride 'em trucks and trains, punching toy.

• Toys to encourage sensory learning—inlaid puzzles, peg boards, geometric insets, Montessori-type dressing frames, lotto games, color-matching games, teleiodescope, flannel board with number and letter cutouts.

• Science-discovery equipment—magnifying glass, magnets, prism, seeds, ant farm, incubator.

NURSERY SCHOOL

When enthusiasm for early learning first became wide-spread in the late 1960s, there was considerable push to get almost all of the nation's three- and four-year-olds into nursery school. Higher-income families were demanding the same kind of advantages for their youngsters that disadvantaged families were expected to get for their children from Head Start programs. Newest research shows clearly, however, that a half-day nursery school program begun at age three or four does little to boost a child's intelligence over the long run, that it's the amount and kind of stimulation in the home from the earliest weeks of life that make the critical difference.

But nursery school programs can add considerably to the stimulation your child is getting at home. And they can provide other social and developmental values.

But nursery schools differ enormously—in approach and in desirability for your child. There are experimental groups in university settings where reading, math, and Dr. Piaget's experiments with conservation are a part of the curriculum and Montessori schools where it's taken for granted the five-year-olds will be reading at second grade level. There are Head Start schools where the emphasis must be on helping children make up for lost learning time, traditional nursery schools where social development is the primary goal, boys-only sports clubs, and play groups intended chiefly as a baby-sitting service.

Should your particular four- or three-year-old attend school? Much depends on whether the nursery schools available to you fit his individuals needs and stage of development, on your neighborhood, on your time schedule, and on the availability of playmates.

A preschooler needs a great deal of experience playing with other youngsters who are approximately his age and at his developmental level. He needs to learn about the rights and feelings of others, about sharing, about being a member of a group.

In some neighborhoods, you can provide your child with preschool playmates simply by opening your door. In others, finding even one friend involves a complex of telephone arrangements and chauffeuring; for such a child, almost any nursery school (which meets established state standards) is a valuable experience.

A preschooler should have the experience of being away from his parents for a few hours during the week to help satisfy his cravings for beginning independence and to ease the transition into formal schooling. Here, too, almost any nursery school with competent, experienced teachers benefits a child.

(For the occasional moppet—usually a three-year-old —who protests sobbingly and repeatedly against going to nursery school, attendance should probably be postponed for six months or a year. Most of these reluctant small fry are delighted at age four with what they feared and rejected so strongly at age three.)

A preschooler needs great opportunity to grow physically, to use large and small muscles, to develop his skills of perception. A well-equipped nursery school, with more outdoor equipment, more blocks and more art materials than a home can provide, can make a major contribution here. Some of the males-only sports clubs do a superb job of helping small boys develop self-confidence and skill in games.

A preschooler needs learning stimuli to help develop his mental abilities—probably in far greater amounts than most parents and educators have realized until recent research. Montessori schools, some laboratory schools in university settings, and a few private nursery schools do have programs based on fostering a small child's inherent drive to learn, his ability to absorb language in both written and verbal forms, and his power of concentrating on what fascinates him. And they do it without sacrificing any of the other beneficial aspects of nursery school experience.

Unfortunately, these schools are still extremely few and inevitably have long waiting lists. (A large percentage of Montessori schools have been started by groups of parents who have, in some cases, even raised funds to train a teacher and provide a building in order to have Montessori training for their offspring.)

But most nursery schools still concentrate on play, on social experiences, on sharing, on group-ism, and on emotional adjustment. Few pay even lip service to mental development and often argue against it because "we are protecting your child's right to be a child," or "thinking doesn't begin until age seven or eight," or "we don't want to duplicate the curriculum of the kindergarten," or "we certainly don't want to start pressuring children at this age." As Dr. Wann pointed out, even equipment and materials which could provide children with mental stimulation are usually used instead to promote group activities, for "play therapy," and for small-muscle coordination.

By rerouting a preschooler who needs mental stimulation back to bead-stringing and the sandbox, many nursery schools actually serve as a holding-back or braking operation on mental development.

An intelligent, interested parent can satisfy almost all of a preschooler's needs—given time, information, space, money, a neighborhood with other small children, some learning materials, and enough freedom from other responsibilities. Since these ideal circumstances are rare, the best course you can follow is to make an objective appraisal of available nursery schools, your child's individual personality and needs, and your family's assets —and choose the school which can best supply what your family cannot.

In most communities, kindergarten programs have changed little for several decades, although small children have—and research is increasingly emphasizing the importance of early learning. The basic purpose of helping a youngster adjust to school often has the effect of convincing him that school is a social place to meet his friends and not a learning environment.

New curriculum ideas for kindergartens, based on the eagerness and abilities of five-year-olds to learn, are being developed in some university centers. Many school systems are experimenting with more intellectual content for five-year-olds. Already, it has been convincingly demonstrated that kindergarteners can learn to read, that they can absorb important concepts regarding history, geography, science, and economics—if taught by teachers who understand their special kinds of learning abilities.

Kindergartens in the future will probably have little resemblance to the traditional, readiness-and-adjustment-to-the-group programs which now prevail in most school systems. Until this happens in your school system, your child will need to go to kindergarten for its value in other areas of development, of course. (If your community does not have public kindergartens, you should make the effort to find a private one for him.) And you will have to do what you can to keep his fascination with learning alive at home.

7. Should You Teach Your Preschooler To Read?

Teaching a preschool child to read is one of the happiest, most worthwhile, and most satisfying forms of early learning. It is also the subject of widespread research —with bright youngsters, culturally-deprived children, three-year-olds, small fry who are mentally retarded, emotionally disturbed, or brain-injured, moppets of average I.Q., four-year-olds, two-year-olds.

Reading is being taught to preschoolers by parents at home, by psychologists in child-development research centers, by educators in nursery schools, and by six-year-old sisters who like to play school in the family room. It's being taught phonetically, by sight-word techniques, by combination methods, and by no method at all. It's being taught with sandpaper alphabets, with newspaper comic strips, by first grade primers, by television, by programmed readers, by phonograph records, and by computer-operated typewriters.

Regardless of method, or motivation, most of those who

163

try to teach preschoolers to read in any consistent way are generally successful. Those who have written about their experiences—in professional journals or in letters to the editors of newspapers—usually comment on the great joy, eagerness, and enthusiasm with which the preschoolers have learned.

Several years ago, the *Chicago Tribune* and a score of other newspapers in the United States ran a thirteen-week series of daily cartoon strips which showed parents how to teach small children to read by a simple, phonetic method. A year later, a mother in a small, northern Illinois town sent this letter to mark the anniversary of the *Tribune*'s series, an event which she said "is celebrated at our house by much reading."

Mrs. John M. Sullivan wrote:

I doubt if you are fully aware of the door to a world of knowledge which the *Tribune* opened to children in the Chicagoland area. I do not see how you can begin to imagine the hesitant and curious way in which two of my little girls and I opened that door. Our doubt and curiosity soon gave way to an overwhelming enthusiasm and eagerness.

The older little girl started first grade this fall, reading as well as her second and third grade brothers. Our four-year-old spends many happy hours each week educating and entertaining herself. In our home there are no longer moans of "What can I do now, Mommy?"

My two little daughters and I have developed an understanding and a closeness that I never dreamed possible from our "association" in the field of education— an unexpected bonus from the reading-strips. I am looking forward to the same delightful experience of opening the door to learning for my other two babies and only wish, dear *Tribune*, that you had been around when the *eight older ones were small*.

Contemporary interest and research about teaching preschoolers to read began in the late 1950s. It was touched off, generally, by new discoveries about the functioning of the human brain itself. And it was fueled, in part, by the growing concern of educators and parents about the large percentage of elementary school pupils who were failing to learn to read.

First grade reading problems have been the subject of worried complaints and public and professional clamor since the early part of the twentieth century, when the teaching of reading was first beginning to be studied by American educators. The development of standardized testing during the 1910s and 1920s gave formal evidence that a substantial percentage of first graders were, indeed, failing in reading. Endless and unresolved cycles of debate began on issues such as phonics versus sight-word teaching methods; oral versus silent reading; grouping within the classroom versus whole-class instruction; experience charts versus standard textbooks.

Although the educators battled each other about methods, they did present a united front to parents in one respect: Don't try to teach your child to read yourself, they ordered. Reading is such an enormously complicated mental endeavor that even trained teachers sometimes fail to teach successfully, parents were told. So how can you possibly succeed? You'll use the wrong methods. You'll pressure your child. You are too involved emotionally to help your youngster. You'll ruin his eyes. Besides, he can't possibly learn until he has a mental age of six—maybe even seven or eight—so you're wasting your time and inviting emotional disaster.

Parents, especially those who were well informed about education, got the message. Many of them even refused to answer their children's questions about letters, words, signs, and labels. Many unwittingly, but effectively, blunted their small fry's spontaneous interest in written words— an interest which first grade teachers are instructed to build again slowly and painstakingly.

After the *Tribune*'s preschool reading series began to appear in print, dozens of parents wrote the paper with comments like this: "We're so glad to know it's all right to help our child with reading. He's learned so much on his own, from watching television commercials and asking us questions about words. But we were afraid the school wouldn't approve."

"I spent most of kindergarten being scared my teacher would find out I knew how to read," commented a young editor at the *Tribune*. "My parents told me not to let on because the teacher thought it was wrong to read before first grade."

The theory that a child needed a mental age of six or six and one-half before he could learn to read was based on several studies made during the early 1920s and 1930s which showed that among first graders, those with a higher mental age learned to read better than their classmates.[1] These findings were generally interpreted to mean that the older a child, the better he could be taught to read, and that youngsters with a mental age of less than six could not read. The occasional moppet who did come to first grade already reading was thought to be so highly intelligent, he learned to read almost spontaneously. Or his parents were suspected of pushing him to satisfy their own neurotic feelings of inadequacy.

Actually, what these studies do show is that the higher the child's I.Q. the easier he will learn to read, say contemporary critics who have reviewed this evidence. Furthermore, they point out, it isn't valid to draw conclusions about preschool reading from research which deals only with six-year-olds taught by a sight-word method in a formal classroom situation.

Several experiments with early reading were done in the first two decades of this century, with promising results. But the implications of these findings were submerged in the wave of progressive education that dominated the schools for decades. The most influential researchers on child development were concerned chiefly with establishing age-level norms for youngsters, with little regard for the environmental influences that produced the behavior they described. Because almost no attempts were made to teach reading before the age of six, almost no children learned before they reached first grade. It was easy to assume that they couldn't.

During this period, too, educators—probably compensating for the harsh learning conditions and rote drill of earlier educational eras—were greatly concerned about social and emotional development, sometimes more so than about mental growth. It was generally considered more important for a child to learn to adjust to his age group and to get along with his classmates than to develop his mental abilities in reasonable proportion to his potential.

But in recent years, the consequences of failing to learn to read adequately have become more clear. Public pressures have helped stimulate educators to ask themselves new and more far-reaching questions. As long ago as 1954, for example, Dr. Arthur I. Gates, professor emeritus, the Institute of Language Arts, Teachers College, Columbia University, said in a symposium on reading problems:[2]

> Certain factors suggest both the possibility and the advisability of helping a child to learn to read long before the sixth year, indeed, perhaps during the fourth year.
>
> Children learn to understand spoken English and to use it long before the sixth birthday. . . . Children are getting an increasing amount of experience with picture books, comics, radio, television, and other visual-auditory media almost from infancy. The result of this is that children are well advanced in getting information and stories of all kinds, long before they learn to read. The difficulties of teaching reading to a large class are so great that the average child learns rather slowly. By the end of the first grade, the typical child cannot read material anywhere nearly as complex as he can secure through other media. This puts reading at a very great disadvantage. . . .
>
> Readers of this article may feel that the writer's comments on the difficulties of learning to read in the first grade are hardly in harmony with the suggestion that children learn to read earlier. The reader is reminded that the difficulties and confusions attending the new and strange group life, the necessity of learning in a

distracting group situation, the teacher's difficulty in giving each child much quiet individual guidance, and the meagerness of the content of what a child can read in the first grade in comparison with what he can get from spoken words and pictures may comprise greater hardships than those attending easy-going guidance and self-employment at a younger age.

Today, the teaching of reading to preschoolers is well underway in many different places in the United States. Today, there is no doubt that preschoolers can be taught to read—in several happy, satisfying, successful ways. A sampling:

In a Montessori school, in Oak Park, Illinois, four-year-old Bobby spreads out his 4- by 6-foot mat on the floor, then takes a collection of simple picture cards from a nearby drawer. One by one, he lines up the pictures in a row, down the side of his mat. He studies the first one, a dog. Slowly, Bobby sounds out the word under his breath. Still repeating the initial "d" sound, he goes to an open rack full of colored letters cut out of sandpaper-covered cardboard. He locates a "d," takes it back to his mat, and places it beside the pictue. Next, he finds an "o" and then a "g," sounding out each letter as he walks back and forth.

Bobby successfully spells out "man" and "cat" and "hat." Then he tries "bus." But he can't remember what letter makes the initial "b" sound. So, for the first time he asks for adult help.

"What says 'b'?" Bobby asks the Montessori directress. She goes with him to a bin of large-size sandpaper letters that are glued on cardboard rectangles. Gently, she guides the fingers of Bobby's right hand so that his fingertips trace the sandpaper shape of "b," while she repeats the sound of the consonant. After learning the "b" sound through his eyes, his ears, and his fingers, Bobby is easily able to find it himself.

Without any more help or supervision, Bobby spells out the rest of the names of his picture cards. Then, he sits back on his heels, contemplates his work for a minute, and then quietly returns all of the materials to their proper place.

No one has instructed Bobby to do the reading-spelling lesson. No one has supervised him or graded him or pressured him or even praised him for doing it. He could have chosen any of dozens of other activities. But he was sounding out and making the words because he enjoys the learning and the sense of competence it gives him.

Dr. Montessori discovered that preschoolers could learn to read and write and enjoy the process enormously when she was developing her first slum-area school at the beginning of the century. Ever since, Montessori schools have taught preschoolers to read and to write. Dr. Montessori's textbooks—now published in several new editions in the United States—are full of descriptions of the eagerness and the enthusiasm with which her culturally-deprived youngsters learned to read. After studying their progress, level of interest, and rate of learning, Dr. Montessori concluded that children learn to read most easily at ages four and five.[3]

The widespread and enthusiastic revival of Montessori schools in the United States has been due in large part to parents' inteest in early reading. For the Montessori method of teaching reading and writing is one of the best and most complete available to preschoolers today. Much of the entire Montessori program aims at educating a youngster's five senses and is designed to culminate in the joyous and exciting discovery by preschoolers that they can communicate by reading and writing.

A child in a Montessori school learns to write before he learns to read. And he learns with such ease and pleasure that most elementary school teachers find it difficult to believe. He begins by learning how to control the muscles in his hand—by manipulating equipment designed for this purpose, by working with geometric form boards and inlaid puzzles, and by tracing and filling in geometric shapes with a pencil. Then he practices tracing sandpaper letters with his fingers as he learns the sounds these letters make. In this way, he learns all of the physical motions necessary to write before he ever risks making a mistake by actually trying to write with pencil on paper. When he is ready to try, he usually succeeds immediately and joyfully.

Dr. Montessori's classic book, *The Montessori Method,* describes the tremendous excitement and delight with which her small preschoolers discovered that they could indeed write real words, as a result of previous training of the senses and having learned the sounds of the letters. "The first word spoken by a baby causes the mother ineffable joy," she wrote. "The first word written by my little ones aroused within themselves an indescribable emotion of joy."

Only after a child has learned to write well does he learn to read, Dr. Montessori believed. He should be taught reading by sounding out the words phonetically, then repeating them rapidly until he understands them. Often reading, too, comes with the same burst of excited joy with which a child discovers that he can write.

Four-year-olds, on the average, take only a month or a month and a half from the first preparatory exercise to achieve their first written words, said Dr. Montessori. Five-year-olds need only about one month. "Children of four years, after they have been in school for two months and a half, can write any word from dictation and can pass to writing with ink in a notebook," wrote Dr. Montessori. "Our little ones are generally experts after three months' time, and those who have written for six months can be compared to the children in the third elementary. Indeed, writing is one of the easiest and most delightful of all the conquests made by the child." Moving from writing to reading takes about two weeks, reported Dr. Montessori.

The same easy progression from writing to reading has also been noted by Dr. Durkin in her studies of youngsters who learned to read at home before they entered first grade. More than half of these children were intrigued with printing words before or at the same time they became interested in reading. Such a child would draw or scribble with an ordinary pencil, or write on a blackboard at home. Then he would start to copy letters of the alphabet. Soon, he would begin to ask questions about words ("Show me my name!") and about spelling. And from this interest, he would advance naturally into reading.[4]

The idea that a preschooler will almost teach himself to read, if given the opportunity to explore freely in an environment that contains the proper stimuli, is also basic to the newest method by which small children are learning to read—the "talking typewriter," developed by Dr. Moore. Dr. Montessori called her schools, with their carefully-designed learning equipment, a "prepared environment." Dr. Moore calls his learning device a "responsive environment."

Just how children can—and will—teach themselves to read if given an opportunity is clearly shown by watching how youngsters use talking typewriters when they are available in a nursery school setting. For example, four-year-old Scott sits alone in a wood-paneled booth, facing an automated, talking typewriter. The machine is dictating to him, describing a photograph shown on a small screen above the keyboard. Scott begins to type. "This is a walrus. Isn't he funny-looking? You may think he looks like a man with a mustache."

As Scott types each letter, the machine pronounces it for him. At the end of each word, the machine repeats the letters and speaks the word. When Scott gets to "m-u-s-t-a-c-h-e" and hears the typewriter call out "mustache," he laughs with delight.

"Mustache! That's really funny. I like that word," shouts Scott with obvious pleasure. He wiggles happily in his seat, hums a bit to himself, and goes on to the next sentence.

The machine now changes photographs and begins dictating again. "Another strange sea beast is the seal."

"Seal? Seal!" says Scott, joyously. "I've never heard that word before. I like that one, too."

Although he thinks of it as just a delightful game, Scott is really discovering for himself the connection between written and spoken language. And he is learning to use in combination the communication arts of reading, writing, listening, and speaking.

The machine that guides him into these happy discoveries looks like a standard, electric typewriter keyboard attached to a large steel cabinet. Keys have been painted in different colors to suggest correct fingering, and Scott's fingernails have been daubed with water colors in corresponding colors to teach him, subtly, to touch-type correctly.

Above the keyboard is a viewer, where letters and words can be displayed. To its left is the screen for pictures. The workings of the machine are covered with a transparent plastic housing that lets Scott see how the instrument works, but keeps his fingers away from the moving parts. The carriage-return is programmed to work automatically; the keys cannot be jammed by too rapid typing, and the paper comes on a continuous roll.

After about twenty-five minutes, Scott tires of typing and raises his hand. Immediately, a booth attendant, who has been monitoring him through a one-way glass, quietly opens the door and says "Good-by, Scott. Will you please tell Mary Beth that it's her turn now." Deliberately, she makes no comment on what Scott has—or has not—accomplished.

In another cubicle, a pig-tailed moppet is telling a booth attendant, who is seated beside her, about a forthcoming trip to Philadelphia. The attendant suggests that she record the story so she can write it down later. Excitedly, Pamela proclaims, "We are going to take an airplane to Philadelphia. We're going to see my cousins and my grandmother and my grandfather. We will have a wonderful vacation, and we will not come home until Wednesday."

"Are there any words that you don't know how to spell and would like to learn?" asks the attendant.

The child lists them: "Philadelphia, cousins, we're, vacation, Wednesday."

"I already know how to spell 'grandfather' and 'grandmother,'" explains Pamela and ticks through them quickly.

The booth attendant then writes out the five new words and has them flashed on the viewer. Pamela copies them on the typewriter. Then, to her own dictation on the tape recorder, she writes her own story.

Pam and Scott are two of hundreds of preschoolers who have learned to read and write by means of the talking typewriter. The machines they used were installed in the second floor of a converted house, the headquarters of the Responsive Environments Foundation, Inc., in Hamden, Connecticut, a nonprofit organization formed to test and develop responsive-environment devices, such as the automated typewriter, and to train others in their use. The foundation also provided a setting for a nursery school attended by childen of average I.Q. who use the typewriter as part of their preschool program.

Three- and four-year-olds attended the morning sessions of the school. Each child, including two youngsters who started at the age of two years, seven months and two years, four months, had a thirty-minute turn with a talking typewriter, a turn he was free to decline or cut short if he wished. It's a central theory of Dr. Moore's that reading and writing are "autotelic," that is, they have intrinsic interest for small children who want to learn solely for the pleasure of learning and not because they are motivated by fear, reward, approval, or competition. So every effort is made to remove pressure of every kind.

Each child's first introduction to the talking typewriter is made by another moppet—not by an adult. The small guide explains only that the youngster need not use a typewriter unless he wants to, that he can leave whenever he chooses, that he must give someone else a turn after thirty minutes, that he need not explain his coming or going, and that if he leaves the booth for any reason, his turn is over for the day although he can come again the following day.

"A child seldom refuses his turn," commented Joseph R. Dunn, administrative director of the Hamden foundation. "But the youngsters do refuse often enough so we know that they feel free to do so, and that we haven't rigged the situation unknowingly in some way. Most of the boys test us out early in the fall to see what we would do if they refuse a turn. Nothing happens. So now they go for months without skipping a chance—and then it's usually because there is a birthday party downstairs they don't want to miss. Occasionally, a child refuses to leave, however, when his turn is over. In that case, a booth attendant simply picks him up and takes him downstairs."

When a child first begins to use a talking typewriter, he is permitted to play freely with the machine, exploring its possibilities and punching keys at random. As he hits each key, the machine calls out the name of the letter or symbol. It's not unusual in this phase for a moppet to type an entire page of ***** or &&&&&. One three-year-old who delighted in dollar and cent symbols often wrote them by the score.

When the booth attendant watching outside detects that a child is beginning to lose interest in random typing, she changes the machine's controls. Now, the typewriter prints a single, large-size letter on the viewer and calls out its name. The youngster suddenly discovers that all of the keys except the corresponding one are locked. With exploration, he finds the correct one. The machine then pronounces this letter again and presents him with a new one. Soon it becomes a game for the moppet to strike the right key and shout its name before the machine can repeat it.

When he's ready for phase three, the typewriter unexpectedly pesents the youngster with a complete word in the viewer. Keys remain locked until the child discovers that he must type the letters in left-to-right sequence, with the machine calling out each letter as he finds it and then the completed word.

After several such sessions, the child suddenly realizes that he has not been typing random series of letters, but actually forming words. He discovers that he can read. At this point, some youngsters jump up in great excitement and rush out of the booth to share their elation.

From single words, the child now progresses to sentences and to stories. Sometimes programming on the talking typewriter is varied so that he can dictate his own stories, then write them from his own dictation. Sometimes the machine is switched so it teaches him phonetic equivalents for letters, or rules for sounding out words. He also learns to write the letters he knows on the blackboard and even to use script after practicing on a talking typewriter with a cursive typeface.

"Even two- and three-year olds, including retarded children, can learn to print and write in a cursive style," notes Dr. Moore.

When a youngster is tired or bored, he merely raises his hand and leaves the booth. He's never urged to try again or to stay a bit longer. He's never praised or scolded. "If you pat him on the head today and then don't tomorrow, you're implying a kind of punishment tomorrow," explained Mrs. Ann Shrader, laboratory supervisor.

No one who is "significant" to the child is told how he is progressing, not even his parents or the teacher who conducts the rest of the nursery school program, emphasizes Dr. Moore. Without being told, the child realizes that no adult who praises him or criticizes him knows how or what he is doing in the typewriter booth—and therefore, he is in no danger of failing to live up to the adult's expectations. There is no competition from classmates, no embarrassing attempt to read in front of a class. No stigma is attached to giving a wrong answer to a machine when it doesn't care and no one else knows. And there is no motivation for learning except that inherent in the activity itself.

Every attempt is made to keep adults from using the typewriters to "teach" the child and to detract in any way from his freedom to discover for himself. That's why the adults observing the children and programming the machines are called "booth attendants," rather than "teachers."

Even though they understand the "discovery philosophy of learning," some adults still have an almost irresistible urge to try to teach a child directly, says Dr. Moore. "It requires constant monitoring by the laboratory supervisor to keep booth attendants from teaching," he points out.

Kindergarten-age moppets attended the afternoon ses-

sion of the Hamden nursery school. Among eleven
youngsters in a group of children with average I.Q.s, at
least one read at sixth grade level, and all enjoyed books
and stories on their own. For fun, they published their
own newspaper, creating and typing the stories themselves, doing editing, artwork, and headlines, and handling the production. The youngsters also wrote poetry
and an occasional play, which they produced themselves.

"It's curious, but when they have been in the program
for awhile, these youngsters begin to act like gifted children," observed Dunn. "They become much more creative. Visitors say to us, 'No wonder you are succeeding
so well; you're working with bright youngsters to start
with.' It's hard for them to believe that the reading, writing, creative children they see were originally chosen for
this program because they had an average I.Q."

Dr. Moore's interest in how learning theories could
be applied to helping youngsters learn the symbol systems
which are increasingly important in our technological
society led him to begin his experiments with typewriters. One of his first subjects was his own daughter,
Venn, a curly-haired moppet who was then two and one-
half years old.

Venn was fascinated by the opportunity to explore her
father's electric typewriter and was permitted to strike
keys at random while her mother, Ruth, a close associate
in Dr. Moore's research, called out the name of each
letter, much as the automated typewriter does now. A
motion picture made when Venn was two years, eleven
months old, shows the little girl happily typing sentences
like this, "Bea is my dog; Maggie is my doll" on the
typewriter and chalking phrases like "Venn is a girl" on
a blackboard. At this point, she could read about 1,000
words, identify many others by phonetic clues, and sail
through first grade books with ease and pleasure.

Another movie made four months later pictures Venn
writing longer sentences on the typewriter and both up-
percase and lowercase letters on her blackboard. Her
intense satisfaction, as she reads from a viewer, is obvious.

From this beginning, Dr. Moore and Richard Kobler,

an engineer from the McGraw-Edison Company, designed the complex, automated, talking typewriter now in use. Its official name is the "Edison Responsive Environment," or "ERE." Dr. Moore describes it as a "computer input and readout device, three distinct memory systems, an audio-recording system, and two visual exhibition systems, all of which are integrated by a central electronic logic and control system."

The first large-case test of the typewriter's potential took place at Hamden Hall Country Day School, a private institution located near Yale University, where Dr. Moore was then teaching. The three-and-one-half-year experimental study was financed by the Carnegie Corporation of New York.

Venn was a member of the first nursery school group to try the talking typewriter, and all of the youngsters experienced her delight in discovering for themselves how to read and write. When this group reached the end of first grade, those who had been in the program at least two years were reading, on the average, at sixth grade level. When they were second graders, one of their teachers recalls, they knew vocabulary words like specious, onomatopoeia, perspicacity, irony, and euphemism, and enjoyed doing adult crossword puzzles, writing stories and poems, and publishing their own newspaper.

None of the youngsters who has learned to write and read via a talking typewriter has had difficulty adjusting to school, although some of them have been bored with too-easy and too-routine workbook assignments when they would have preferred more creative work.

"I doubt that real competence, per se, produces trouble in school," comments Dr. Moore.

Careful follow-up reports on children who have used the typewriters in nursery school, then advanced into public schools, confirm this finding. "In one way or another, every follow-up letter that comes to us says, 'This youngster enjoys school.' Children who have any kind of verbal skills do not plateau when they go out to other schools," said Dunn. "The longer they have been in the program and the more they have absorbed, the easier is their adjustment to school. A child who has been used to learning on his own is not tied to a teacher in order to progress. When he finds himself in a large class, he is able to keep going on his own, without the teacher's constant help and supervision."

In 1964, the Responsive Environments Foundation moved its laboratory from Hamden Hall into its own headquarters, so that experiments with the talking typewriter could be carried on with a wider variety of children than those attending a private school. The machine has now been used there and elsewhere with great success, by youngsters described as average, gifted, retarded, culturally deprived, brain-injured, mentally ill, and physically handicapped.

The youngsters who have used the typewriters in experimental groups have had complete and repeated evaluations of their vision, speech, hearing, general health, I.Q., and emotional status by experts in each field. No damage of any kind has been found to be related to the children's experiences with early learning.

In one group of five children, all certified by the State of Connecticut as retarded and awaiting openings in state institutions, two were able to attend regular public school after working with the talking typewriter. Two were admitted to special educational classes in public school. Only one, a youngster with severe convulsive disorders, actually entered the state institution. Talking typewriters have also been used with success to help bring autistic youngsters back into contact with people.

Culturally-deprived moppets respond with great enthusiasm to an opportunity to learn language skills by discovery, too. In a Mount Vernon, New York, project designed to give the mentally stimulating aspects of preschool education to as many children as possible, a talking typewriter was placed in a store-front "nursery-mat" in a commercial area. (It was so named because mothers could drop off a child for a morning session that took just about as long as washing a load of clothes in a laundromat.)

In the pilot study, one of the twenty-four culturally-deprived four-year-olds who used the instrument for short periods during these hour-long school sessions learned to read well enough to skip kindergarten completely. Others started school with a greater chance of success than such youngsters usually have.

Ten talking typewriters have been used to teach reading skills to 106 three- and four-year-olds from public-aid families in Chicago's Project Breakthrough, backed by funds from the Office of Economic Opportunity. The youngsters had I.Q. scores ranging from 55 to 112, with a median of 85. Almost all of their parents were functionally illiterate. Few of the children had ever been read to at home. Most had limited verbal skills and it seemed likely they would have great difficulty in school and would repeat their parents' pattern of school failure, unemployment, and poverty.

But, the Chicago study demonstrated, even children chosen as least likely to succeed can teach themselves to read using a talking typewriter and can improve their verbal abilities in the process.

Billy, for example, would have been the despair of any sensible reading teacher when the program started. He was hyperactive, negative, uncooperative, and rebellious. He refused all efforts by teachers and classmates to be friendly. He lived in a public-housing project with an illiterate mother on ADC. His speaking vocabulary—the rare times he could be persuaded to talk at all—was meager and generally mispronounced. Furthermore, he was only four years old.

With other children recruited by a social worker from public-aid lists, Billy was bused daily to a Chicago vocational school, where a nursery area was set up and the talking typewriters installed in individual booths. Each shift of three- and four-year-olds stayed an hour, participating in standard nursery school activities until they were invited to take a turn with a typewriter. The only professional teacher involved in the program directed these nursery school activities; the typewriter booths were staffed by attendants with only a few weeks of training.

Billy refused his first two invitations to try the typewriter. But then he became intrigued with the machine and explored it vigorously. In his ninth session, after having spent a total of two hours in a booth, he began to recognize the shapes and sounds of letters. After 37 minutes more, he learned to write the first four letters of his name. Soon he was able to add the final letter.

After 46 sessions—or 18 hours—Billy could recognize letters when he saw them outside of the typewriter booth. He could write many letters himself and knew most of their phonetic equivalents. He could recognize some sight words, and he was ready to start reading unfamiliar material independently with great joy and pride.

A fringe benefit of the talking-typewriter sessions was a notable improvement in speech patterns of the children, many of whom used only a limited southern black dialect, according to the project's director, A. Louis Scott. Researchers studying the program also noted that the youngsters became much more sensitive and open to learning stimuli of all kinds in their environment as their language skills increased.

That a talking typewriter would stimulate the minds of culturally-deprived youngsters is not as surprising to many who have seen Dr. Moore's experimental groups as is its success with youngsters of average or higher intelligence who come from good homes. Dr. Moore believes that the great potential for learning—especially in the area of symbol systems and inductive thinking— inherent in preschool children has been largely overlooked in all youngsters.

"If we have a positive effect on a child who comes from a home conducive to learning, it really shows the power of this theory," commented Dunn.

There is a history of early-childhood stimulation, usually by a parent, in the case of every extremely bright young person for whom records exist, points out Dr. Moore. He says no harm can come from such stimulation, "as long as there is a safety valve by which the child can turn it off when he wishes."

The talking typewriter can also be programmed to help youngsters discover basic mathematical concepts, to teach any of six foreign languages, and to introduce children to ideas in other areas, such as geography and social studies.

In itself, the typewriter is not some sort of magical gadget that automatically educates and stimulates children, Dr. Moore emphasizes. Rather, it is an essential part of an over-all program of mental stimulation based on sociopsychological principles of learning.

The typewriter is just one of a whole new class of machines being developed which are responsive to a child's learning activities, he explains. He feels that one of education's greatest challenges is to find new ways in which children can learn to master the complicated symbol systems upon which our technological society is increasingly dependent.

The high cost of the talking typewriter has limited its use in early-learning programs, but it has demonstrated clearly that, given a chance, young children will help themselves learn to read eagerly and happily.

"The future will demand more in terms of abstract understandings," he says. "We need better methods of imparting skills in information processes. And we need to learn how to make the most of the early years of life, when learning ability is so high." The big question for the future, notes Dr. Moore, is, "Can we use modern technology, the behavioral sciences, and mathematics to create new ways of teaching which will give youngsters creative challenges and a sense of enjoyment, or must we drive them with pressures?"

Both Dr. Moore and Dr. Montessori have taken great precautions against pressuring a child into reading. The youngster's only reward, in both situations, is the joy of discovery, the feeling of accomplishment and mastery, the fun of knowing. Yet even skeptics who aren't convinced of the value of preschool reading acknowledge with surprise the intensive interest, concentration, and delight with which children use the sandpaper alphabets and the talking typewriter.

The warmth, praise, and enthusiasm of human teachers play a greater role in some of the other ways in which preschoolers are being taught to read today. This is particularly true of methods designed for parents to use at home—without the abundance of Montessori materials, or the expense of the talking typewriter.

Best known of the sight-word methods intended to teach small children with parents' help is the system developed by Glenn Doman and Dr. Carl Delacato, who didn't start out, originally, to teach reading to small children. They were concerned with treating brain-injured children and experimenting to find the most effective methods possible of pouring sensory stimuli of all kinds into the damaged brains of their patients, in hopes of activating unused and uninjured brain cells. To their surprise, Doman and Dr. Delacato discovered that their four-, three- and even two-year-old brain-injured patients could learn to read and do it with enormous excitement and joy.

These researchers at the Institutes for the Achievement of Human Potential then began to encourage parents to teach normal, unhurt preschoolers to read. They learned, too—at the ages of four and three and two. What impressed their parents and the researchers most was the great delight and enthusiasm with which they learned.

With the Doman-Delacato method, a youngster is shown a large-size card with red lettering two inches high, preferably when he's being cuddled close by a loving parent. He's told what the word says, casually, and without fuss. Next time he's handed the card, he's asked what it says. If he responds correctly, he gets a hug and a joyous burst of enthusiasm from his mother or father. If he doesn't remember it, he's merely told again what the word is, casually, and without further comment. When the youngster has learned several dozen words, he begins using word cards of a small size, until eventually he's reading from primer-size type. From here, it's an easy step into easy-read books designed for children who have learned to read with typical sight-word vocabulary in first grade.

The two- or three-year-old who is taught to read is much happier than one who is not, says Doman. He is far less hyperactive and much easier to control because he has been given one excellent way in which to satisfy his insatiable hunger for learning.

However, phonetic reading methods, which teach a child from the very beginning that printed words are just written-down sounds which he can easily learn to decode, do a better job of teaching reading than sight-word techniques, like Doman's. (Debate does still persist on the sight-word versus phonics issue, however. But nineteen out of the twenty-two best-conducted and most complete research studies on the subject show a clear-cut and continued advantage for youngsters who learned by techniques that introduce phonics at the beginning of instruction. The three remaining studies are inconclusive, but none favored a sight-word method or a sight-word method with gradual introduction of phonics.)[5]

So when the *Chicago Tribune* decided to develop a comic-strip feature to help teach preschoolers to read at home, a phonetic plan was chosen. This one was developed by a nursery school teacher, Mrs. Dorothy Taft Watson, and included several games and learning activities.[6]

"This is a game to teach you what the letters say," a parent begins by telling a preschooler. Showing the child the large letter "h" in the comic-strip panel, the mother points out, "This letter looks a little like a chair."

The next panel shows a little boy running. The mother reads, "Harry ran home so fast, he was out of breath." With the next panel, "He fell in the chair, and all he could say was 'h - h - h - h - h.'"

Then, the parent encourages the youngster to run across the room, pretend he's out of breath, and collapse in a straight-backed h-shaped chair as he makes the out-of-breath "h" sound.

Finally, the mother suggests that the child listen for the "h" sound as she says such words as hat, helicopter, heart, and hammer. If the child is still interested, she asks him to think of words he knows that begin with an out-of-breath sound, and she writes them down for him.

"A very young child usually does better if he doesn't

even know the names of the letters at first, except for the vowels, which sometimes make the sound of their own name," explains Mrs. Watson. "Later on, you can easily teach your youngster the alphabet by means of the familiar alphabet song," she tells parents.

The second comic strip teaches "m," linking the sound with Mary, moon, mouse, milk, and monkey and the shape with a pair of child's mittens held together, thumbs outside. Next comes "p," associated with the noise Papa makes puffing on a pipe. This time the parent writes down a series of words starting with "p" and asks the child to draw a circle around each "p" as she sounds out the words.

Parents are advised by Mrs. Watson to play the game of letter sounds with a child for only a few minutes at a time. She suggests that each session be no longer in minutes than the youngster's age in years—three minutes for a three-year-old, five minutes for a kindergartener. But the game can be played several times a day, provided the moppet is interested and enjoying it.

As a child learns the sound of a letter, he is encouraged to look for it in places other than the comic strip—on cereal packages, highway signs, labels, headlines. Many mothers wrote the *Tribune* that they had invented games to be played in the car, or while doing dishes, which involved the child's listening for initial consonant sounds in strings of words or sentences concocted by the parent.

"Remember that for preschoolers, phonics is still very much a game—just as learning to walk and to talk were games," advises Mrs. Watson. "Keep it light, happy, and relaxed. Your child has no deadlines to meet, no tests to pass, no possibility of failure.

"Your child will often forget the sound of the letters, particularly at first," explains Mrs. Watson. "Just tell him the right answer at once. Don't make him guess or wallow. Do praise him delightedly for each sound he learns and each word he sounds out. Your child will learn far faster when he's motivated by praise. And most important, do share his excitement at his own cleverness and the new world that is opening to him."

Next, "s" is taught, linked with snake. Then comes "w" with its windy sound, emphasized by having the moppet hold his hand in front of his mouth as he says witch, wild, wagon, wolf.

The letter "t" is learned in association with the *t-t-t-t-t-t* tick of a clock, and "r" becomes the *r-r-r-r-r-r* sound made by a big, cross dog, which a child can have ferocious fun imitating.

When a preschooler has learned the sounds and shapes of these six consonants, all of which make a consistent sound, he's ready for his first vowel. Mrs. Watson tells preschoolers that vowels are "fairy letters" because they can do magic tricks with other letters, and because every word must have one. She teaches the short sound of "a," as in apple, first.

Then comes the exciting minute when a preschooler is ready to roll consonants and a vowel together to make his first word, "hat." To emphasize the smoothness of this procedure, the *Tribune*'s comic strip shows a snow-suited moppet rolling the "h" and "a" and "t" into a snowball.

Starting with the eighth comic-strip lesson, a pre-schooler is able to read a very simple comic written for him, using only the sounds he has learned to identify and blend together. For the rest of the thirteen-week newspaper series, he gets a new comic every day to read by himself, as well as instructions in a new sound or reading technique.

"When your child begins putting consonants and vowels together to make words, it's important that he learn to do it smoothly and quickly, so he will recognize the word he is sounding out," stresses Mrs. Watson. "You may have to work with him several days before this comes easily and naturally. Tell him he need not sound a word he already knows. He should just read it right off."

As the lessons proceed, a preschooler learns the sound of "j," "l," "z," "b," and "d," reading easy comics and playing simple games based on letter shapes or sounds. (For example, a child can act out "d" by marching about, making the *d-d-d-d-d-d* sound on a pretend drum.)

The fairy letter, "e," as in egg, comes next. The letters "ck" together are taught as "k" sound. With "g," a preschooler learns the hard sound, as in "gag." But he is also told that sometimes "g" sounds like a "j," and if he can't make sense out of the word using the hard "g," he should simply try the other one.

Parents are encouraged to make up simple games to play with their children, using these basic sounds. For example, a sixteen- or twenty-square bingo-type card can be drawn, using letters instead of numbers and raisins or small gumdrops as markers. A mother can be washing dishes or sewing as she calls out the sounds for the youngster, who shouts out his own name when he has succeeded in marking a row up or across, and then he gets to eat the markers.

After a youngster has learned the consonants and short vowel sounds, the *Tribune*'s reading program begins to teach him shortcuts. First, he learns a few common digraphs—two letters which join together to make a special sound of their own, such as "ch," "sh," "qu," "ph," and "th."

Linguists point out that "th" actually makes two different sounds, as in "then" and "thin." But this is a subtlety that doesn't trouble preschoolers. Almost always, without being told, they will choose the correct pronunciation without realizing the difference.

After the common digraphs, Mrs. Watson introduces phonograms, groups of letters which almost always sound the same, such as "ook," "ank," "ink," "all," "ight," "atch," "or," "er," "aw," and "oy." These word patterns make it easy for small children to learn some of the most irregular vowel sounds and consonant combinations. And by blending these parts of words with initial consonant sounds, a preschooler can increase his reading vocabulary rapidly and easily. This technique is an important part of the new linguistic reading programs.

At this point, Mrs. Watson advocates teaching a preschooler the names of the five vowels. He is taught one

simple rule about when a vowel says its own name:
When two vowels come together in a word or have only
one other letter in between in a short word, the first
one usually says its own name and the second one keeps
quiet. For example, if a youngster already knows how to
ponounce "at," this rule makes it easy for him to learn
"ate" and "eat." And it gives most moppets a wonderful
sense of mastery and competence to be able to apply
this rule to read "rob" and "robe," "kit" and "kite,"
"hat" and "hate," and "bat" and "boat" and "bait."

Critics of phonetic reading methods always point out
the inconsistencies in the English language, such as the
different sounds of "ough" in "cough," "rough," "bough,"
"dough," and "through" (the worst single example of
sound-spelling inconsistency in English), and subtle shades
of difference in the pronunciation of vowels. But advocates
emphasize that 85 percent of all English words are
completely phonetic and almost all of the rest are at
least partially so. And it's far easier to learn the spelling
of the forty-four basic English sounds and a few rules
about when to use which than it is to memorize every
word by its total shape, as some reading methods teach.

When a child does discover such an inconsistency, a
parent should merely tell him that it is a "naughty letter"
that doesn't follow the rules, suggests Mrs. Watson. Most
preschoolers are delighted at this idea and have no
further difficulty.

As he begins to read easy books (many of which
are still being written from word lists used with look-say
methods, rather than according to phonetic principles),
a child will encounter a few common words which don't
follow the phonetic rules he's learned so far. It's easiest
just to tell him what each word says when he comes
across it and have him learn it as a sight word, advises
Mrs. Watson. Such words include: could, father, friend,
once, one, pretty, said, says, shoes, sure, there, to,
too, very, where, would, and you.

Once a preschool child has learned the sounds of the
consonants, the sounds of the long and short vowels and
rules about when to use which, and a dozen common

sight words, he can proceed independently in reading. Eventually he should be taught the names of the consonants. And he should learn the alphabet (it's easiest with the familiar song that follows the "Twinkle, Twinkle, Little Star" tune). But from this point on, he'll absorb almost everything else he needs to know from practice.

"Julie was four when your first lessons started," one mother wrote to the *Tribune*. "She whizzed through about sixty of the lessons, but then lost some interest. She just wants to read books instead. Now she has very little trouble reading her sister's third grade reader. And she's trying to teach her little three-year-old brother to read. Thank you for making reading such a wonderful experience for our little girl."

"Parents should not be afraid of helping their children with reading," emphasizes Mrs. Watson. "The subject has too frequently been surrounded by a maze of technical terms and suggestions. Too many people think of reading as being far more complex and difficult than it really is and tend to find deep and complicated reasons for any simple mistake a child may make.

"Teaching a child to read is actually quite easy," she says. "You can hardly go wrong. Anyone can easily learn the simple, basic letter sounds suitable for a preschool child. And it is surprising to see how easily and enthusiastically an extremely young child will often learn them. Phonics can be started—as a game, of course—when the child is just learning to talk.

"My own children began as babies, running in and out of my kindergarten and picking up their letter sounds along with nursery rhymes. If they saw a picture of a cow, they knew the cow said 'moo,' and if they saw a printed 'm' they knew it said 'm-m-m.'

"It is easy to teach a child the rudiments of reading," comments Mrs. Watson. "It is also a privilege and such an enjoyable experience that it would be a pity to miss it. Moreover, these early years are usually periods of high intellectual curiosity in the child. His interest is keen. He wants to learn. And he will do so more easily than he may later on. A four- or five-year-old who discovers the magic of letters will often spend endless hours experimenting with every bit of printed matter he can lay his hands on. Presently, he will discover that he can read—and then the world is his."

Giving parents a preschool reading program for their children via a newspaper comic strip was such a revolutionary concept in education that it might stir up a controversy, *Tribune* editors thought. First grade teachers, especially, would disapprove of the suggestion that part of their primary job could be done at home by a parent.

So the great burst of enthusiasm that greeted the preschool reading series caught the paper by surprise. What was intended as a public-service feature suddenly became one of the hottest circulation ideas in years. More than sixty thousand parents asked the *Tribune* for reprints of parts of the series they had missed, or mislaid. Forty thousand bought paper-covered reprints of the reading strips soon after the series ended. The entire thirteen-week reading program has been published in many other newspapers and repeated twice since in the *Tribune*. Thousands of delighted parents have written the *Tribune* about their experiences using the material with their youngsters.

"My three-, four- and five-year-old children are learning so much about reading from your comic strips," wrote one mother. "Our two-year-old listens and our nine-month-old baby eats whatever she can reach—the reason why we are missing two of the lessons. Can you replace them, please?"

"We need the last four comic strips," wrote another parent. "We were out of town for the weekend. The neighbors were saving the papers for us, but decided to keep the reading strips for themselves."

The mother of a four-year-old boy and a two and one-half-year-old girl describes her experience with the reading lessons this way:

Jimmy, my oldest son, will be five in December. He was very enthusiastic about learning to read. Last summer, he was more interested in going over his comic strips than playing outside with his friends. "Reading" his new sound was the high point of each day.

The time spent daily in learning each new sound and going over the old ones varied from two or three minutes to fifteen. I found it very important for the child, as well as myself, to find a time when there were few distractions, such as a favorite TV program for him, or demands of caring for the two youngest children for me. When either of us was tired, rushed, or had our mind on something else, nothing was accomplished.

I had some difficulty in convincing him that the sounds could be put together to form words. Jimmy has now reached the point where he can recognize on sight most of the common short words and is not afraid to tackle the long words.

After the first eight weeks, I purchased a beginner's dictionary, which I found was very helpful in building up Jimmy's self-confidence. Now he is reading books in the easy-read series. He reads to anyone who will listen to him—his father, sister, friends, even delivery men cannot escape without listening to a sentence or two. Another side effect of learning to read is that his speech has improved; each word is said clearly and mistakes in pronunciation can be corrected easily.

Linda was only two and one-half when the reading strips started, and like most younger children, she tries to imitate every word and action of her older brother. I intended to use the series with her next year when Jimmy starts kindergarten, but I have already shown her several of the comic strips to teach her sounds that she was unable to say. I now believe that she will complete the entire series and be able to read long before next September.

I have recommended the series to three mothers whose children are having difficulties with reading in the first grade. One of them even offered to buy the scrapbook I made of the comic strips. But I wouldn't part with it for the world. It will always have an honored place in my home. My son is a walking, reading testimonial to its effectiveness.

Kindergarten and first grade teachers did, indeed, make up the largest group of individuals writing the *Tribune* about the preschool reading program. But contrary to expectations, almost all of them had high praise for the idea. This was particularly true of former teachers who retired temporarily to rear small children of their own.

"I am a first grade teacher in an Indiana school," wrote one. "I think you'll be interested in knowing that my best student is also one of yours. Would you kindly send me the entire series so I can use it with all my pupils?"

"Would you please send me the first weeks of your how-to-read series?" asked another parent. "I resisted the idea for some time for fear my daughter would be bored in school and her teacher would object. Now my daughter's teacher has convinced me of my folly in not helping Lisa to read before school. By now, of course, my back issues of the *Tribune* have been hauled away by the junk man. (His children, no doubt, are all reading well!)"

In some schools, kindergarten and first grade teachers sent notes home to parents, suggesting the use of the reading strips. Explained one, "with the schools becoming more crowded, this kind of idea certainly helps the teacher of the first grade. The children entering the class then have some idea of phonics and reading, and they aren't so lost."

"We have a kindergartener in our house, and I am also a first grade teacher," wrote an Iowa mother. "I was overjoyed to find your excellent series. Now my five-year-old girl is delighted that she can read as well as her third grade sister. I only wish my own pupils had this same opportunity. This is certainly not pushing a child —but helping him develop his own potential. These children in my first grade class have good minds, but no one has encouraged them to use their minds. It is like having an arm in a sling; if it's never exercised, it will eventually become unusable."

What accounts for the remarkable success of these different reading programs, carried out in different ways, under different circumstances, by people with such varied interests and training?

One explanation may be this: All language, whether written or spoken, is a function of the brain, not of the ears or the eyes which receive it, or of the tongue and hand which produce it. Neither ear nor eye can comprehend the meaning of abstract symbols; it merely passes them along as electrochemical impulses to the brain, where they are interpreted. Recognition and understanding are in the brain, regardless of where the sensory stimulus originated.

We have long taken it for granted that every child, except the most severely retarded, will learn to speak the language used in his immediate environment and to speak it quite well before the age of five. He will also acquire the accent, vocabulary and grammar—good or bad—he hears most frequently. And he will accomplish this learning with little apparent effort, without formal training, without pressure, and usually with considerable enthusiasm and satisfaction. He will also acquire this language more easily than ever again in his life because of the physical state of his developing brain.

Because understanding and use of language are activities of the brain, it should be just as easy for a child to learn printed symbols as it is for him to learn spoken symbols, say many researchers. In fact, small children of deaf parents do learn sign language, with its intricate finger movements, more readily than verbal language.

In explaining why first graders sometimes fail to learn to read, some educators blame the fact that young minds are not able to deal with the abstract nature of printed words. These educators fail to realize that the spoken sound, "cat," is just as abstract as the printed letters, "c-a-t." Both are merely symbols for a small, furry feline. If a child's brain has developed to the point where it can understand that an arbitrary symbol represents a cat, it should make no difference whether the symbol is first perceived by the ear or the eye for transmission to the brain.

In fact, it's likely that the printed word—which remains visible and constant for as long as a child wishes to study it—may be even easier for him to grasp than a spoken word, which vanishes in a fraction of a second and varies in tone and in volume.

Suggesting that most children could learn to read in their fourth year, Dr. Gates noted, "they learn to understand spoken language quite well by their second year and psychologically, there is little difference learning, as it were, 'to read' spoken words and learning to read printed words. Spoken words come to the child through sound waves and printed words through light waves. The main reason they learn to understand spoken words first is merely that it is more convenient for parents and others to use them than to present printed material. . . . There is no evidence that printed words are more difficult to perceive or distinguish than spoken words." [7]

From the very first weeks of his life, a baby is surrounded with spoken words. He hears again and again, one at a time, simple words which are related intimately to him. His efforts to duplicate these words bring obvious pleasure and praise from those around him.

But printed words are kept hidden away from him for the most part. Those he sees in books, magazines, and newspapers are so small and jumbled together, he hasn't a chance of separating them and deciphering them.

Often the first words that a child learns to read are those which he sees large, clear, and one at a time—labels on cans, gasoline-station signs, brand names in the supermarket, key words in television commercials. These are all he's had a fighting chance to learn.

Because learning to read and learning to speak are similar as a brain activity and all normal children master speech as a matter of course, the reason why some children fail to learn to read, or have great difficulty in doing so, must lie with the way in which adults present reading to children, suggest psychologists Dr. Arthur W. Staats and Dr. Carolyn K. Staats.[8]

They point out three differences. First, speech is acquired very slowly. Learning sessions are short, frequent, and distributed throughout the day. No one expects the child to succeed immediately, or to keep working at the learning task.

Second, when a small child does learn to speak a new word, his learning is quickly and strongly reinforced. If he says "water," he is usually handed a drink. If he calls "bye-bye," someone usually bye-byes back at him. If he asks for a "cookie," he usually gets one—at least until his mother is sure that he knows the word.

Third, these reinforcements of learning are immediate.

Yet none of these learning principles apply to the teaching of reading in typical first grades, note these psychologists. Compared to the teaching of speech, spread out over all the early years of life, reading comes with great suddenness, despite readiness programs in kindergarten. And when a teacher must deal with twenty-five or thirty or thirty-five first graders, all learning to read, reinforcement of successes can rarely be strong or immediate.

The learning theories presented by the Staats in professional journals and in textbooks are complex. But generally they make the point that small children can learn to read with no more effort than they learn to talk, provided they are given ample opportunity and encouragement.

The debate about whether children younger than six *can* learn to read has generally been resolved. It's obvious that preschoolers can read and read fluently. But some influential critics still contend that even though it's possible, it's not a good idea to help a youngster learn to read before he starts first grade.

The opposition to preschool reading uses several arguments. First, the critics charge, too much pressure is bad for preschoolers, and it must take pressure to get children younger than six to accomplish first grade level work. For example, commenting on the program of Denver public schools to give parents television instruction on how to introduce reading to four-year-olds at home, one professor of education wrote in a professional journal, "We shudder at what can happen when thousands of eager parents launch an attack on their young children."

Pressure *is* bad for small children. Furthermore, it's usually ineffective. Even greenhorn parents who might be inclined to pressure a youngster discover long before their firstborn is one or two years old that pressure doesn't work—in getting a child to nap or to use the toilet or to eat peas or to wave bye-bye or to say thank you to the nice lady for the cookie.

The Denver program reported no evidence of pressuring from parents.[9] (This sixteen-week experiment which gave parents instruction on how to teach their small fry about beginning consonant sounds, letter forms and names, and letter-sound associations for some consonants brought much enthusiastic response. Of parents participating, more than 80 percent said that the instruction was helpful to them and important for their children. And about 75 percent said they would appreciate having more help in early reading, and that they intended to continue beginning-reading activities with their offspring.)

Observers who have studied other early-reading programs have not discovered any evidence of pressures or negative emotional reactions. Even in the cases of four preschoolers, now reported in professional literature, who have failed to learn to read in research programs —all twins with low I.Q., emotional difficulties to start with, and a culturally-deprived family background— researchers found that the youngsters enjoyed the program and scored better on psychological tests afterwards than they had previously.

Actually, an earlier start in reading reduces the pressures of learning by introducing a youngster to reading at the age when his brain is most able to acquire language and his fascination with words is at its peak. When reading is taught individually and informally by a parent at home, a child isn't pressured by first grade competition. He doesn't have to try to make the top reading group, or feel humiliated in the lowest section. He doesn't need to be concerned about grades or tests or keeping up with anyone else. He is free of the fear of making mistakes in public.

Every first grade reading method requires much repetition of words and/or sounds. The writers of primers often boast about how many times they can use the same word on a page or in a story. The total vocabulary introduced in first-year sight-word reading programs ranges from about 110 to 300 words. It's no wonder it takes rules and discipline to keep a six-year-old's eager, active, space-age, television-conditioned mind on "Run, Spot, run."

But two-, three- and four-years-olds enjoy repetition. What is boring at six can well be fascinating at three. What a first grader does only at a teacher's insistence, a three-year-old may easily do by his own choice and initiative.

The critics who still think no one but a trained teacher can help a child read ignore not only the new research on the subject, but also a youngster's ability to learn spoken languages. They also ignore the skill with which a majority of parents learn to adjust their child-rearing methods and teaching techniques to the individual personality of their child.

In studying the backgrounds of forty-nine youngsters who read before entering first grade to find out how they learned, Dr. Durkin found a surprising factor. Sixteen of the youngsters said in interviews that they had been taught to read by an older brother or sister. Checking out these statements with parents, Dr. Durkin learned that the older child had been solely responsible for the teaching of reading in only four cases. For twenty-four other youngsters, however, an older brother or sister did contribute part of the reading instruction. Having a sister about two years older who likes to play school has a great deal to do with early-reading ability in a preschooler, suggests Dr. Durkin.

Parents who are teaching reading at home are routinely cautioned to stop the instruction the second the youngster seems bored or frustrated or inattentive or uninterested. Most parents do this quite naturally and successfully, as letters to the *Tribune* indicate. One mother wrote:

You should have seen how interested and excited

my three-year-old boy was to learn the sounds of the letters. I believe now that if a child can tell a knife from a fork, he can tell an "a" from a "b." It's that simple.

I never pushed my children. Rather, they kept after me to teach them another sound. I only gave them one at a time and added another only when they could identify the last one on cereal boxes, newspaper headlines, and the like. I think we mothers don't always realize that we are really the child's first and most important teacher.

The wife of a missionary temporarily stationed in Portugal taught her four-year-old to read, using the reading strips from the *Tribune* mailed to her by the boy's grandmother. She wrote:

> Jon just turned four in October. We began in September. Every day, five days a week, he wants a new letter. And we review from the beginning each time! His enthusiasm overwhelms me. My mother has been sending me a week's comic strips at a time, and if Jon happens to see them, he is quite insulted that he cannot learn the new ones right away. Tonight, as he went to bed, he asked, "Tomorrow will I learn a new letter?" Outside, he calls our attention to signs, and many times a day he can be heard muttering letters and words, "h - a - m—ham!" and "f - a - s - t— fast!"
>
> I am thoroughly enjoying teaching him, despite the fact that I have never had any training. In fact, I've never had any college work.

A Wisconsin mother said, "Our kindergarten son has just turned five. I have not pushed him into learning these comic strips. In fact, I have to hold him back, and now he has only two more letters to go. He has really enjoyed learning, and he has read at school for his kindergarten teacher and principal, who were delighted. Do you realize that you are not only helping children learn to read, but bringing parents and the child closer together."

"Many thanks to you and the *Tribune* for the reading lessons from a two-year-old and forty-one-year-old," a Nebraska mother wrote. "I don't know what other mothers have done, but I made the series into a scrapbook for Lynn. We have had much fun. For the minute it becomes no fun, we put it away for another day. Two years of age is young and the attention wanders. Ten minutes was all that we have ever spent in a single day. But I do want you to know how much Lynn and her mother enjoy the whole project."

A mother who had taught her daughter to read long before the *Tribune*'s program began wrote:

I read with great interest the first article in your new series on reading. I taught my daughter to read a few years ago when she was three and one-half. She is now seven and has completed first grade. She is able to read your articles herself.

Many people told me I was making a mistake when she first began reading. But she was the one who insisted on reading. When she was younger and I would read fairy tales, she would say, "Please, Mommy, show me the words you are reading." I always pronounced all the words, with emphasis on the sounds of the letters, and it was a breeze teaching her to read. I hope all mothers will try it.

"I am having very wonderful results with my little boy," a Georgia mother wrote. "Not only is it improving his speech, but it has sparked his interest in books, and he is very enthused over being able to read words. We are both having a marvelous time. Our littlest boy, age thirteen months, leans over his crib when we make the 'magic sounds' and imitates us. Also, when we are not studying, we talk about sounds and words as we see them on signs and on food boxes or in the grocery stores."

Another mother said:

Thank you for the joy of teaching my little five-year-old girl to read. We have been working for about four months, whenever we had time and felt like it. She thinks in sounds and now is reading little books, although she may ask me about one or two words.

She does attack big words as well as little ones, simply because things like "spray starch" and "frosted flakes" are as easy to read as baby words when you see sounds instead of alphabet letters.

My four-year-old knows all her consonant sounds well and a few vowel sounds, but so far hasn't made much progress putting the sounds together. I have not had too much time to spend with her. Even our two-year-old daughter goes around making the sounds, and I'm sure someday, will enunciate more clearly because of it.

Sometime we play "M and M" bingo. I give my five-year-old a card with words and my four-year-old a card with letters. The girls eat the "M and Ms" when they are through.

A former teacher had this comment:

Our five-year-old is reading second grade readers with very little assistance, and when he doesn't know a word, he can at least make an intelligent guess.

We spent very little actual time on each day's lesson. We usually did them at the breakfast table, and he eagerly looked forward to each day's lesson. Other than encouraging him to read various labels and signs that he was interested in, I used no additional aids or techniques. We merely went through each strip and read the words a few times. His eagerness to learn to read and his subsequent desire to read as much as possible have been my greatest satisfaction.

A Nebraska mother put her feelings this way:

Our five-year-old boy is an average sort—flashes of brilliance liberally mixed with die-hard ignorance. His excitement over lessons has been considerably less than fever pitch. Nevertheless, he is pleased over his many little victories and to be solving the reading mystery. When he shows signs of bogging down, we just put the lessons aside.

I work with my boy daily, except week-ends, and I also take a week off now and then for assimilation, as he seems to need such breaks. We have completed forty lessons, and he can use all of these ideas with confidence. It is a true pleasure to be able to be his partner in this new adventure. It definitely enhances the parent-child relationship.

Many parents are troubled about what happens when a youngster enters first grade able to read competently and independently. They fear that such a child will be a problem for the teacher and out of lockstep with the educational processes.

One mother expressed her worry like this in a letter.

I have taught my preschool child to read by a combination of sounding out most words and remembering non-phonetic ones. She is four and one-half and reading quite well.

The problem is this, what will happen when he starts school? At kindergarten registration yesterday, we were given a little booklet that said to let the teacher— with teacher underlined—teach the ABCs. Here is my child reading already. I thought perhaps I would not continue the reading. But she has already reached the point where she picks up books, spells out the words to me that she can't read, and goes on by herself when I am busy and can't sit with her.

Do I tell the school she is reading or instruct the child to sit patiently through it all again? Except for this one concern, teaching my child to read has brought a great deal of pleasure to both of us.

Most kindergarten and first grade teachers are elated to find a pupil who is already able to read. Primary teachers are continually urged on to try to meet the individual needs of their pupils—and it is easier to help the first grader who can read than the one who cannot.

Almost all first grades are divided into first, second, and third reading groups, with two groups working independently, while the teacher gives reading instruction to the third. As enthusiasm for preschool reading continues to grow, chances are that most first grades now contain more than one child who could read fairly well before the beginning of the school year. These two or more youngsters can form their own reading group. Or, if one moppet is far advanced beyond the top reading group, it is quite easy for the teacher to keep him occupied and interested—just by giving him a library book to read. The fast-spreading ungraded primary plan will also make it easier for early readers to continue working at their own pace.

But what if an early reader draws a poor teacher, one who resents his accomplishments and lets him know it? It's difficult to conceive of an adult worthy of the name of "teacher" who would penalize a six-year-old for already knowing how to do something he is supposed to be learning. But it has happened, and it can happen again.

If a first grade teacher is so insensitive to the feelings of a child and so unenthusiastic about achievement in learning, the whole class is probably in for a difficult and unhappy year. A first grader who draws such a poor teacher—and there are some among the hundreds of thousands of elementary teachers in this country—will probably have unusual difficulty in learning to read in class. Parents can count it a blessing that a youngster already knows how to read, if he's trapped in such a situation.

Since a majority of youngsters do learn to read in the first and second grade, why encourage a child to read at age three, four, or five? It isn't worth the effort, even assuming it succeeds, critics also contend.

On the contrary, a preschool reader gets a head start in first grade and maintains his advantage all through elementary school, according to increasing and well-documented evidence. His I.Q. is likely to be increased permanently.

An earlier start in reading is an advantage for children throughout elementary school, according to studies made in California and New York public schools by Dr. Durkin.[10]

In her first study, in California, forty-nine youngsters entered first grade able to read at grade levels ranging from 1.5 (fifth month of first grade) to 4.5 (fourth grade, fifth month). The median grade level was 1.9. Their I.Q.s ranged from 91 to 161. Five years later, fifteen of the children had been double-promoted. Of these, twelve were still attending school in the same community and were available for further testing. Their mental age ranged from 10.9 to 17.2, with a median of 14.0.[11]

The earlier the youngsters started reading, the greater the advantage they gained, Dr. Durkin's research shows. For example, twelve of the youngsters began to read at age three; their reading level at the time of the last follow-up averaged 9.2. Fourteen children were five years old when they started to read. Although the average I.Q. of this group differed from that of the three-year-old readers by just one point, they were only reading at the 7.6 grade level.

The lower the child's I.Q., the greater he profits from having a head start in reading, Dr. Durkin's research also suggests.

Preschool help with reading does not lead to problems of learning in school, Dr. Durkin stresses, in summing up the findings of her five-year study. None of the children involved in her research had an academic problem. And a majority of the bright, preschool readers did better in reading after only five years of school instruction than nonearly readers of the same I.Q. level did after six years of schooling.

No learning problems resulting from an earlier start in reading were detected, either, in a major, long-term study of the teaching of reading in kindergarten conducted in the Denver public schools between 1960 and 1966. The study involved about 4,000 youngsters, who were followed closely from kindergarten through fifth grade.[12]

Organized reading instruction in kindergarten for youngsters in all ability ranges and from all types of backgrounds did not produce any harmful social or psychological results, the extensive Denver research shows. It did not trigger problems of school adjustment or create dislike for reading. No more of the early readers developed visual defects or reading disabilities than did the control-group youngsters who followed a traditional timetable for learning to read in school.

The kindergarten reading program did have many positive advantages, however, especially when the early readers were given the opportunity to move ahead faster, later on in school.

The kindergarten readers who got an accelerated reading program later on had significantly higher reading rates at the end of fifth grade than did the youngsters who followed the traditional program or who got a stepped-up reading program without the kindergarten head start. The kindergarten readers had a larger vocabulary. They did better on reading comprehension tests. And they also scored higher in word-study skills, in arithmetic concepts, language, social studies and, to some extent, in science.

Reading can be "quite effectively" taught to large numbers of typical kindergarten pupils in a big-city public school system, the Denver study concludes. Pupils in all ability groups benefit proportionately. And the earlier start in reading has a measurable, lasting effect at least through fifth grade, provided the school program is adjusted to take advantage of the early start.

However, the benefits of the early start tend to be lost after first or second grade, if the traditional school program doesn't give the early readers a chance to build on their skills at a faster-than-usual rate, the Denver researchers found.

A preschooler can't see letters well enough to read, and he will ruin his eyes if he's pressured to try, some critics have also charged. This has been a common and persistent assumption, but researchers who have studied early readers have not been able to find any evidence of eyestrain or damage. Parents who know how fast very young children can discover tiny objects—pins, beads, buttons—on the floor usually discredit the theory that preschoolers can't see well enough to read. New studies about visual abilities of newborns are leading doctors to revise their traditional concepts about vision in young children. Early reading, particularly if the letters are large and clear, may actually be good training in visual perception, some advocates of early reading explain.

The eyes of most children are physiologically ready for reading at the age of twelve months, says Dr. Jules H. Shaw, a Boston ophthalmologist and the head of the eye clinic at Beth Israel Hospital. He says that most normal children can focus and accommodate by the time they are a year old, and that if a youngster has normal eyes, good health, and good intelligence, he can read at an early age.[13]

Teaching a child to read will rob him of his childhood and prevent him from achieving the social and emotional growth which is the chief developmental task of the preschool years is another argument critics hurl at advocates of early reading.

But how many moppets have a life so full of fascinating toys and happy play that they can't spare even ten minutes for reading? (The Denver reading program found that youngsters made significant gains in reading ability if parents spent as little as thirty minutes per week working with them.) A toddler screaming his impatience at being imprisoned in a playpen is a more typical picture of early childhood. So is the four-year-old whining, "Mommy, what can I do now?"

There are other arguments that are often used against early reading: Preschoolers won't read for meaning; they'll only call words or recite them like a mechanical robot. Young children don't hear well enough yet to discriminate between words. And, they may not know the precise meaning or range of meanings of words.

All of these sound just like arguments against permitting

a child to learn to talk. Yet no one worries about "talking for meaning." No one claims that a child is too young to handle the abstractions of spoken language, or that he may use a few words he doesn't completely comprehend. No one even frets very much when a baby who has just learned to say "Daddy" applies his precious new word one bright morning to the milkman. Even the critics who contend that a preschooler can't understand a book if he reads it himself still urge parents to read to their children, yet they express no concern that the small fry may not understand precise word meanings.

Some questions about preschool reading do, however, remain to be answered by extensive research in the future. For example, if six and one-half is not the minimum mental age at which a child can learn to read, is there in fact a minimum age at all? Dr. Fowler thinks that perhaps a child requires a mental age of four to be able to read, although he taught his oldest daughter to read when she was just two and his second and third daughters at age three—all with considerable success.

Dr. Fowler was not successful, however, in an experiment to teach everyone in a group of five three-year-olds to read in a nursery school setting. Three of the children were each one of a set of twins, and two of the youngsters were part of a set of triplets. Two of the children, who had I.Q.s in the 120 range, learned to read happily in just a few months. A third child with an I.Q. of about 100 also made considerable progress. But two others, who came from culturally-deprived homes seriously lacking in intellectual stimuli and had I.Q. scores of about 85, did not learn much, although they obviously enjoyed the reading games and activities and could recognize a few letters.[14]

When Dr. Fowler was director of the University of Chicago Laboratory Nursery School, reading was taught to three- and four-year-olds using a method he developed which stresses sound-letter relationships, word patterns, play orientation, and careful programming. He notes that in his research, he's found that bright three-year-olds often do as well and in some ways better than bright four-year-olds.

The Denver public school research suggests that the average child should be about four and one-half to profit from instruction in reading, although youngsters with special aptitude and interest could begin earlier. Doman urges that a start be made at two, or even younger. And Montessori schools begin prereading sensory stimulation at about three.

Dr. Durkin suggests a simple way in which to tell when a child is ready to read: Give him interesting opportunities to learn and see what happens.

Although well-planned research studies show that phonetic methods of teaching reading do a better job than sight-word or combination techniques, these research projects have largely been done with first graders. Similar research with preschoolers would be valuable.

Can the advantages of preschool reading instruction be made available to all children, even those whose parents are not willing or able to help them at home? The experiences of the Montessori schools and the experiments with the talking typewriter suggest that reading can be taught in a carefully-prepared environment, without the one-adult-to-one-child relationship that is ideal for informal teaching at home. Television programs like "Sesame Street" and "The Electric Company" also help to give millions of children some exposure to reading fundamentals.

If you have a preschooler now, you can't wait a decade or more for research to answer these questions beyond any argument and for reading instruction to become available at the nearest nursery school. What should you do?

You should teach your preschooler to read—because research to date shows he has much to gain and nothing to lose. Everything you teach him will help him, even if you begin teaching him and don't follow through to the point where he can read independently. Even if he learns only a few words or a few sounds, it will profit him. No matter which method you chose, he will not become confused later on in first grade if the teacher uses a different technique.

But don't try to teach your preschooler to read unless you really want to, unless both of you will enjoy the process. Don't pressure him to learn so much every day. Don't drag him away from any other fascinating occupation to read. And don't attach any penalties to his not learning if he isn't in the mood. Stop the minute he acts the least bit bored or restless—or before, if you can manage it. Most people who have taught small children emphasize that you're more likely to bore a child by going too slowly than by proceeding too fast.

If you were not taught to read by a phonetic method when you were in first grade, you'll probably be surprised at how logical and simple a modern phonetic or linguistic reading program is. Investigate a program of this kind before you begin helping your child. You should use reading materials with large-size type, preschool educators say.

Your moppet may be one who enjoys making reading a formal game of "school," especially if he's itching to go to school with older brothers and sisters. Unless this is so, don't attempt to make reading instruction anything formal. Just cuddle your child up close, as you do when you read to him. Show him a new sound or a new word. Review a few of the ones he already knows. Be enthusiastic about what he remembers. Tell him matter-of-factly what he has forgotten. Then give him a happy, loving hug before he goes back to other activities. You probably won't spend more than ten minutes a session. After your child has learned a few sounds or words, you'll find reading games are a delightful way in which to keep him happy.

The more you expose your child to printed words, the quicker and easier he will learn to read. Some parents have used the technique of hanging labels on a table, a toy box, a bed, a doll. Buy your child all the books you can afford. Make your local library a regular stop and let him choose his own reading materials.

Do read to your child, happily, lovingly, frequently. The children who did best in the Denver preschool reading program were those whose parents read to them at least sixty minutes per week. A love of reading is one of the best legacies you can give your child—and one of the best assurances that he will be able to keep up with the future.

8. How You Can Encourage Your Child To Be Creative

Kim, four, spends a busy November morning digging up black dirt in the backyard and filling little cardboard boxes with it. When her mother asks her why, Kim explains that these are to be her Christmas gifts for her brother and the other boys she knows.

"What boys like best is to get dirty and play in the mud," Kim tells her mother. "When the snow covers all the ground, they can't find any mud. So I am going to give them some for Christmas."

Gregg, five, is a tinkerer. In the last month alone, he has tried to take apart the toaster, rejuggle the tubes in the radio, find out what makes the hands on the clock move, and discover how fast you have to slide back and forth in the bathtub before the water swooshes out.

Randy, three, asks questions almost nonstop every minute he's awake. "Where does the night go in the morning?" "Why is the sky always up?" "Where was I before you had me?" "Why amn't I Johnny?" "Why doesn't it rain up sometimes?"

All of these preschoolers give evidence of possessing creative intelligence to a high degree—as do most young children. Yet, according to recent research, it's likely that this gift will be blunted or ignored or misdirected or discouraged or punished out of the youngsters long before they reach high school, and their promise will be only partially realized.

"Creativity" is a name now given to a particular component—probably several components—of intelligence. (Researchers have identified dozens of separate intellectual talents comprising over-all mental ability and estimate there may be almost as many more factors not yet recognized. The usual type of I.Q. test measures only six to eight of these elements.) Educators and psychologists have become especially concerned with creativity in children in recent years because it seems to be the essence of genius—and an essential characteristic of those individuals who make original contributions to the world.

Creativity means far more than talent in art or music. It includes the whole range of creative and adventurous thinking in every field: scientific discovery, imagination, curiosity, experimentation, exploration, invention. It is the ability to originate ideas, to see new and unexpected relationships, to formulate concepts rather than to learn by rote, to find new answers to problems and new questions for which to seek answers.

A creative child has intelligence of the highest order. But he may or may not score well on an I.Q. test, which measures chiefly academic areas of mental ability. Research on creativity in children is far from complete, and most of what is known has been learned in studies of school-age children. Valid tests of creativity are difficult to develop because by definition they are concerned with producing many fresh ideas and unorthodox solutions, rather than one "right" answer. So the tests are hard to score and evaluate.

But most researchers agree on these points: (1) Almost all small children possess a considerable amount of creativity. (2) Creativity can be increased by deliberate encouragement, opportunity, and training. (3) It can also be dulled almost out of existence by some child-rearing and educational practices.

It is important that parents understand how to identify and cultivate creativity in very young children. For the tender sprout of creativity needs to be encouraged and guided almost from birth, according to Dr. E. Paul Torrance, chairman of the department of educational psychology at the University of Georgia and an expert on creativity in children. (In some cultures—and to a lesser extent in some cultural groups in the United States—certain kinds of stifling, early environments produce individuals who are not open to new ideas and whose production of good innovations is very limited.)

"If we observe how infants handle and shake things and twist and manipulate them in many ways, we find some of the earliest manifestations of creative thinking," says Dr. Torrance. "Since the infant does not have a vocabulary, he can learn little by authority. Thus, by necessity, much of his learning must be creative; that is, it must evolve from his own activity of sensing problems, making guesses, testing and modifying them, and communicating them in his limited way." [1]

Beginning about age three, a child's creativity usually begins to increase, note Dr. Torrance and other researchers. It seems to reach a peak between four and four and one-half. Then it drops suddenly about age five, when the youngster enters kindergarten (probably because of pressures from teacher and classmates to be more conforming). Creativity then rises slowly in the first, second, and third grades, says Dr. Torrance, until there is a sharp drop in the fourth grade.

What are the signs of creativity that you can watch for in your small child? Several researchers have compiled descriptions of creative children you'll find useful. For example, an enormous bump of curiosity is typical of a creative youngster. He loves to experiment, to test the limits of situations. He questions constantly and usually in a penetrating way or on an offbeat tack that can annoy a busy parent or a preoccupied kindergarten teacher who doesn't understand this special type of intelligence.

A creative child isn't often put off by an overly-simple answer, or at least not until his basic creative instincts have been blunted. He is particularly sensitive to answers that don't make sense in relation to other facts he knows. Often he invents long, complicated explanations for phenomena he doesn't understand.

A creative child is particularly sensitive to what he sees, hears, touches, and experiences. You'll notice this sensitivity not only in the pictures he draws or finger-paints, but also in his surprising understanding of other people and other people's problems. He delights in learning precisely the right word for an object or a feeling or a color. And he enjoys sharing these special observations with an adult who is also aware of them. Because sensitivity is considered somewhat feminine, a highly creative boy may seem a bit less masculine than his friends.

A creative child generates new ideas like sparks, many of them offbeat or silly, but a few are surprisingly original and good in relation to his age. He often gives uncommon answers to questions, suggests unusual solutions to problems. He finds unexpected uses for common objects, like the four-year-old who used peas to be baked potatoes in her doll-house dining room and the five-year-old who constructed a "nutcracker" for her father's birthday present out of an empty paper tube, a heavy bolt, and a string.

In one test of creativeness designed for school-age children, youngsters are told to list all the uses they can for a brick, other than building. An extremely creative boy or girl may think of thirty-five or forty.

The imagination of a creative youngster is unusually active, delightful, and full of humor. Many preschoolers can turn this vivid imagination on deliberately and do so with great delight. For example, Mindy, a highly creative little girl, just five, enjoys spinning fantasies about what kindergarten will be like when she is finally permitted to attend in September. Mindy knows what school is really like, of course. Her big brother has told her. She's played many realistic games of "school" with the first grader across the street. Her mother has read to her several times the introductory material supplied by the school. She's even gone to visit.

But Mindy enjoys elaborating on her own imaginary version. For example, there are no boys in her pretend kindergarten. "But the kindergarten does have a private-eye detective school," Mindy points out. "That's where we learn how to watch boys. You have to keep track of what the boys are doing, you know.

"Every day we have vanity class in kindergarten," continues Mindy. "The teacher gives us make-up to put on and powder, perfume, and lipstick, and sometimes we put curlers in our hair.

"Then we go into the bead room. That's where you sit and try on beads after beads after beads until you find the best ones. You get to keep a whole string of beads every day. The school pays for them.

"Next we go into the bride's room," says Mindy. "That's a whole room full of fluffy things brides wear. You get to put on all of them you want. You get a diamond wedding ring, too. The teacher gives it to you because there aren't any boys in kindergarten, you know.

"After that comes the birthday room, where you get cake and squawkers and different presents every day. Everyone has a birthday every day. And you can put just as many candles on your cake as you want. You can be just as old as you want to be. The school pays for everything, so you can have all the presents you want."

In Mindy's kindergarten, there's a puppy room ("You sit there and cuddle up baby white puppies"). There's a baby room ("You sit there and cuddle up babies—real babies, not dolls—and they give you a baby to keep forever").

There's a sticky-paper room, "where you stick things on the walls and the rugs and the mirrors and the chairs and on all kinds of woodwork." And there's a cotton room, "where the walls are made of pink, cotton candy, and you can stick it all over your dress to make a pretty costume, or you can pick it off the walls and eat as much as you want without getting sick."

Mindy has spent about three months collecting her "school supplies." As her fantasies about kindergarten have grown, she's added item after item to what she calls her "worksactivity bag" until she needs a pillowcase to hold it all.

Among the school supplies in the worksactivity bag are: an old birthday party invitation, a plastic fish, a Japanese fan, a broken badminton birdie, toy opera glasses, a rattle, a bathing cap, measuring spoons, a cake of soap from the Mark Hopkins hotel, a harmonica, a Hawaiian lei, old Christmas cards cut up and pasted into a booklet, a bell without a clapper, an empty candy wrapper, a hair band, a bottle for a doll, a souvenir pin from the Ice Follies, a bent paper clip, a half-burned birthday cake candle, a roll of crepe paper, a stuffed dog, a toy egg beater, a rubber band, a sugar Easter egg, modeling clay, a pearl bracelet, and one of the birth announcements her parents sent out when she was born. Mindy can explain precisely what she intends to do with every item when she gets to kindergarten.

It is characteristic of a creative youngster to attempt tasks far too difficult for him. But instead of considering his failures frustrating, he accepts them as challenges—at least some of the time. His attention span is longer than usual for his age. And he may become so preoccupied with his own thoughts or projects that he may not pay attention to what his parents are saying to him.

Unusual flexibility is another mark of a creative youngster. He is open to suggestions, new ideas, to almost any activity an adult describes as "a new experience." Research shows that in comparison with others, a creative youngster tends to be more self-sufficient, resourceful, stubborn, industrious, introverted, complex, and stable.

Because creativity implies independent thinking, a creative child often seems to be in conflict with his teachers in nursery school or kindergarten, or with his parents. He may ignore or be ignored by many of his preschool or kindergarten classmates. Teachers may consider him disruptive and impertinent. Deciding to what degree he will give in to social pressures toward conformity may cause him emotional upset, even before he reaches first grade.

This uncommon degree of independence may make a creative girl seem somewhat more masculine than her classmates. Social and family pressures to act more feminine may be one reason why girls do not continue in scientific and engineering fields, in which they often show creative abilities when very young.

Dr. Torrance, a pioneer in developing tests for creativity in children, often hands a youngster a toy and asks, "How could you change this toy to make it more fun to play with?" He reports that girls are often reluctant to deal with science toys and with a fire truck, objecting that girls don't know anything about toys like that. Boys, in turn, frequently refuse to make suggestions about a nurse's kit, on the grounds that boys don't use girls' playthings. Some boys change the name of the kit to "doctor," and then they feel quite free to produce ideas about improving it, notes Dr. Torrance.

Because he enjoys being independent, a creative child often objects strenuously to what he considers unnecessary rules and controls. He usually prefers to work by himself on his own projects, rather than to participate all of the time in the group-work that dominates so many nursery schools and kindergartens.

How can you encourage and increase your child's creativity abilities? Although research in this field is still incomplete, many positive recommendations can now be garnered from numerous studies. Many of the suggestions for increasing creativity in small children are virtually identical with recommendations already made in previous chapters in regard to over-all intelligence. By stimulating a small child to see, to hear, to touch, to manipulate, to explore, and to try for himself you can foster creativity. A parent who talks happily with a small child—and listens seriously in return—is helping creativity to grow. So is the parent who is enthusiastic about his child's achievements and projects and who encourages his innate curiosity.

In addition, experts on creativity make these recommendations:

• Help your youngster to feel and value his uniqueness, to find satisfaction in expressing his feelings, to experience the joy of creation. Too often, a child feels that he could not possibly think up a worthwhile idea, and so he doesn't follow through on the ideas he does have.

A child needs what Dr. Carl R. Rogers, of the Center for Studies of the Person in La Jolla, California, calls "pschological safety" to express his ideas in new and spontaneous ways. A parent who laughs at a youngster's ideas, even in an indulgent way, or who pushes off suggestions with a what-could-you-know-about-it-you're-only-a-kid attitude usually convinces his child quite easily that his thoughts couldn't possibly be valuable or worth developing. Of all the image-makers in our society, none is more powerful or more damaging than the adult who casually derogates his own child.

• When you can, let your youngster plan some of his own and your family's activities, and use his ideas when it's possible. Even a two-year-old can sometimes decide whether he'd rather picnic in the backyard or eat indoors as usual. A four-year-old should be permitted to select which of two or three play dresses to buy (after you have restricted the choice to those suitable in price, size, fabric, and style). Preschoolers should have occasional opportunity to plan family menus ("Which meat shall we have? What vegetables? What for salad?"), weekend activities, and treats.

Permitting a child to make such decisions not only makes him feel that his ideas are worth consideration, but it also helps him realize that decisions have consequences. If you recognize and respect your child as an individual, you'll find that his urgent drive for independence will not be so likely to erupt in undesirable ways.

• Encourage your child to become more sensitive to his environment, to ask questions, to experiment. Many of the suggestions already listed in the section on science in Chapter 6 are useful in this context, too.

• Science activities provide good opportunities to help your child understand that not all experiments succeed, and that an experiment that doesn't succeed isn't necessarily a failure.

"Most parents find it extremely difficult to permit their children to learn on their own—even to do their school work on their own," comments Dr. Torrance. "Parents want to protect their children from the hurt of failing."

It is important to teach children how to avoid failure when possible, of course. It is urgently necessary when their physical safety is involved. "But overemphasis may deter children from coping imaginatively and realistically with frustration and failure, which cannot be prevented," says Dr. Torrance. "It may rob the child of his initiative and resourcefulness. All children learn by trial and error. They must try, fail, try another method and if necessary, even try again. Of course, they need guidance, but they also need to find success by their own efforts." [2]

If this sounds like too rigorous a concept to impose on your child, remember the process by which he learned to walk. How many times did he fail and fall? How long did he try without giving up? How much of the process did he do by himself without active help or motivation from an adult?

As you study your own child and his reactions to experiences, you'll come to know about how much adult help he needs to function creatively, and when he is apt to get discouraged and quit.

• Don't be deterred by traditional concepts of "readiness." New research shows that they are often inaccurate. If you constantly wait to introduce your child to new experiences and new materials until you detect signs of "readiness," you will keep him from being creatively challenged and stimulated.

"Readiness" too often becomes what Dr. Torrance calls a "holding-back operation." He says that this reluctance to let children try for fear of failure is one of the most powerful inhibitors of creativity operating in the early childhood years.

"The usual defense of holding-back operations is the

fear that the child will become frustrated by failure," says Dr. Torrance. "The ability to cope with frustration and failure, however, is a characteristic shared by almost all outstanding individuals. Certainly, almost all highly creative scientists, inventors, artists, and writers attempt tasks that are too difficult for them. If they did not attempt these overly difficult tasks, their great ideas might never be born." [3]

• Invite your child to try what one educator calls "creative calisthenics" with you. These aren't formal lessons, but games you can play while riding in the car, or ironing, or waiting in the dentist's office.

For example, play "How many ways could you use a pencil?" with your youngster. Take turns thinking up as many different, nonwriting uses as you can, for example, a mast for a toy boat or a perch for a birdhouse. Then substitute other common objects for the pencil, such as an empty milk carton, a paper cup, a spool, or an old tire. Be encouraging and happy about his responses—not critical.

• Apply the old necessity-is-the-mother-of-invention gambit. Give your child the need to think creatively by handing him an occasional mind-stretching problem or tough question to ponder: "What would you do if you were lost in the shopping center?" "How could you make a birthday party more fun?" "What can we make with the leftover lumber in the garage?" "How can we find out which is the shortest way to the park?" "What could we use to make trees around the doll house?" "What would help George stop being such a bully?" "What would you do if you had to be the teacher in kindergarten tomorrow?" "Can you invent a good game to play in the car?" "If you had a television station, what kind of programs would you put on?"

• Encourage your youngster to appreciate new experiences—from watching a carrot top sprout in a dish on a windowsill to solving a new problem; from observing the subtle shadings in a sunset to learning a new scientific concept (ice cream melts at room temperature; chocolate melts if left in the sun).

Sandy's mother used this approach so often and so successfully that when her five-year-old got into the car to be driven to the hospital to have his tonsils taken out, he asked her in a shaky little voice, "Mommy, is this going to be one of my new experiences?"

His mother felt like crying, but she managed to answer in a calm voice, "Yes, Sandy, it will be a new experience for you. Part of it won't be very pleasant, and you will feel uncomfortable some of the time. But there are two ways to take this kind of new experience. You can look for all the interesting new things you can find—the way in which the doctors and nurses do their work, the funny kind of bed, the breathing gadget that helps you go to sleep so you won't hurt when your tonsils come out. This way you'll discover some interesting things about hospitals and doctors, and you won't pay so much attention to the uncomfortable feelings.

"The other way to face a new experience is to let yourself get scared instead of interested—and being scared is no fun. Being scared makes everything seem worse than it is. And you miss seeing all the new, unusual things."

Sandy did have a few bad moments in the hospital, of course. But he recovered his poise and characteristic curiosity sooner than his mother expected. He had no emotional aftereffects. And his doctor said that he was one of his most cooperative patients.

• See that your child has a quiet place and time to work on his own, without having to participate in a group, even a family group, all of the time. Most nursery schools and kindergartens, as well as elementary schools in general, place heavy emphasis on sharing and on group activities. Without your active efforts, your youngster may have almost no private time for individual creative activity. Yet all good ideas begin in a single, individual, human brain.

Richie, a four-year-old attending a university lab school, was working with great concentration on discovering the relationships between number rods. He placed a four-unit rod next to a six-unit one, thought for a minute, and was reaching for a two-unit rod when Peter snatched the

materials away. Richie shouted in protest and tried to
wrestle the rods back. At this point the teacher intervened.
She divided the rods between Richie and Peter and lec-
tured Richie on sharing. But Richie's moment of discovery
was lost.

"Don't interrupt a child who is working even to praise
him," is a principle emphasized in Montessori schools to
protect this irreplaceable instant of creative discovery.

• Motivate your child to follow through on his ideas.
Too often, brilliant innovations are lost because their
inventor did not have the self-confidence or self-control to
complete their development. During the preschool years,
you can often encourage follow-up by questions like,
"How are you going to finish your picture?" or, "Are you
going to make a hat to go with that beautiful costume?"
Sometimes you can offer additional raw materials, "Can
I help you find some cloth to make a rug for your lovely
doll house?" Or, "I like your idea about rearranging
your room. If you'll help, we can fix it your way right
now."

• Don't worry if your preschooler enjoys making up
stories, or weaving fantasies, or playing highly imaginative
or imitative games. It's a normal part of preschool development. You'll probably be more comfortable about
your youngster's use of his creative imagination in these
ways if you help him label his stories "made-up" or
"pretend" when they are. Set an example yourself by
telling him whether the books you read to him are nonfic-
tion or fiction.

• Often you can spur creative activity in a youngster
by giving him a good reason for trying to be creative. Plan
a backyard art fair, for example, with moppets' master-
pieces clothes-pinned to a clothes line for relatives and
neighbors to view, and you may stimulate a minor Renais-
sance on your block. Start a young marching band, and
interest in rhythm instruments among preschoolers will
double. Introduce word games on long car trips, and your
offspring's awareness of words and their usage will
sharpen. Write down some of your youngster's imagina-

tive stories to paste in a scrapbook, and the quantity and quality of the stories will increase.

• Don't teach your child how to do everything step by step, but leave room for his imagination to flourish and for his brain to function. This doesn't mean, of course, that you let your youngster flounder with no preliminary guidance or instruction at all, or that you let him try to work out his own method for such basic physical maneuvers as tying shoelaces. Your youngster does need to learn, for example, the rudiments of using paint and brush, how to hold a pencil, how to manipulate scissors. But his creative feelings will be stifled if you insist on holding his hand to show him how to draw a horse, or if you correct his drawing yourself when he has finished.

• You can make positive suggestions when your youngster seems to need them. Often these can be in the form of questions that stimulate his own thinking. If he crayons a horse, you might ask, "Where is the horse going?" "Is someone coming along to ride him?" "Is he standing in a field or beside a barn?" If your young artist is unhappy about the looks of his horse and asks for help, suggest that the two of you find some pictures of horses to give him more ideas, rather than tell him specifically what to do.

If your moppet is making up a story, you can say, "I'd like to know more about that pirate; what did he look like?" Or, "Where do you suppose that spaceship came from?" Or, "How did that boy feel inside when the giant grabbed him?"

One good way in which to encourage creative story-telling is to play "Round Robin Story" with your offspring. He begins a story, starts to develop a plot and then stops, often in mid-sentence, for you to pick it up. You carry the story line a little further, then toss it back to him.

You can set a pail of water in the corner of the sandbox to make sand-castling more successful. You can locate a big, empty cardboard packing box for your backyard cowboys and Indians to turn into a fort or a jail, or for your miniature Martians to use as a spaceship. You can suggest costumes and props when your small fry need new ideas for imaginative play—paper bags, empty cartons, and canned goods for playing store; colored paper pads, a punch, and suitcases for playing train; books, stamp pad, and index cards for playing library.

With practice and observation, you'll develop considerable skill in this type of creative encouragement.

• Recognize that creative efforts are often messy. Paints spill. Bug collections add clutter. Experiments with seedlings take space and time. Cherished leaf collections gather dust and crumble. A preschooler who is constantly pricked by fear of being scolded or spanked for making a mess isn't going to feel much of the adventurous excitement of being creative. It's much safer and easier just to watch television.

You will need rules about cleaning up afterwards and limits about where in your house finger paints may be used and rock collections displayed. But it may help to remind yourself that no one wins prizes or scholarships or fame for being neat. One mother comments, "I used to fret about how messy my children's rooms are most of the time. Now I just call them 'creative' instead of 'messy,' and I shut the doors when we have guests. I feel much better, and my children are happier."

• Do reward your youngster for his creative efforts— by praise, encouragement, and interest; by sharing with him the inner joys of creation; by valuing his creative results, even if they don't come close to adult standards. Your surprise and pleasure at what your youngster has discovered or thought or made or said will encourage him to keep trying; your indifference will damp his innate creative sparks.

• Enjoy being creative yourself and share your feelings with your child. Talk about the color scheme you are trying to create for the living room; the effect you want to achieve in your garden; the solution to a problem you've just worked out; the new recipe you're experimenting with for dinner. Let him know when your efforts to be creative aren't spectacularly successful. If the new dessert sinks out of shape or the new casserole seems too dry, you can be casual about it and comment that at least you've learned something, and the next one will probably be better. This will help your small fry to feel that he need not be assured of success before he undertakes a project, and it makes it easier for him to experiment.

Provide your child with plenty of good, simple art materials. Encourage him to use these experimentally and without constant supervision, discouraging criticism, or fear that he will make a mess for which you will scold him.

All forms of creativity, even in scientific and engineering fields, are related, many researchers believe. Stimulating your child to be creative with art materials helps him develop sensitivity, originality, flexibility, and imagination —talents necessary for creative thinking in all fields.

Knowing just how much to supervise and suggest is a creative art itself. But if you study your child's individual reactions to your suggestions and comments, you'll soon discover just how best to encourage his efforts and his originality. This is one major reason for being aware of your offspring's need for creative stimulation—you are in a position to know him better than any teacher can and to work with him individually.

You should, of course, show your child the basic ways of using these art materials. But you shouldn't insist that he make his sky blue just because it is, or form his clay dog into better shape yourself. It helps to spur your child on if you comment favorably on what he has produced. But your remarks should be sincere, specific, and enthusiastic, in proportion to the effort your youngster has expended.

"You always say what I have drawn is 'interesting,' and half the time you don't even look at it," complained one perceptive five-year-old. "I hate that word 'interesting'!"

Raw materials for preschool art range far beyond mere crayons and paper, although these will probably be the first craft materials your child uses. Creative art can also be inspired by:

—A package of white paper plates, to decorate with crayons, to turn into picture frames, to make into clocks by adding numbers and hands, or to edge with bells for a tambourine.

—Peanut shells, to paint or ink with faces and to use as fingertip puppets.

—Paper lace doilies, to color for place mats or to crinch around flowers for nosegays or to trim with ribbon for bonnets or to use as clothes for clothespin dolls.

—Large sheet of white, dull-finish oilcloth, to map out the streets of your neighborhood. Encourage your small fry to crayon in the houses he knows, or to build them with blocks. Add toy trucks, cars, tiny dolls for a working community.

—Assortment of small, multicolored pads of paper, to mark for parking tickets, train tickets, paper money, or just to stimulate drawing.

—Old sheeting, to cut up and crayon for place mats or doll-house bedspreads or costumes. Colors will last longer if you place the sheeting color-side down on newspaper, cover with a damp cloth, and press with a hot iron.

—Finger paint in the three primary colors, to stimulate freewheeling art and experiments with color. You can buy it ready-made, or mix your own, using liquid laundry starch and food coloring, or powdered poster paints. Apply to white shelf paper dampened with a sponge, or use it directly on a laminated plastic table top, which you and your pint-size Picasso can sponge-clean quickly afterward.

For new varieties of paint, combine food coloring with a squeeze of toothpaste or a daub of hand lotion. Both make a delightful finger paint.

As an alternative to fingers in finger painting, try a comb, a small rag, a notched piece of cardboard, or an old hair-roller. To add a new dimension to a finger painting, let it dry, then add more color with a paint brush, or make a second finger painting on top, using a different color. Or, try adding a few small dabs of finger paint to a piece of paper, smear slightly, fold in two, and open to discover an unpredictable, double design. Or, finger-paint over squiggles of crayon.

One mother plopped her rambunctious Rembrandt into

the bathtub, made "finger paint" by adding two or three drops of food coloring to several squirts of father's foamy shaving cream and afterward cleaned up both art and artist easily with a soapy bath.

—Long lengths of brown wrapping paper, to make magnificent murals.

—Chalk, to use on bright or black construction paper, as well as on sidewalks and slate. Or, soak sticks of colored chalk in cold water and rub on a sheet of paper that has been soaked or sponged wet, too. (Newspaper does nicely.) You can draw with the sides or ends of the chalk, or even rub the chalk about with fingers. Lay the finished design on a fold of newspaper to dry—and preserve it by spraying it with a fixative. (Hair spray makes a good one.)

—Collage collection, for young pop art. In a box, assemble a big assortment of bright paper, bits of ribbon, interesting fabric swatches, trimmings, headlines, old Christmas cards, string, cotton, seals, stickers, colored pipe cleaners, scraps of glittery wrapping paper, buttons, old postcards, magazine pictures. Your moppet Michelangelo glues or rubber-cements his choices to construction paper or cardboard to make original designs, or unique birthday cards.

—Potatoes, to slice in half and use with paint or ink to stamp out patterns and designs. To make other unusual prints, walk fingers across the paper in paint patterns. Or, try fork tines, bottle caps, half an orange, a celery stick, corks, carrot halves, clothespin heads, a spoon, checkers, or small blocks dipped into paint.

—Poster paints, for paintings. For unusual variations, instead of a brush, try a feather, a small sponge, a toothbrush, a wad of paper towel, a piece of string or yarn. Or, put poster paint and a little laundry starch into an empty plastic squeeze-bottle and use it to apply paint to paper, varying the amount of squeezing, the distance from the paper, and the speed of hand movements. Combine with other colors, in other old bottles.

Or, suggest that your child arrange small daubs of paint on paper with a squeeze-bottle or a spoon. Before they can dry, he blows on them gently through one or two straws, holding the end about two or three inches from the paper. (Do see that his working area is covered with newspaper before you begin.)

—Clay or its equivalent, for sculpturing. A five-pound bag of ceramic clay from an art store is most fun. But children also enjoy the homemade kind (equal parts of salt and flour, with water added gradually to the right consistency and powdered paint or food coloring mixed in too, if you wish). Using cookie cutters, tongue depressors, pipe cleaners, orange sticks, and a rolling pin with clay may stimulate fresh ideas.

—Crayons, basically for drawings. Or, your moppet can make crayon rubbings by laying an object with an interesting texture—penny, wood, leaf, corrugated paper, string design, sandpaper, or checker—flat on a firm surface. Cover with paper and rub over it, using the flat side of the crayon.

Or, he can shave (with a dull knife or grater) flakes of old crayons onto a sheet of shelf paper. You can cover this with another paper and press with a warm iron to melt the crayon. Then, your child can add more to the picture, if he wishes, with black crayon, or he can scratch lines into the colors.

—Waxed paper, to make translucent pictures. Spread out a sheet of waxed paper, and on it arrange colored shapes and bits of bright tissue paper in overlapping designs. Add crayon shavings and wiggles of colored thread. Top with a second sheet of waxed paper, cover the whole creation with a piece of plain paper, and you can press it for your child with a warm iron.

• Enrich your preschooler's life with music in every way you can. Case histories of gifted musicians show that some of them began having lessons at the age of three or four. But in these instances, the child's family almost always contained at least one professional musician, and there is evidence that the youngster probably inherited a high degree of musical talent. A Japanese musician has successfully taught preschoolers to perform surprisingly well on the violin. But to date, there just isn't enough research in this area to justify recommending lessons to very young children.

Your preschooler will enjoy and profit from having an opportunity to use simple musical instruments, such as an octave of bells, xylophone, rhythm sticks, finger cymbals, a triangle, drums, a tambourine. Or, he may also enjoy simple experiments with an autoharp, a piano, or an electric organ, if you have one.

A phonograph he can operate himself, plus his own records, gives a preschooler great delight and a good introduction to music. He will also enjoy and appreciate some classical music that has a definite melody, especially if you tell him something about the composition. Records which introduce the instruments of the orchestra are also helpful.

You've probably been singing lullabies to your baby since you brought him home from the hospital. Gradually, you can add other songs, folk tunes, ballads, musical comedy tunes. He'll enjoy learning a song in a foreign language and singing games and songs with accompanying finger plays.

You can help your preschooler discover more about music by talking about how music makes you feel or want to move about. Good examples: *Peter and the Wolf;* almost any Sousa march; *Swan Lake;* "The William Tell Overture," with its storm and quiet aftermath; "The Skater's Waltz"; "The Flight of the Bumblebee"; Dvorak's "Largo."

• Encourage your child to let stimuli from one artistic field suggest creative activities in another, related area. For example, suggest that he make up a dance to go with ballet music; or paint an illustration for a favorite poem; or make a dust-jacket design for a book you've just read to him; or dictate a story for you to write down about a painting he's just made; or finger paint to music.

Nurturing your child's creativity is one of the most delightful privileges of parenthood. Many of your happiest hours with your child will be the times when you share his adventurous thinking and work together on creative projects.

It is urgently important that your child's creative abilities be firmly established before he starts first grade and encounters the stifling, stunting effects of groupism or encounters a teacher who makes it clear to him that he'll get along better if he just obeys orders and doesn't ask questions. Perhaps your youngster will be fortunate enough to have a teacher who knows how to stimulate and value creativity; but even so she must deal with twenty-five or thirty other pupils and cannot give your child what *you* can. The conforming pressures of classmates will also begin to inhibit and blunt your child's creativity. Unless he has already been sold on the delights of thinking and creating for himself, he will find it easy to fall prey to demands for conformity and mediocrity and the desire not to be different in any way.

9. Montessori Ideas You Can Use at Home

What do little children like to do most of all? To learn.

What should nursery schools teach preschool children?

To read, write, understand mathematical concepts, be self-disciplined, self-reliant, courteous, orderly, and love learning.

Why?

Because the years between three and six are the time when such learning can be absorbed most easily and happily by a child's developing mind.

These tenets, basic to much of the new research about early learning, were also held by Dr. Maria Montessori, an Italian physician, who put them into practice in the early 1900s with great success. Long in eclipse in the United States, although not in Europe and India, Dr. Montessori's ideas, techniques, and equipment were rediscovered in the 1960s by American educators and parents who see in them a practical and successful way in which to put into operation what the early-learning theorists are talking about. For Dr. Montessori not only formulated many of these theories herself half a century ago, but she also worked out the best and most complete educational methods to date for implementing these concepts.

"Today, many educators go to great length not to admit they are plagiarizing and mining Montessori for ideas in the field of preschool education," commented a school superintendent. (Dr. Montessori, for example, developed child-size furniture, educational toys, inlaid wooden puzzles, programmed instruction, and much of the other equipment now used in modern nursery schools.)

Even today, Dr. Montessori remains the single best source for practical ways in which to stimulate the mental development of preschool children. There is still much in Dr. Montessori's books and concepts and in the Montessori schools that you can mine for use at home with your child, whether or not you wish to consider sending him to a Montessori school.

Maria Montessori's first job, after her graduation from medical school in 1894, was working with children in Rome who were classified as mentally retarded. So successful were the methods she developed to stimulate their learning abilities that many of these youngsters equaled or surpassed the records of normal children in school examinations.

So Dr. Montessori asked herself the logical question: What are we doing wrong with normal children that they can be outperformed by the mentally retarded?

Eagerly, Italy's first woman doctor accepted the offer of a job to start a nursery school in one of the early Italian housing projects in an extremely poor area. The sponsors of the school had only one goal—to provide supervision for preschool youngsters while their parents worked and to keep them from damaging the buildings. But Dr. Montessori saw in the school an opportunity to test out her theories about how the minds of very young children learn.

So poor were the youngsters, that Dr. Montessori told

their mothers that if they had only bread and water to eat, they should make hot bread-and-water soup, so it would seem more filling. The curriculum also had to include such basic instruction as how to take a bath.

In this "Casa dei Bambini," teaching children from the most appalling slums, Dr. Montessori developed the educational philosophy and techniques which were to prove so successful with youngsters from every kind of socioeconomic background. Among the principles she worked out are these:

1. A child, unlike an adult, is in a constant state of growth and change, and the ways in which he changes can be modified greatly by his environment.

2. A young child wants to learn. The task of the adult who loves him is to encourage, to provide opportunities for learning, to permit him to learn by himself.

"Who doesn't know that to teach a child to feed himself, to wash and dress himself is a much more tedious and difficult work, calling for infinitely greater patience than feeding, washing, and dressing the child one's self," Dr. Montessori wrote. "But the former is the work of an educator, the latter is the easy and inferior work of a servant. Not only is it easier for the mother, but it is very dangerous for the child, since it closes the way and puts obstacles in the path of the life which is developing." [1]

3. The mind of even a very young child has great capacity for absorbing a tremendous variety of experience, even though he can't express it verbally. "The most important period of life isn't the age of university studies, but the first one, the period from birth to the age of six," said Dr. Montessori. "For that is the time when man's intelligence itself, his greatest implement, is being formed."

4. A young child absorbs almost all of his early learning from his environment. To foster learning, his environment should be "prepared" so that he can choose freely from it the learning activities for which he has developed a readiness.

5. The very young child learns much through movement, and his movements should not be restricted any more than is necessary for his physical safety and to

avoid interference with the rights of others. He needs great opportunity to move about, to explore, to learn through every sense organ of his body.

6. A youngster goes through specific stages in development when it is easier to acquire certain types of learning than it ever will be again. This is true, obviously, in the development of speech.

"Children pass through definite periods in which they reveal psychic aptitudes and possibilities which afterwards disappear," said Dr. Montessori. "That is why, at particular epochs in their lives, they reveal an intense and extraordinary interest in certain aspects of their environment to the exclusion of others."

7. Sensory-motor activities play a great role in a child's learning. The more opportunities a youngster has to feed sensory stimuli into his growing brain, the more his intelligence will develop.

8. Children learn best in an atmosphere of freedom combined with self-discipline and in an environment prepared to help them learn. The child, said Dr. Montessori, must be free within the classroom to follow his own interests, to move about, to work freely at activities of his choice. But freedom cannot exist without self-discipline and without the development of skills which make a child relatively independent of help from an adult. Limits also must be imposed to protect the rights of others.

9. The teacher must not impose learning upon a young child and must not intrude upon what the child is learning by himself. She should not substitute her will for the child's or rob him of the satisfaction of working on his own tasks.

10. A youngster should be able to learn at his own rate, at his own level of readiness, without being forced to keep up with or wait for a group.

11. A child develops a sense of his own worth by doing any simple task well—whether it is scrubbing a table, pouring water from a pitcher without spilling it, or multiplying 15 times 8. He needs great opportunity for such successes.

12. When a child is given a chance to learn when he is

ready to learn, he not only increases his intelligence, but he also gains contentment, satisfaction, feelings of self-confidence, and a desire for further learning.

The great success Dr. Montessori had with her slum-area children drew distinguished educators and visitors from many parts of the world to the "Casa dei Bambini" during the 1910s. Montessori schools sprang up and flourished in many parts of Europe, and later in India. A few were started in the United States. But teacher-training in this country was generally inadequate. The movement ran headlong into the educational concepts of John Dewey; it was often misinterpreted and misunderstood, and it quickly withered.

Dr. Montessori continued to teach, lecture and write in Italy, throughout Europe, and in India until her death in 1952. It was not until late in the 1950s that interest in the Montessori method began to revive in the United States, sparked by new research into the importance of early-childhood learning and by the urgent need to find better ways of educating slum-area children.

Montessori schools have mushroomed in the United States in recent years, many of them organized by groups of well-educated parents in university communities who feel that their three- and four-year-olds are ready for something more mentally stimulating than bead-stringing and fingerpainting. The biggest brake on the growth of Montessori schools has been a lack of qualified teachers. (A college graduate needs a year of special training for certification by the American Montessori Society.)

The swift spread and obvious success of Montessori schools in the last few years have been major factors forcing hard new looks at this country's traditional concepts of preschool education. Not every nursery school teacher agrees with Montessori concepts, however, or with the way in which they are implemented in Montessori schools.

Some preschool educators are still strongly opposed to the idea of a nursery school that is concerned with mental stimulation, rather than the traditional social and emotional adjustment, or just random play. Others feel

that all of the valid Montessori ideas were long ago in-
corporated into nursery school programs here.

It is true that some of the Montessori equipment, such
as inlaid puzzles and pint-size furniture, have become
part of standard, early-childhood education. But these
critics have taken the tools, while missing the blueprint
for what the tools are expected to accomplish. They have
not grasped the Montessori concepts about the absorbent
mind, sensitive periods, freedom to work individually at
learning tasks of a child's own choice, and the importance of intellectual work at an age when youngsters are
so eager to learn.

Controversy about Montessori methods is also aug-
mented by the fact that Montessorians are divided into
two groups. One faction tries to follow as closely as possible the precise techniques started by Dr. Montessori, and
it is sometimes charged with being too rigid and ritualistic
for middle-class American children. The other group
adapts Montessori ideas to contemporary youngsters and
adds more art, music, and creative activities to the curriculum.

Except for the size of the children, almost everything in
a Montessori school differs from what is found in a usual
nursery school. And everything in a Montessori school—
from the colors of the learning materials to the tone of
the directress's voice—is precisely planned to stimulate a
preschool child to learn.

For example, when Eric, four, bounces into his
Montessori school, he begins the morning by hanging
up his own coat. First, he spreads it out on a low table.
Then he inserts a hanger into the shoulders, fastens the
buttons, and hooks the hanger over a low rod. He learned
this technique through the programmed instruction which
breaks down activities into small steps that he can master.
The purpose is to capitalize on a preschooler's fierce
desire to "do it myself" and to help him gain as much
independence as possible from adults in his personal care.

Then Eric changes his shoes for bedroom slippers to
help him feel comfortable and to keep down the level

of noise which might distract youngsters from their learning projects.

After a quick "Good morning" to the directress, Eric is free to choose any of the learning activities he wishes. He can use the material as long as he desires. And he is never urged to share it with any other child who happens to want it at the same time. His activity is respected seriously as "work," and no other youngster is permitted to interfere, in contrast to other types of nursery schools where sharing is emphasized regardless of what a child is attempting to accomplish by himself.

In a Montessori school, learning is an independent —not a group—activity. Each child works at his own speed, in his own way, with materials he chooses because of his own ability level and interests. He doesn't compete with any other child. He is neither held back nor pushed for the sake of keeping pace with the group.

The adult in charge of a Montessori classroom is called "directress" instead of "teacher" to emphasize the different kind of relationship she has with the children. Her function is to prepare the environment in which a child can learn, to guide his self-teaching, to answer his questions. She is a "catalytic agent," explains Dr. Urban Fleege, professor of education at DePaul University. She does not impose learning upon a youngster, but stimulates him to learn for himself. She seldom praises his accomplishments, so that he learns to look for satisfaction in his work and to learn to please himself, not someone else.

Eric walks quietly around his classroom for a few minutes. Then he pulls out a small piece of rug from a cubbyhole, spreads it on the floor and picks up a set of number rods, marked off in alternating red and white units. With them he begins to set up a problem in subtraction. When he has arranged the rods to his satisfaction, he gets sandpaper numerals and a minus sign to illustrate his mathematical operation.

Jane, three and one-half, has chosen one of the "practical-life" activities. Using a plastic pitcher, she dips water from a big plastic container marked "nice, clean water," and with a sponge and cloth cleans the table tops. When she's finished, she'll pour the water into a second container labeled "dirty, old water" and put her equipment away.

Over by the long row of windows, Jack, four, is arranging a "1000-bead chain," hooking strips of ten beads each together until they number 1,000. At each 100-bead interval, he lays out identifying numerals. Jack's project is taking him almost an hour, but he doesn't tire of it. When he encounters large numbers later on in elementary school, he'll have a concrete idea of what these symbols mean.

Toby is taking apart and reassembling an inlaid wooden puzzle that is a map of the world, saying the names of the continents under his breath as he handles them. Julie is matching an assortment of bells with eight other bells arranged to make an octave. Two five-year-olds are reading quietly to themselves. Another is writing words in his notebook.

Three-year-old Marcia is carrying a pile of graduated pink blocks over to her rug to build a tower. Like most of the Montessori equipment, the blocks are self-teaching and self-correcting. The youngster using them can tell for himself when he is right and when he needs to correct an error.

When each child has finished a project, he usually smiles in satisfaction, pauses for a minute or two, then puts his equipment carefully away in its special spot. After that, he chooses another activity. Occasionally, the directress stops by his rug to see what he's accomplishing. But usually, the inner feeling of achievement is the child's only motivation and reward.

After the youngsters have been working with great concentration and interest for about ninety minutes, the directress quietly begins to walk along an oval stripe painted on the floor of the classroom. Soon, most of the children are following her, except for a few who are still too intent on their own projects. Gently, the directress leads the youngsters in activity games designed to strengthen their muscles and give them more mastery of their bodies. They sing two songs in French and play a counting game in French.

Then comes the silence game. Seated around the oval, the children squeeze their eyes shut and sit as motionless as they can. The silence game has two purposes: to show a youngster his progress in self-mastery and to increase his auditory sensitivity.

When all is still, the directress calls each youngster softly by name. One by one, each tiptoes silently to his own little table, painstakingly pulls out his chair and sits down.

"We teach the children to be silent, not because an adult says so, but in order that they can hear better," explains the directress. "We teach them how to pull out a chair quietly because it gives a child great pleasure to be able to control the chair and himself well."

Juice-break comes next at a Montessori school—but it differs from juice-time in other nursery schools. Here, the children take turns pouring the juice themselves, carefully, with great control, and no spilling. With great concentration and a tiny smile of pride on her face, a three-year-old carries a tray of little glasses to the other children and distributes them.

The Montessori emphasis on self-discipline has raised doubts and opposition from some critics, who may be confusing self-control and inner discipline with the rigid control imposed by adults. But Montessorians explain that only through inner discipline can an individual become truly free to learn. Only when he has mastered learning techniques and materials is he free to be creative. Only when he understands reality can he be truly imaginative.

If there is a Montessori school near your home, you may want to consider enrolling your child. (Most schools start youngsters at the age of three, or two years, nine months, in some cases.) Even though the basic learning techniques used in these schools are more than half a century old, Montessori classes still do more to encourage a preschooler's love of learning than all but a few experimental nursery schools.

You may also want to read some of the books by or about Dr. Montessori which are listed in the bibliography. Parts of most of these books are obviously out of date and do not apply to contemporary children. But they still contain a wealth of ideas and insights into the gentle ways which can foster the learning development of small children.

Not all Montessori activities are applicable to homes and parents. Some depend upon the establishment of a large, "prepared environment" in which a child is free to choose his own learning tasks. And a mother can't maintain the same type of low-key, rather impersonal relationship that a Montessori directress has with a child. Some of the equipment is almost impossible for parents to obtain because it is expensive and sold only to recognized Montessori schools. Montessorians warn that the equipment itself is no guarantee of success; it's essential that a parent know how to use it and when to introduce it to his child.

But many Montessori ideas and techniques do work splendidly at home. Much of the equipment is now available to parents in accurate, well-made copies. Other materials have been adapted into games and equipment quite similar to the Montessori originals. Parents who understand Montessori purposes can often make equipment and use learning techniques that will accomplish the same result.

In adapting Montessori ideas for your child, it helps to keep in mind these guidelines, which have been worked out for parents by Montessori directresses:

• Teach your child with real things. If you take time to show him how to handle materials and equipment carefully, he will be capable of far more than you realize.

• When you want to teach your preschooler a new activity or skill, plan it out first as a programmed, teaching exercise. Break it down into small, precise steps. What points of interest does the activity hold for your child? How can possible error be controlled by the activity itself, not by your verbal directions? (In helping a child learn how to polish shoes, for example, a Montessori directress slips a piece of white paper under the shoe. The youngster can tell immediately when the polish is not going on the shoe because of the marks on the paper.) Can you isolate a single learning element you want your youngster to absorb?

• When teaching a small child, slow down your movements. Use as few words as possible. Let your movements guide your youngster's eyes to what he is to learn. (For example, in teaching a child how to use scissors, show him how to pick them up safely, to hand them to someone else, and to cut a straight line. Then let him practice, progressively, on thick straight lines, thinner lines, curves and angles, and finally on pictures.)

The purpose of this type of teaching is not to direct every move your child makes or to enforce your methods on him. It is merely to give him a successful way of doing something he wants to do urgently at this stage in his life. He can do it other ways if he wishes. But at least he will know one sure way that he can count on.

• Cultivate the art of not helping your child whenever he can do a task for himself. "Any unnecessary aid is a hindrance to learning," commented Dr. Montessori decades ago.

• Whenever you can, arrange your home and equipment so that your child can manage for himself. Make his table and chair low enough, his toy-storage shelves accessible, his clothing equipped with fasteners he can work, his closet rod the right height. Then, don't do anything for him that he can do for himself.

• Give your child enough time to do a task without hurrying. He usually works at a slower, more deliberate speed than an adult, and needs to repeat activities often, even after he appears to have mastered them.

• See that your preschooler has as much choice as possible over his own activities and learning. He can't live up to his potential unless he has the opportunity for independent work.

• Don't insist that your child try a new activity

if he isn't interested. Don't make him stick at a learning task when he doesn't want to.

One reason for the great success of the Montessori method is this freedom of choice offered to the child. For a youngster's responses and interests are the best guide adults have to his level of readiness for learning. And this technique is a parent's best protection against undesirable pressuring and pushing.

• Make discipline interesting whenever you can. Say, "See how quietly you can close the door." Or, "See if you can spread the peanut butter all the way to the edge of the bread."

• Don't ever rob a child of the feeling of satisfaction of having done a job all by himself. Don't do over any activity that he has done while he is watching. If he is not succeeding and is becoming frustrated instead of continuing his efforts, suggest a more simple, but related game or project that will help him acquire the necessary skills. For example, if he is having trouble controlling a pitcher when he wants to pour a glass of water, encourage him to try pouring easier substances, such as sugar or rice, from one container to another until his muscular control has improved.

• Whenever you can, protect your child from interruptions while he is concentrating on any activity, even if it seems pointless and repetitious to you. His learning is work of the highest importance, and if you have respect for him and what he is trying to do, it will be much easier for you to teach him respect for others and their work.

• A useful Montessori way of helping a child learn the exact name of an object is called the three steps of Seguin (based on a teaching technique of Dr. Edouard Seguin, a nineteenth-century philosopher and educator who had great influence on Dr. Montessori). First, put three objects—for example, a paint chip of red, one of blue, and one of yellow—in a row in front of the child. First, point to the red and say, "This is red." Then, pointing, say, "This is blue." And, "This is yellow." Then tell the child, "Point to blue. Point to red. Point to yellow." In the third step, the parent or teacher changes the order of the objects and pointing to each one asks the child, "What is this?"

Some learning activities based on Montessori techniques and ideas have already been described in this book. But here are others which you and your child will enjoy and which will help educate his senses and aid in his mental development:

• For a happy game that develops motor skills, draw a wide circle or an oval on the floor with chalk or paint. First, let your child walk it, placing one foot directly in front of the other and precisely on the mark, until he can balance well. Then, encourage him to try it carrying a glass of water without spilling it as he walks, or a bell without letting it ring, or a bean bag on his head without letting it slip.

• To stimulate your child's tactile sensitivity, cut out matching pieces of cloth having several different textures —velvet, silk, seersucker, corduroy, chiffon. When your child can match them easily by sight and touch, blindfold him and let him try it by touch alone.

• Put a dozen simple objects in a paper bag, with the top tied just tightly enough to let your youngster slip his hand in. He is to identify each object by touch before taking it out.

• For a game to foster visual perception, you can get two sets of paint "chips" from a hardware store and mount each one on cardboard to make a color-matching activity. (Some mothers use two sets of spools of thread in a range of hues.)

A two-year-old can begin by matching just the three primary colors. Later, various shades of each color can be added to make the game more challenging. As he becomes more skilled, a child can learn to arrange the shades in order from lightest to darkest. (Children in Montessori schools learn to match and arrange sixty-four different shades.) Finally, in a color-memory game, you can show your youngster one shade, then send him into another room to choose the matching hue from a pile of all the colors.

• To sharpen your child's auditory abilities, take small, empty salt shakers or little cardboard boxes and fill pairs of them with different substances—sand, gravel, rice, pebbles, for example—that make a noise when your child shakes them. First, he should learn to match the pairs of sounds. Later, he can arrange them in order of loudness.

• Obtain four small medicine-type bottles of opaque glass with droppers. Into one, put lemon juice and into another, vinegar. Into the third, put sugar and water; and into the fourth, a diluted syrup. Drop a little from one bottle at a time onto your child's tongue and ask him to identify whether it is sweet or sour. Most preschoolers delight in making appropriate faces for the sour substances.

• Buy two sets of bells, each of which makes an octave. First, have your youngster learn to match the bells which have the same note. Then arrange one set in proper musical order and encourage him to match the scale with the second set. Finally, challenge him to line up the bells correctly, from lowest to highest note, just by listening to them without the guide set.

• This basic technique can be adapted to help your child learn many different types of things. For example, you can buy or collect two identical, inexpensive sets of mineral specimens. First, have your child learn to match the minerals. Then teach him their names. Later, he can learn to arrange them according to hardness, or group them into other classifications.

• Lotto cards of different kinds can be used to help your child learn about animals—first by matching, then by discovering their names, and finally by classifying them according to families or habitats. Other subjects you can use in this way: leaves, trees, dinosaurs, flowers, unshelled nuts, insects, birds, geometric shapes.

• To help your youngster learn more about himself, have him lie down on a large sheet of wrapping paper and trace around him with a thick pencil. He can then crayon in his features and his clothing and cut out his outline.

• To stimulate his ability to observe accurately and record his observations skillfully, let your youngster use a windowpane instead of paper for drawing. He can trace the shapes that he sees through the glass on the window with crayon and learn easy lessons in perspective, shapes, comparative sizes, and structures by himself. He'll even enjoy polishing the window clean again with a commercial cleaning solution.

10. How To Safeguard Your Child's Brain

Douglas was a bright, eager, outgoing infant, who walked at the age of ten months and talked in three-word sentences before his second birthday. Then, he had encephalitis, an inflammation of the brain.

When his fever had subsided and his parents were permitted to bring Douglas home from the hospital, the little boy had to begin learning all over again. He had forgotten the torrent of words he used so excitedly before his illness. He couldn't remember how to walk. He could no longer feed himself, or pull on his socks, or wind up the music box in his toy puppy.

"It was as though we had a different child," Douglas's mother told a neurologist at a clinic for mentally-retarded children. "It's not so bad having to start over with him. But now he doesn't seem to want to learn, as he did before." Doctors are hoping that Douglas can be helped enough so he will eventually become eligible for public school classes for the educable mentally handicapped.

Just how much intellectual ability a child has at any given time is the result of three interacting factors, explains Dr. Richard Masland, former director of the National Institute of Neurological Diseases and Blindness, of the National Institutes of Health.[1] These factors are:

1. The basic, genetic quality of the youngster's brain and the rest of his central nervous system, which he inherits.

2. Changes in or damage to this central nervous system by injury or disease, either before or after birth.

3. The impact upon the child's brain of his environment and his experiences.

You can't change the first factor—the quality of brain that your youngster possesses. This is determined by the complex of genes carried within the egg and sperm that joined at his conception. These in turn reflect his biological heritage from both his father's and his mother's families for innumerable, preceding generations. The third factor has already been discussed at length in this book.

This chapter will be concerned with the second of Dr. Masland's factors—what you can do to protect from injury and disease the brain your child has inherited, so that it will develop optimumly and function effectively. Chapter 11 will detail a dozen steps that you can take during pregnancy to increase the likelihood that any future baby you have will be born with the best possible, uninjured, healthy brain.

In the United States today there are at least five million individuals who have been diagnosed at some time in their lives as being mentally retarded, according to the American Medical Association. An even larger number of people probably function ineffectively throughout their lives because of a lesser degree of mental retardation, or slight, unidentified brain damage, or dysfunction.[2]

The concept of minimal brain injury, or minimal brain dysfunction, is relatively new. Medical researchers are discovering that a large percentage of boys and girls who have behavior problems, who have trouble learning to read in school, who are overactive, hard to discipline, poorly coordinated, easily distracted, and who have perceptual difficulties, really suffer from minor brain damage or dysfunction. Often this damage is so subtle that it can't be detected by the limited diagnostic techniques doctors now have. But it can sometimes be assumed because the child's symptoms match those of youngsters with proven brain injury and because the case history indicates when the damage probably occurred.[3]

Children with minor brain damage are usually average, or above, in over-all intelligence. But because of their difficulties and distortions in perception and because of their behavior, they usually have a struggle learning to read, and aren't able to make full use of their intelligence. Often these learning disabilities trigger secondary emotional problems, too.

At least 50 percent of all mental retardation can be prevented, even with the limited knowledge now available, emphasizes the American Medical Association.[4] So can much of the minimal brain dysfunction. Many of the known ways to prevent brain damage lie chiefly within the control of parents. That's why it's important for you to learn about possible dangers to your child's brain and the ways in which you can protect him from learning disabilities and mental retardation—just as you guard his physical health from injury and disease as much as possible.

Odds are excellent that your child will be born with a normal, healthy brain, which will continue to grow and develop throughout childhood without injury. But a youngster's mental abilities are not something to leave to chance. You owe it to your youngster to learn all you can about the preventable causes of mental retardation and minimal brain damage and to give him all the protection you can.

Here are some of the most important ways:

1. *See that your youngster never has measles—the*

regular, "red," two-week variety which doctors call rubeola.

Parents used to consider measles a childhood nuisance, a necessary but rather minor evil. But measles can kill and is also the most serious cause of mental retardation of all the common childhood diseases, research has shown; even physicians have been underestimating the extent of its damages. Now that measles can be completely prevented by vaccination, doctors are willing to talk more freely about its dangers than they did when the disease was considered an inevitable part of growing up.

Until 1965 measles had been killing about four hundred to five hundred children annually in the United States—and far more in primitive countries, where as many as 20 percent of its victims die. This is only a small part of the problem. Physicians also were beginning to realize that this disease, even in mind form, may be a cause of mental retardation, learning difficulties, and personality or behavior changes.

About four million children had been having measles every year in the United States, until the effects of the vaccine began to be seen in 1965, and the total began to drop. Doctors have long known that about one in every one thousand measles victims suffers a serious complication, such as pneumonia or encephalitis, and that one-third of these would be left with severe, permanent brain damage.

Such a child is Katie Baret, whose teacher had told her mother that she was the brightest girl in her first grade class. Later, when the teacher notified parents in Katie's room that two first graders had measles, Mrs. Baret called the family's pediatrician, who gave Katie a shot of gamma globulin in hopes of preventing the disease, or making it less severe.

Katie did develop what doctors called "modified measles." She wasn't very sick. She had only a faint rash. Her temperature didn't go higher than 101 degrees. And she felt like staying in bed for just one day.

But four days after the rash broke out, Katie felt

drowsy. That night she had two convulsions and slipped into a deep coma. For three weeks in the hospital, she remained unconscious, suffering innumerable convulsions. When she at last appeared to become conscious, she could no longer talk, only grunt and cry. She couldn't recognize anyone, not even her mother and father. And she acted like a wild animal, ripping her clothing, biting, scratching; she was completely out of touch with reality.

Katie's desperate, loving parents tried everything possible to keep her at home and make her life comfortable. Unable to restrain her from hurting herself in her violent rages, they finally had a padded room built for her in their house, where her uncontrollable activity did only minimal damage to herself. But inevitably, the Barets decided to send Katie to a state institution, where she lives in a nightmare world of terror and rage, beyond the reach of love, or reality, or medical help.

"Unfortunately, the immune globulin doctors have been giving children after exposure to measles does lighten the usual symptoms of the disease, but does not lessen the effects of measles on the brain," points out Dr. Frederic A. Gibbs, emeritus professor of neurology at the University of Illinois School of Medicine.

Few youngsters are so tragically affected as Katie, of course. Yet there are enough that the National Association for Retarded Children launched an all-out, nationwide campaign against measles and the mental retardation it causes in June, 1966. The 1966 poster child for the association was a pretty four-year-old who was born normally intelligent, but became mentally retarded at the age of two as a result of measles.

Measles also leaves lesser brain damage, resulting in learning and behavior problems, in countless numbers of children.

Abnormal readings on the electroencephalograph (EEG) occur in about 51 percent of all children during measles, Dr. and Mrs. Frederic Gibbs and their associates have found in years of research. This indicates that the brain has been affected, even though there may be no symptoms of encephalitis, and even in cases without high fever.

These EEG readings usually return to normal later on. But in some cases, the brain disturbances continue and change, and eventually, perhaps years later, lead to epilepsy. Without the continuing evidence of brain abnormality from repeated EEG readings, doctors would not have been aware of the connection between the measles and the epilepsy.

In a large percentage of cases in which epilepsy does not occur and the EEG returns to normal, the children still experience learning difficulties, a reduction in intellectual power, emotional instability, and behavior problems, explains Dr. Gibbs.

"I think the doctors or nurses must have dropped my child on her head while she was in the hospital with measles; she's been kind of stupid since she got home," one mother told Dr. Gibbs. The youngster had been hospitalized because of a family difficulty, not because of the severity of the illness. The hospital had considered the child's case routine; but the EEG had revealed brain abnormalities developing in the course of the illness.

Measles "can knock the edge off children's I.Q.," warned Dr. James L. Goddard when he was commissioner of the Food and Drug Administration. "I've personally felt for a long time that we underestimate the seriousness of measles in terms of the dulling it may cause."

Brain damage from measles is highest among preschoolers, particularly three-year-olds, Dr. Gibbs's findings show. And it is preschoolers who need protection from measles the most.

Today, there is no need to risk even the most remote chance that measles could take the edge off your child's intellectual abilities. Effective measles vaccine has been available for general use since 1963, and your baby should be vaccinated against the disease as a routine part of his well-baby care during the first year of his life. The vaccine gives long-lasting, apparently permanent protection against the disease.

Doctors hope that with the cooperation of parents, measles can be eliminated as a hazard to children. But despite widespread, intensive campaigns in many communities and in some states, despite low-cost (and often free) vaccine, too many susceptible children remain unprotected against the disease.

2. *Arrange to have your child in the care of a skilled and up-to-date physician who will give him regular medical checkups and all recommended immunizations.*

Besides measles, there are other infectious diseases and disorders which can damage the brain of a child who was born healthy and normal, and thereby limit his intelligence. Most of these, fortunately, are rare. Others are uncommon complications of diseases as ordinary as mumps and chickenpox. Some of these afflictions, like cretinism, can be corrected rather easily if diagnosed and treated early in life. Some can be prevented completely by routine shots on standardized schedules. Some come on insidiously, slowly; others start with convulsions and fever and fear in the night.

No layman can hope to know enough about all of these brain-damaging hazards to children. You don't need to. But it is important that your child be under the regular, routine care of a good physician who keeps informed on new research and who is as close as your telephone.

It's safer today to raise a child in the United States than ever before in history. Good, routine care and preventive medicine are two major reasons why. But it is still up to parents to take the initiative to make sure these are available to their children.

3. *Take reasonable precautions to prevent accidents which can injure your child's brain.*

Sometimes you feel as if only a wrestler could keep your seven-month-old squirmer from wiggling off the table while he's being changed. Or, only a professional athlete could supervise a two-year-old explorer closely enough to stop him from tumbling down the stairs or off the top of the bookcase. Or, only a Marine sergeant could bellow emphatically enough to make a four-year-old sit safely still in the car while you're driving.

But you must protect your child against accident. For injuries involving the head can cause brain damage, which is reflected in a loss of intellectual ability.

"If parents could see what happens to a child's EEG when he's hit on the head or falls down stairs and is knocked out for a minute or two, they wouldn't take accidents so casually," says Dr. Gibbs.

Almost all head injuries can be prevented. But it takes a parent's foresight and effectiveness. The dangers of head injuries are greatest, of course, in cars. And in most family autos, children have less protection from possible injury than do the adults. Thoughtless parents permit their small fry to lie on the ledge under the back window, or to scuffle in the car, or to climb at will from front to back seat, or to stand up on the front or back seat, leaving them frighteningly vulnerable to head injuries resulting from sudden stops or accidents.

Seat belts the the quickest single way to reduce the number and severity of car-accident injuries. But parents are often careless about buckling their moppets in every trip, especially when they're tired and rushed and only going a short distance. And parents sometimes feel that seat belts are just one more thing—one thing too many— to nag children about.

It's easiest to convince your children that you mean what you say about seat belts if you begin when they are very young, by refusing to start the car until everyone, including the driver, is strapped in. If you're consistent, you can make the force of habit work for you, and you can usually avoid daily hassles about it.

If your moppet isn't big enough for a seat belt to fit properly across his pelvis (it's dangerous if it holds him around the abdomen), get a safety harness. A good one, designed for youngsters between about eight months and six years of age, must be anchored securely to the structure of the car itself to be effective. The usual type of car seat that hooks over the front seat and often

has a plastic steering wheel is not safe for the toddler,
safety experts emphasize. Car crash tests show that such
a seat won't hold a baby in place if sudden impact occurs
at a speed of more than ten miles per hour. The steering
wheel can cause facial injuries, while the seat's metal
bar can injure the youngster internally. National safety
organizations have approved a few car seat designs, however, and your child should be reasonably safe in one of
them.

If your baby isn't old enough to sit up, he is safest
riding in a bassinet, according to safety experts. The car
bed should have rigid sides. And it should be wedged
in between front seat and back seat, parallel to the
car's length. A baby isn't safe sitting on an adult's lap
and strapped into the adult's seat belt.

Two cardinal principles to remember in protecting your
baby or toddler from falls are these: He's stronger and
quicker than you think. And every day he can do more
than he did yesterday.

Starting the day you bring your infant home from the
hospital, make it a habit not to leave him alone on
a table or counter or in a bathinette, even for the second
it takes to turn around for a fresh diaper. Even before
he learns to roll over, a baby can dig his heels into a
table top and shove himself off.

Every pediatrician can tell you about the babies who
fall off examining tables while they and their mothers
are waiting for him to come in. The flustered mothers
inevitably say, "But, doctor, he's never rolled over
before."

Never leave your baby alone in a high chair, either,
even for the minute it takes to answer the phone. The
day your baby crawls the first inch—or even before—put
up gates at the top and bottom of every staircase. Police
other members of your family to make sure that everyone locks the gate behind him. And be ready to get new
locks or safety catches the minute your baby learns to
pick the old ones. As soon as he can learn, teach him to
go up and down stairs safely, holding on.

Train yourself to put up the sides of your baby's crib

without fail. And when your toddler is old enough to begin climbing out by himself, keep an old mattress beside the crib to cushion tumbles. Or, promote him to a youth bed. He may get up and inconvenience you sometimes, when he's supposed to be sleeping. But he will be safer from falls. Be sure, too, that your windows are safely screened, especially above the first floor.

When your youngster reaches the jungle-gym-tree-climbing stage, teach him to maneuver safely. It's better strategy to find safe, secure spots for him to do his climbing than to issue blanket orders against it.

4. *Protect your child from brain-damaging poisons.* Of all the substances that can accidentally poison a small child, the one most likely to leave permanent brain damage is lead.

Lead poisoning is still a major public health problem, especially in many big cities with large poverty areas. The possibility that your child could be a victim of lead poisoning, with its brain-damaging effects, is remote. But it's a danger that you should know about, so you can keep the possibility remote.

The lead that poisons children and damages the brain usually comes from lead-based paint—on carelessly-repainted toys or cribs or other furniture, but usually from old, peeling paint in slum-area buildings. Occasionally, parents in very poor areas have burned old battery casings for warmth in the winter, and the fumes have given whole families lead poisoning. And rarely, a child has been poisoned by licking old-fashioned toys made of lead.

Lead poisoning usually develops slowly, over several weeks or months, as the damaging substance accumulates in the body, especially in the brain. First symptoms are unusual irritability, followed by digestive upsets and tiredness—and often by convulsions and death. Even when a child recovers, the chances of permanent brain damage are high—inevitable, according to some doctors.

The usual victims of lead poisoning are toddlers and preschoolers who live in deteriorating slum houses, who are often unsupervised, and who have the habit (called pica) of eating inedible matter, like chips of peeling paint and plaster. But any child who lives in an older home, regardless of its cost, and licks the paint on a windowsill or chews unobtrusively on it over a period of time, could develop lead poisoning.

Paint designed for indoor use now contains only a minimal amount of lead. But some paints intended for outdoor use can have extremely hazardous amounts. That's why you should check the label on paint you use inside your home and in repainting toys and not let your teething toddler chew on anything that has been coated with exterior paints.

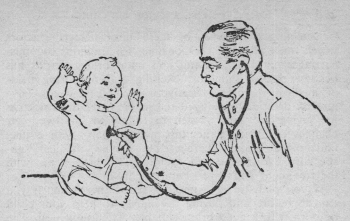

11. How To Care for Your Baby Before Birth

"Is it a boy or a girl?" is the first question a new mother asks. The answer seldom matters for more than ten seconds.

"Is he all right?" is invariably the second question, although a mother may not be able to put it into words. The answer could mark the beginning of a lifetime of heartbreak for an entire family.

Most mothers receive a happily reassuring, "He's just perfect," from the doctor. But there are more than 100,000 babies born every year in the United States with defects so obvious that they can be identified as mentally retarded at birth. And an "overwhelmingly larger number" of children born with injured or malfunctioning brains are not identified until later, says the American Medical Association[1]—until they are slow to talk or unable to keep up with their classmates in school. At lease one infant in every sixteen born annually in the United States has a birth defect of some kind.

Detecting the causes of these birth defects (factors which may also be responsible for millions of miscarriages) and of prenatal and natal brain injuries has become one of the most exciting and promising fields of medical research. Discoveries in recent years have already drastically changed the recommendations doctors are giving pregnant women to follow to improve their chances of having a healthy, normal baby with a fine, undamaged brain. There's even a new medical sub-specialty evolving called "fetology," which deals with the treatment and care of unborn infants.

If you plan to have another baby, there's much you can do before and during pregnancy to help your child be born with a good brain capable of learning well. The care you take of your developing infant in the nine months before he is born is as important—perhaps even more so—as the care you give him at any other time in his life.[2]

American women haven't been taking pregnancy, labor, and delivery seriously enough, the American Medical Association's committee on maternal and infant health has charged. This is one major reason why the infant mortality rate in this country is not as low as doctors think it could be and why so many babies are born with defects and damaged brains.

Much still remains to be learned about the causes of birth defects. Many of the known causes are still beyond medical prevention, resulting from inherited disorders, or mistakes in cell division just before or at the time of conception. But based on current knowledge, you can improve your chances—already great—of having a baby with a good-quality, healthy brain, by following these general rules:

1. *Choose a good doctor who keeps up to date on new medical research and is affiliated with a reputable hospital to see you through pregnancy and the birth of your child. Then follow his advice.*

Joan Adams' husband is a district sales manager who was recently transferred from Phoenix to Baltimore.

Joan's been so busy getting the family resettled that she hasn't bothered to find an obstetrician in her new community, even though she's almost six months pregnant. Why hurry, Joan shrugs. She's already had four children, and it's such a nuisance to get a sitter just to go to the doctor for a five-minute checkup. There's still plenty of time before the baby's due. Meanwhile, she has taken some weight-reducing pills that she borrowed from a new neighbor. She has tried to cure a nagging cold with some antibiotics left over from her oldest child's tonsillitis. And she's using tranquilizers when the pace of her strenuous life seems overwhelming.

Amy Parker is seventeen, a high school senior, unmarried—and three months pregnant. She's too scared to tell her parents or arrange for an abortion. The boy responsible has brushed her off with "That's your problem; don't come whining to me about it." She has had no medical care and isn't likely to get any until her changing figure arouses her parents' suspicions.

Sandra Smith and her husband have just moved to Chicago from Mississippi. No one in either of their families has ever had regular, prenatal care. Sandra knows nothing about the free facilities available in the city and hasn't thought of inquiring, even of her neighbors. She will probably have her baby at Cook County Hospital—one of hundreds of women who come to the hospital in labor, never having seen a doctor before in the course of pregnancy.

Mrs. Adams, Mrs. Smith, and Amy are all taking a dangerous gamble with the health and intelligence of their babies. For some of the causes of retardation can be detected and minimized, or even eliminated, in the course of good, prenatal care by a skilled physician.

Whether it's your first or second or fifth baby, you need medical supervision all during the nine months your baby is growing within you. Even if you've skated through it happily before without a complication, even if your budget is tight, even if you have to wait an hour for a brief checkup with your doctor, it is important for your baby.

The reason is that you not only provide half of your baby's heredity, you also furnish his total environment during the fast-growing, first nine months of his life. His environment—you—must be as healthy as possible. And the environment—you—is not ever quite the same with each baby that you have.

Doctors used to call the placenta—the organ which forms inside the uterus, or womb, to nourish the unborn infant—a "barrier." They assumed that it filtered out infectious agents, drugs, and other substances which could harm an unborn child. It was believed that even if the mother wasn't healthy or well-nourished herself, the growing infant could deplete her body of necessary baby-building materials and be born healthy and normal.

Now, however, the standard textbook ideas about the biological relationship between a pregnant mother and the baby she is carrying are changing. Physicians now know that injurious as well as nourishing substances can pass through the placenta into the developing child. Some of these materials—particularly certain viruses and drugs—have far greater effect on the immature tissues of the unborn baby than they do on the mother herself. And because the baby's major organs and other bodily structures grow from just a small cluster of cells present in the earliest days of pregnancy, the injury or death of only a few cells can cause major damage.

A baby's brain begins to form about the second week after conception—before a woman has any sign that she might be pregnant. The brain's most critical period of development lasts until about the eleventh week. That's why factors which cause birth defects during the critical first few months of pregnancy so often cause mental retardation.

Because the most serious damage to an unborn infant can occur during the first three months of pregnancy, you should have your first checkup with your doctor just as soon as you suspect that you might be pregnant. Most women wait until they are quite sure that they have missed two periods. Yet by that time, all of the baby's major organs have been formed, and much of the most crucial part of his development has already been completed.

It's even better if you plan to have a complete medical examination before you become pregnant, so you'll be in the best possible health from the very first.

Many conditions in a mother which can harm her unborn infant are now known and can be prevented, or detected and treated by a doctor. For example, there's evidence that a mild urinary or vaginal infection, so slight a prospective mother would not even be aware of it, can cause damage to an unborn infant. If a mother's thyroid gland is over- or underactive, her baby can be damaged, even if she isn't affected. Another mother whose baby may be in danger without her realizing it is the prediabetic. Her baby may be born injured, even though she herself may not develop actual diabetes for many more years.

In studying the case histories of mentally retarded children, it is frequently found that their mothers suffered complications of pregnancy, such as bleeding or toxemia. When these complications are associated with premature birth, the baby runs a high risk of cerebral palsy, epilepsy, and mental retardation, notes the American Medical Association. If the baby is not born premature, he still has a greater-than-usual chance of having minor types of brain damage, resulting in learning disabilities and behavior problems.

One major purpose of prenatal care is to check for the likelihood of toxemia and other complications and to prevent them, if possible.

Because prenatal care is so important, most family doctors and obstetricians charge parents a flat rate for prenatal care, delivery, hospital visits, and postnatal checkups, regardless of how much time the doctor spends with the mother. The rate is usually based on the husband's income, and if a couple wish, an installment type of payment program is sometimes worked out during the period of pregnancy.

Because of the new knowledge about the relationship of prenatal care to mental retardation and birth defects, major efforts are underway by both private and public agencies to make good prenatal care available to all women, particularly those in the lowest socio-economic groups and to "high-risk" mothers. In most cities, the local health department sponsors free prenatal clinics, and so do most county hospitals and many teaching hospitals connected with medical colleges.

Educational campaigns are also underway in many cities to encourage poorly-educated, low-income women to seek out free prenatal care. The National Foundation-March of Dimes has set up pilot programs to demonstrate that women living in underprivileged areas can be taught the importance of prenatal checkups and will report regularly for care, particularly if transportation and sitter-service for other children in the family are provided.

Since 1963, the U.S. Children's Bureau has made grants totaling millions of dollars to state and municipal agencies and to hospitals for special projects that provide free or low-cost prenatal care for low-income families. Many of these projects include the establishment of neighborhood clinics, free transportation, and health and nutrition education. The aim of the program, says the agency, is "lowering the incidence of mental retardation, which can be caused by premature births or other complications associated with pregnancy."

2. *If possible, plan to have your children when you are between the ages of eighteen and forty.*

Teen-age mothers and those over forty have more complications of pregnancy, such as toxemia, than do women in the optimum childbearing years between eighteen and forty, and their babies are more likely to be born premature. They run more risk of having a difficult delivery, with possible injury to the baby at birth. All of these factors are related to mental retardation and to minimum brain damage.

This doesn't mean that you can't bear a normal, intelligent, healthy baby if you are seventeen or forty-three. Countless women have and many women will in the future. But the odds are better for your baby when you are between eighteen and forty.

One of the biggest risks that a baby runs when his mother is older than forty is being born with an abnormal number of chromosomes, the rod-shaped structures within each cell which carry genes that determine hereditary characteristics. Each human cell normally contains 46 chromosomes. Special laboratory techniques now make it possible to photograph and identify these 46 chromosomes, which are paired and numbered from 1 to 22, with two sex-determining chromosomes identified separately.

For reasons not yet understood fully, the presence of an extra chromosome, or part of one, causes abnormal development, which usually includes mental retardation. It's now known that many different types of birth defects can result when a baby's cells contain more or fewer than 46 chromosomes. Medical journals are frequently reporting new relationships between chromosome count and abnormalities in physical and mental development.

Best known of these chromosomal defects is Down's syndrome (mongolism), a condition characterized by short stature, a somewhat oriental look about the eyes, abnormalities in internal organs, and marked mental retardation. Mongolism is the most common single cause of mental retardation, accounting for 5 to 6 percent of all mentally retarded individuals and 10 to 20 percent of all the retarded in institutions in the United States. Most mongoloids have 47 chromosomes, instead of 46, with an extra one similar to the pair numbered 21.

In most cases, the extra chromosome occurs because of a mistake in cell division, probably during the production of the ovum (egg) in the mother's body before conception. During the normal process of cell division, the two chromosomes in pair 21 fail to separate properly, resulting in an egg cell with an extra particle—enough to condemn the about-to-be-conceived infant to mental defectiveness.

Why the mistake in cell division occurs is not yet known. There is some evidence suggesting that it might be triggered by radiation, or chemical factors, or even by viruses. But it is a fact that most mongoloid children are born to older mothers, indicating strongly that maternal age affects the cell-division mechanism in the formation of the ovum. The age of the father can also be a factor in some cases of chromosomal abnormalities, some research suggests.

A mother's chances of having a mongoloid baby begin to increase when she reaches the age of thirty-five and rise rapidly after she's forty. Odds are only one in 2,500 that a woman of twenty-five will have a mongoloid baby. But a woman between forty and forty-four has one chance in 100. One mother in every fifty who becomes pregnant when she is forty-five years of age or older bears a mongoloid child.

When a mongoloid baby is born to a mother younger than forty, doctors suspect that a hereditary factor may be at work. Many mongoloid babies born to young mothers have a chromosome count of 46, which appears normal at first. But one chromosome—usually in the pair numbered 13, 14, or 15—is larger than usual and is believed to represent an extra number 21 attached to a normal chromosome.

Chromosome counts made of parents of these babies usually show that one parent has only 45 chromosomes, one of which is a combined number 15 and number 21. When a sperm or an ovum containing the combined chromosome unites with a normal sperm or ovum at conception, the fertilized egg cell contains the disastrous extra number 21 particle, and a mongoloid child results. Young parents who have a mongoloid baby are now advised to have chromosome studies made and to seek genetic counseling before they plan to have another child.

Research on chromosome abnormalities in human babies is still only in its beginning stages. It's known, for example, that at least half of the babies who are miscarried very early in pregnancy, or who die before birth, have an abnormal chromosome count. Researchers hope some day that they will be able not only to detect chromosomal abnormalities before birth, but also to devise means of correcting these mistakes.

3. *Be sure you have had German measles (rubella) or are effectively immunized against it at least two months before you become pregnant.*

For generations, German measles was considered a mild and minor disease of childhood. Parents call it "three-day measles." Doctors label it "rubella." Typically, its victims suffer from a slight rash, a mild sore throat and swollen glands in the back of the neck—nothing more. If they have a fever at all, it is seldom higher than 100 or 101 degrees, and it rarely lasts more than two or three days. It was thought that there were almost never any serious complications.

The first hint that German measles was a serious threat to an unborn baby, when contracted by a mother during early pregnancy, came from Australia, in 1941. There, a brilliant bit of medical detective work by an eye specialist, Dr. Norman McAlister Gregg, ferreted out the first link between a virus disease in a pregnant woman and a birth abnormality in her baby.

Dr. Gregg noticed a sudden and sharp increase in the number of babies brought to him with cataracts. Many of these infants also had congenital malformations and were deaf. Questioning their mothers at length, he learned that almost all of them had had German measles early in pregnancy.

During the next two decades, doctors established that rubella occurring in the first three months of pregnancy could indeed damage a mother's unborn infant. When the disease strikes during the first month of pregnancy, about 50 percent of babies are born with defects, which can include brain damage, deafness, eye damage, and heart abnormalities.

Twenty-two percent of babies whose mothers have rubella in the second month of pregnancy and 7 percent in the third month are born with malformations. There is some evidence that rubella just before conception, or in the fourth month, can also trigger birth defects.

In addition, at least 15 to 36 percent of the pregnancies in which German measles occurs end in miscarriage.

But not until the great German measles epidemic of 1964–65 in the United States did doctors learn the full extent of the damage that rubella can do during pregnancy. More than 30,000 defective babies resulted from that epidemic, despite the fact that doctors in many major hospitals performed abortions on mothers who had German measles in early pregnancy. Some of these babies had severe and different symptoms never before recognized as being due to the German measles virus.

It is now known that many babies whose mothers have German measles early in pregnancy don't get over the disease quickly, as their mothers do. They may continue to be actively infected with rubella all during the seven or eight months of pregnancy remaining and are born with active, severe, and contagious illness. This fact was not realized, or confirmed, until new techniques of identifying the rubella virus became available in 1963.

About 30 percent of babies born to mothers who have German measles in early pregnancy are now known to be born with such chronic infections. These babies may have extensive hemorrhages into the skin, enlarged liver and spleen, lung disorders, jaundice, bone abnormalities, or infections of the liver, heart, or brain. They may—or may not—also have malformations.

These babies have been called "the typhoid Marys of rubella" because they can continue to spread the disease to other people for at least six months, perhaps longer. In one case, for example, a pregnant nurse was infected while she was taking care of such an infant. Later she, too, gave birth to a baby damaged by German measles. Another child was found still to be contagious at the age of twenty months.

Rubella can be such a mild disease that many individuals have it without any symptoms at all. In one large study, only one case in every three detected by lab tests was recognized by symptoms.

But even these undetected cases without symptoms among pregnant women, can cause severe damage to an unborn infant. Babies have been born with chronic measles—and/or with birth defects—to mothers who were not ill during pregnancy and were not even aware of being exposed.

Some medical researchers now suggest that some birth defects, for which no cause could be found in the past, are really due to undetected German measles. For example, in one hospital, a mother brought her baby back several months after birth for a routine check of a congenital heart defect. The mother did not remember being ill during pregnancy. No one had any reason to suspect the disease in her baby, until a nurse who helped with the examination developed German measles. At this point, lab tests showed that the baby had indeed been infected with rubella virus and was still contagious.

Dr. Saul Krugman, chairman of the Department of Pediatrics at New York University School of Medicine, studied three hundred forty-four babies whose mothers had German measles during pregnancy. Only seventy-three of these infants were normal. Of the affected children, 52 percent had heart defects; 52 percent suffered hearing loss; 40 percent had eye defects; and 40 percent had brain damage.

Forty-two of these babies were born to mothers who did not know that they had had German measles—yet all of the infants were carrying the rubella virus. Forty of these children had defects. Without the specific test for rubella virus, the cause of these defects would have been listed as "unknown."

There's still another complication to the rubella problem. Other viruses can cause a mild, rash-y disease which imitates German measles, and some women who think that they are immune to rubella may not actually have had the disease. Laboratory tests for antibodies prove that a substantial number of women are mistaken about whether or not they had had rubella.

Some of these copycat illnesses may even occur in the midst of a German measles epidemic. For example, during an outbreak of rubella in one southern hospital, several student nurses had verified German measles. But one nurse suffered a similar illness with a rash at the same time, which was identified by lab tests as being caused by a different virus. Had she been a prospective mother, she would have had seven or eight months of unnecessary worry about bearing a defective child, or might even have considered an abortion.

A new test to determine whether or not an individual has had German measles was announced by the National Institutes of Health in late fall, 1966. The test is simple, reliable, and inexpensive. And it can tell within three hours whether or not an individual has antibody protection against rubella.

A new, effective vaccine against rubella was licensed in 1969, and large-scale programs of immunization were begun almost immediately in hopes of preventing a future German measles epidemic. Young children have been the primary targets of these mass vaccination campaigns, on the theory that such youngsters are the chief sources of infection among pregnant women. Rubella immunization has also become a routine part of well-baby medical care.

Since 1969, the number of reported cases of rubella has decreased steadily (except for a small increase in 1973), according to statistics from the National Center for Disease Control. But thousands of cases still do occur every year, particularly during the traditional peak months of February through May. Recent outbreaks of the disease have been chiefly among students in junior high schools, high schools, and colleges. From 12 to 19 percent of women of childbearing age are still reported as being susceptible to rubella, never having had the disease or the vaccine. And babies badly damaged by congenital rubella acquired early in prenatal life are still being born.[3]

To safeguard any future baby you might have, it's essential that you make absolutely sure you cannot have rubella during pregnancy. Your doctor or the nearest hospital can arrange for the simple blood test that can tell you for sure whether you have had the disease. Or ask your doctor to immunize you with the new vaccine. Because the vaccine does contain live rubella virus, although in a greatly weakened form, it is theoretically possible that the vaccine could cause congenital rubella in an un-born baby if his mother were immunized early in the pregnancy. So doctors have been advised not to give the vaccine to any woman of childbearing age unless it is certain she will not become pregnant for at least two months.

4. *Do everything you can to keep yourself well during pregnancy and to avoid exposure to contagious diseases.*
If a mild disease like German measles can do so much damage to an unborn infant, what about other viruses and bacteria? Evidence is scarce and often contradictory. But long-range, nationwide studies are under way to discover the exact relationship between illness in a mother during pregnancy and miscarriage, birth defects, or mental retardation in her baby.

Any severe illness caused by a virus within the first three months of pregnancy—especially in the first eight weeks—may possibly injure the unborn infant, reports the American Medical Association. In the last three months of pregnancy, a severe virus infection may trigger premature birth, which is often related to learning diffi-culties later on in childhood.

Infectious diseases in a mother—often so mild that she has no symptoms at all—cause more birth defects than was previously realized, according to the U.S. Collabora-tive Perinatal Project's reports. Researchers urge that better methods of detecting and treating these diseases in pregnant women be developed.

Mothers who have influenza during early pregnancy seem to run a higher risk than usual of having a baby born with defects or later learning difficulties, some studies are showing. Many physicians advocate giving flu vaccine to pregnant women, especially when a widespread outbreak is expected and when the vaccine available cor-responds to the particular virus causing the epidemic.

Polio has also been implicated as a possible cause of birth defects, miscarriage, stillbirth, and prematurity. Measles (the "two-week" variety) may result in miscar-riage or stillbirth. You should be protected by vaccine against both of these diseases before you become pregnant.

Coxsackie virus, which causes an illness most people call "some kind of flu," or "that bug that's going around this month," can also trigger birth defects in babies whose mothers are infected during pregnancy, many doctors now believe.

In one six-year study directed by Dr. Gordon C. Brown, at the University of Michigan School of Public Health, 6,200 mothers were given blood tests frequently during pregnancy to check on the presence of viruses. Defects which could be detected at birth occurred in two hundred fifteen of the babies (forty of them heart abnormalities). Of all the mothers who had virus infections during pregnancy and whose babies had defects, Coxsackie virus was implicated most often.

Strong evidence also exists that birth defects and mental retardation can be caused by another virus few parents know about called cytomegalovirus, according to Dr. Donald Medearis, of the University of Pittsburgh School of Medicine. Cytomegalovirus produces a disease in adults so mild there are no symptoms whatsoever. Yet it is associated with a variety of birth defects including deafness, seizures, spasticity, brain malformations or hemorrhage and jaundice.

Other viruses, when they occur during pregnancy, are also under suspicion and study as possible causes of birth defects and death before birth. These include mumps, chickenpox, ECHO (which causes a flu-type illness) and herpes simplex (which results in cold sores and fever blisters). Syphilis, tuberculosis, and infectious hepatitis in a prospective mother can also be harmful to her unborn infant and require a doctor's careful supervision and treatment during pregnancy.

Mild virus infections during pregnancy may also result in minimal brain dysfunction and learning problems, many doctors now suspect. This subtle brain damage may not become obvious until the age of five or six or even later, when the youngster is unable to learn in school at a rate consistent with his I.Q.

Among all of the children born each year with birth defects and with damaged brains, there is no known cause, no explanation for the tragedy, in at least half of the cases. Viruses are the most logical suspects in many of these unsolved cases, many researchers believe.

Pregnant women are more susceptible to viruses than other adults, researchers explain. Viruses do greater damage to the young, rapidly growing tissues of an unborn infant than they do to adults, as experience with German measles illustrates. Viruses can cause an infection without symptoms in a mother—leaving no evidence of disease except antibodies and a damaged or dead baby.

Much more will certainly be learned in the next few years about the effect of infectious diseases on unborn infants. With the current state of knowledge, doctors' advice can be summed up like this: Before you become pregnant, establish immunity to as many infectious diseases as possible by vaccination. During pregnancy, avoid exposure to disease. Should you become ill, contact your doctor immediately.

5. *Do not take any drug or any medicine, not even aspirin, during pregnancy—and especially during the first three months—unless absolutely necessary, and then only under doctor's orders.*

News that the drug thalidomide had caused thousands of infants in Germany, Great Britain, and Australia to be born with deformed limbs and other defects, in 1961 and 1962, rang a loud alarm in the medical profession. Doctors were as shocked and as grieved as the rest of the world about the plight of the crippled babies. They were also stunned that such a tragedy could be caused by thalidomide, a sedative so mild and so apparently safe that it was sold without prescription (at a twenty-million-tablet-a-month-rate in Germany alone). It was even credited with saving the lives of would-be suicides, who simply could not take an overdose.

Immediately, the fearful question arose: If one tablet of a drug as mild as thalidomide taken at a critical time during early pregnancy could deprive a baby of his arms or legs, how many other drugs taken by pregnant women might also be responsible for miscarriage, stillbirth, mental retardation, and malformation?

Doctors still don't know the answer to this question. They probably never will, precisely and completely, despite their urgent and continuing efforts.

Dangers from drugs are greatest during the first twelve weeks of pregnancy, when the unborn baby's organs and basic bodily structure are being formed. The earlier the damage to the growing infant, the more severe his birth defect.

Doctors now know, almost to the day, when each organ is being developed during the early weeks of pregnancy. From the type of defect existing at birth, they can often determine just when damage to the unborn infant took place.

Germany's Dr. Wido Lenz, who studied the thalidomide-damaged babies, reports that a complete absence of arms was produced in infants whose mothers took the drug between the thirty-ninth and forty-first days after menstruation. Those who swallowed thalidomide between the forty-first and forty-fourth days gave birth to babies with no legs. Interference with development on the thirty-fifth day resulted in a child without ears. After the fifty-second day, thalidomide could apparently have been taken every day for the rest of the pregnancy without harming the infant.

For example, one German mother of a boy with shortened arms and bent hands is certain she took only two thalidomide tablets. She could pinpoint the day precisely, even months later, because she was trying to calm her nerves after her father died of a heart attack. Another mother took only half of one tablet. But because it was a critical day in the development of her baby, he was born deformed months later.

One reason doctors can't tell you now precisely what drugs may damage your unborn infant is that unborn laboratory animals do not always react in the same way to drugs that unborn human infants do. Thalidomide, for example, was tested and found to be safe in experiments with the usual species of pregnant laboratory animals.

Hereditary factors may also be involved in whether or not a particular drug is harmful to a specific unborn infant. This is true with experimental animals, but of course is impossible to track down with individual human beings.

"The fact that a drug has been given in one case during the first trimester without any serious effects does not imply that this medication is safe for all mothers," warns the American Medical Association. That's why you should never try any drugs prescribed for a friend or another member of your family.

Thalidomide was easier to track down than most drugs which may be causing birth defects. The damage was easy to spot immediately at birth, unlike much brain injury which doesn't become obvious for many months or even years. It was widespread, because the drug became popular so quickly and was taken in such large quantities by millions of people who did not need a doctor's prescription to get it. And it occurred over a relatively short period of time.

Most important, not even one of the 32,000 babies born to United States military personnel stationed in Germany during this period had similar defects. The drug was not given to armed forces families because it had not been approved for sale in the United States. This sparing of American babies made it possible for medical researchers to rule out quickly such possible causes as radioactive fallout and disease epidemics.

Usually, in medical detective work, it's much more difficult to link precisely cause and effect, drug and defect.

Eventually, long-term statistical studies relating the condition of babies to the history of pregnancy may help to pinpoint dangerous drugs more exactly. These records will have to be kept as the pregnancy progresses, before the baby is born. It's too inaccurate to wait until a malformed infant has been delivered, and then ask a mother to recall everything that affected her during the previous nine months, down to the last aspirin tablet, emotional upset, and headache.

Meanwhile, the federal Food and Drug Administration is forbidding the sale of medicine suspected of causing birth defects. Even when evidence is slight and involves only experimental animals, the FDA issues warnings that these substances should not be taken during pregnancy.

But these steps may not be enough to protect your baby, if you are pregnant now. That's why doctors have issued new and stringent rules for all pregnant women: Do not take any medicine at all during pregnancy, unless it is ordered by your doctor and is absolutely necessary.

To spell out the warning even more clearly, to underline it and emphasize it, doctors add:

• Don't continue to take medicine prescribed for you before you became pregnant, unless you tell your doctor that you think you might be going to have a baby, and he again says the drug is essential.

• Do remember that some of the most crucial weeks of your baby's existence occur before you ever make your first prenatal visit to your physician. That's why the responsibility for safeguarding your unborn infant lies primarily with you. Some doctors even advise that every married woman of childbearing age should refrain from taking any medicines, without strict supervision by a doctor, because injury to a baby might take place before she even suspects she might be pregnant.

• Avoid a general anesthetic during pregnancy, if at all possible. It comes under the heading of "medicine," too. If you need to have dental work done during pregnancy, be sure that your dentist knows about the baby, so he will give you only a local anesthetic, if it's necessary.

• Do be sure you realize how much that word "medicine" includes. It means not only pills, but every type of medicinal spray, ointment, salve, and liquid—even aspirin. It includes fizzing powders, baking soda, and home remedies for "heartburn." Digestive "aids," nose drops and sprays, laxatives, pep pills, sedatives, tranquilizers, mineral oil, "nerve tonics," reducing medicines, and even vitamin supplements are also on the list. Some doctors even warn against insecticides you might spray around a room and inhale in small quantities.

Of course, millions of women have taken tens of millions of drugs during pregnancy and still have given birth to healthy, normal babies. But there is grave risk involved, new medical research shows. And the stakes you are gambling with are terrifyingly high—your baby's future.

6. *Avoid X-ray examination or radiation treatment, especially in the abdominal area and particularly during the first three months of pregnancy.*

The danger that radiation could deform an unborn infant and damage his sensitive brain during the first three months after conception was first detected in 1929. In that year, it was noted that some mothers who accidentally had been overexposed to X-rays during treatment for pelvic disease gave birth to babies who were brain-damaged. Studies of infants born after the atom-bombing of Hiroshima and Nagasaki confirmed this discovery. So has extensive research with laboratory animals.

Today, it's a routine precaution to avoid X-ray exposure to the pelvic area of any woman who is pregnant. Good hospitals and careful physicians make it a firm rule that in every woman of childbearing age, X-rays of the abdomen are to be made only during the first ten days following the start of a regular and normal menstrual period, except in serious emergency. The reason for this strict regulation is that the danger to an unborn infant from diagnostic X-ray is greatest between the second and sixth weeks after conception—a time when a woman may not yet even realize that she is pregnant.

Even in the last few weeks before birth, the use of X-ray to determine the baby's size and position has been drastically limited to cases of necessity.

Some doctors now advise women to avoid X-ray exposure to other areas of the body during pregnancy, even for dental purposes. But most medical authorities say that only the pelvic areas need to be protected from this type of radiation. If you are pregnant, or even suspect that it might be a possibility, you should tell any doctor or dentist who is planning any type of X-ray examination or radiation treatment so that your baby can be protected.

Direct irradiation to the sex organs—either in a man or in a woman—can apparently destroy or damage chromosomes in egg or sperm cells before conception takes place, researchers point out. In most cases, such injury causes miscarriage very early in pregnancy. When there is lesser damage to the chromosomes, the baby may survive, but it will be born with defects or brain damage. Or, the abnormal hereditary material can be passed on to grandchildren or great-grandchildren before its effects become obvious.

This danger, of course, is remote for most individuals. But careful doctors and hospitals do take precautions to guard the sex organs of men and women, boys and girls, from large doses of X-ray, and during radiation treatment.

7. *Don't smoke cigarettes during pregnancy.*

When the National Institutes of Health set up a long-term nationwide Collaborative Perinatal Research Project in 1959 to study the relationship between what happened to 50,000 women during pregnancy and the health and intelligence of their children during the early years of life, one of the first discoveries concerned cigarette smoking. The project's findings confirmed several other studies on these points:

1. Women who smoke cigarettes during pregnancy give birth to more babies classified as "premature" than nonsmoking women.

2. Babies of smokers average about one-half pound less in birth weight than infants of nonsmokers.

3. The more a mother smokes, the less her baby is apt to weigh at birth.

It isn't just a lack of fatty tissue that makes infants of smoking mothers weigh less, investigators have found. These babies also tend to be shorter in length, indicating that their over-all growth and development has been retarded during pregnancy. This may be a result of the nicotine which is known to pass through the placenta into the body of the growing baby before birth, or because the high level of carbon monoxide in the mother's blood reduces the amount of oxygen carried to the unborn child.

A premature baby faces many hazards and difficulties, both at the time of birth and for years afterwards. A majority of preemies have at least some learning difficulties in school. These problems will be discussed in greater detail later on. But they are serious enough to make it well worth the effort it takes to stop smoking.

It's true that nervous, high-strung mothers are more likely to smoke than other types of women. But even when this factor is taken into account in research, a direct relationship between smoking and prematurity is still evident. Both smoking and nonsmoking mothers in these studies gained about the same amount of weight. So investigators are sure that the baby's smaller size is not due to a lower intake of food by the smoking mothers.

You may find it easier to give up smoking during the early months of pregnancy than at any other time. The taste of cigarettes and the odor of cigarette smoke are high on the list of things that trigger nausea in a substantial percentage of pregnant women. You can consider it a lucky break for your baby if you experience this powerful reaction against smoking and are able to stop.

8. *Maintain an adequate diet—rich in proteins, vitamins, and minerals—not only during pregnancy, but before.*

Because you are your baby's total environment during the first crucial nine months of his existence, you must make sure that you are as healthy and as nourishing an environment as possible. This means that your diet must contain all the essential building blocks your baby needs to lay the foundation of a strong and healthy body, plus all the foods essential to keep your own body functioning well.

Much medical research is being done to link specific birth defects and brain damage with specific diet deficiencies. Experiments with laboratory animals do demonstrate that depriving them of certain essential food elements will cause their offspring to be born with malformations and damaged brains. Many doctors expect that soon some of these specific findings can also be applied to human beings.

Women who have an inadequate diet do have more miscarriages, more stillborn babies, and more premature infants than those who are well nourished, many studies have shown. But because such women usually come from homes where living standards in general are low and usually have little or no prenatal care, it's difficult to know precisely the role the diet has as the specific cause of an unborn infant's failure to develop normally.

What should you feed your baby the months before he is born? The Food and Nutrition Board of the National Research Council recommends a 2,300-calorie daily diet for the average woman during pregnancy, including the following:

- Milk—three or more cups.
- Meat—six ounces of cooked meat, poultry, fish, cheese, or eggs.
- Vegetables and fruits—six servings, including a serving of a dark-green or deep-yellow vegetable for a source of vitamin A and one or two servings of citrus or other fruit containing vitamin C.
- Breads and cereals—five or more servings, whole grain or enriched, including potatoes and legumes.
- Fats and sweets—in amounts to fill calorie requirements.
- Supplementary vitamin D, if fortified milk is not used, and if ordered by physician.

Women who can afford to eat an adequate diet during pregnancy may still not get sufficient nourishment for the health of their unborn infant, simply because they try to limit their weight gain too drastically, new research is showing. A three-year study by the National Research Council concludes that cutting calories too much during pregnancy may hurt the unborn baby's neurological development and make his birth weight dangerously low. Recommended weight gains during pregnancy have been liberalized considerably, and the ideal increase is now considered to be about 24 pounds, or within the range of 20 to 25 pounds, according to the council.

9. *While you are pregnant, don't eat any undercooked meat or handle any cat that might be a source of toxoplasmosis infection.*

One of the newest links between an organism that infects a pregnant woman and a birth defect in her baby involves the comma-shaped toxoplasma organism. Normally, in adults, this infectious agent causes a mild disease that may include a brief rash, cough, swollen glands, and other cold-like symptoms; sometimes the infection is so slight it goes unnoticed. A woman who has toxoplasmosis during pregnancy recovers quickly from the disease. But, as with rubella, her unborn infant may continue to have active infection all the rest of his prenatal life and after birth. About 20 percent of these infected babies are born with major defects such as mental retardation, epilepsy, eye damage, hearing loss, and hydrocephalus.

The chief sources of human infection by toxoplasma organisms seem to be raw or undercooked red meat and the feces of cats. The organisms can be killed by heating meat to at least 140 degrees—the "rare" reading on a cooking thermometer. So it's safe to eat rare lamb and beef, provided you can be sure all of it has actually reached this temperature. In a restaurant, it's safer to order meat well-done to avoid the possibility that some of it may be dangerously undercooked. Raw meat, such as steak tartare, should be avoided all during pregnancy.

Toxoplasma organisms also live in the digestive tracts of cats, where they produce oocysts, another infectious stage of the organisms; these are then excreted in the feces. The usual disinfectants aren't effective against these oocysts and they can remain hazardous for as long as a year, specially in moist soil or water. Cats acquire the organisms by eating raw meat, mice, or other animals, or by coming in contact with infected cats.

You can guard against the possibiilty of toxoplasmosis by taking these steps: don't bring any new cat into your home while you are pregnant. Any cat you already have should not be fed raw or undercooked red meat or allowed to hunt or come in contact with other cats that might be infected. (Commercial or canned cat food is safe because the canning or drying process destroys the organisms.) Don't empty your cat's litter box if you are pregnant; it should be cleaned daily, however, by someone who wears rubber gloves, and the litter should be burned or dumped away from any area where you could come in contact with it. You should not garden in any place where cat litter has been deposited, and if you have a backyard sandbox, it should be covered at all times it's not in use.

A cat that isn't allowed to hunt and has been in your family for several months should be quite safe. But if there's any possibility of infection, you can ask a veterinarian to test your cat for toxoplasmosis infection. Your doctor can also give you a blood test to determine whether you have had the disease and are immune, or whether you are still at risk of getting it.

10. *Do everything you can to help prevent your baby from being born premature.*

A premature baby is usually defined as one weighing less than five and one-half pounds at birth. This can mean that the baby was born a few weeks before his expected day of birth, before he had time to grow enough to equal the average birth weight of a little more than seven pounds. Or, it can mean that the baby was born full-term, but because of some condition existing during pregnancy, his growth was slower than normal. In either case, he is a "high-risk" baby.

It has long been known that a premature baby requires extra care, that he needs more frequent feedings, better protection from infections and more careful control of temperature and humidity, and that he is more likely to suffer from medical problems than full-term, full-size infants. Gradually, doctors have also discovered that prematures are especially susceptible to medications, that even oxygen in excess can cause severe damage. But once the hazards of early infancy are passed, parents are often assured that a premature baby will "catch up." This isn't necessarily so, particularly in the area of intelligence, new research is showing.

Catching up does not tend to occur in children with low birth weight; in fact, the opposite seems to be true, according to long-range studies by Dr. Gerald Weiner and his associates at the Johns Hopkins University School of Hygiene and Public Health.[4]

Prematures show more of a lag in I.Q. at age ten than they did at age six, according to Dr. Weiner. Those who had weighed less than four and one-half pounds at birth had an average I.Q. of 87, while those with a four and one-half- to five and one-half-pound birth weight had an average I.Q. of 90. The I.Q. of infants weighing more than five and one-half pounds who were included in the study was 96.

By the age of twelve and one-half, some of the former prematures were behind as much as three years in school. Many had learning difficulties, particularly in arithmetic.

Low birth weight seems to be associated with neurological impairment later on in life, especially for what doctors call "small-for-date" babies, those that weighed less than expected given the length of the pregnancy. The findings hold true regardless of the social class of the children.

Intelligence among children who are premature is distributed in a curve, just as that of youngsters of normal birth weight. But the whole curve is slightly lower than the normal one, with a larger percentage of youngsters clustered in the lower-than-average part. Among those who weighed less than three pounds, five ounces at birth, almost none are found with "superior" or "high-average" I.Q., while a large percentage are classified as "defective," "border-line-defective," and "dull-normal."

"Follow-up studies indicate that 70 percent of premature infants weighing less than three pounds, five ounces at birth have various physical and mental disorders, such as spastic diplegia, mental retardation, speech and hearing difficulties, visual disorders, and behavioral problems," says the American Medical Association. "While the specific role of socio-economic class, and prenatal and perinatal complications remains to be clarified, prevention of prematurity has high priority in prevention of mental retardation." [5]

Prematurity is related to many other factors affecting a baby's development before birth, such as poor nutrition and illness in the mother, poor living conditions, and lack of prenatal care. (Many of these environmental influences also tend to limit the intellectual development of the baby after birth.) So, many different measures are necessary to reduce the dangers of premature birth.

How can you help prevent your baby from being born before he reaches optimum development? Don't smoke during pregnancy. Get good prenatal care early and follow your doctor's advice. Eat a proper diet. Get sufficient rest. Avoid exposure to infectious diseases. Take extra good care of yourself if you are older than forty, if you are pregnant with twins, if you've already had a baby born premature.

11. *Know your blood group and your Rh type. If incompatibilities are possible between your blood and your husband's, be sure that your doctor makes the necessary checks and takes the steps that will protect your unborn infant—and any future children you have—from Rh disease.*

The Rh factor is one of the best known—and most feared—causes of brain damage and death before birth. Several years also, a few doctors were even suggesting that couples who had Rh incompatibilities should not marry. But within a few years it will be possible to prevent Rh disease almost completely, and already most women can be protected from having a baby with this problem.

Basically, the Rh factor is present in the blood of about 85 percent of the population. It is an inherited trait, with the Rh-positive gene dominant and the Rh-negative gene recessive. Problems are possible only when an Rh-negative woman, married to an Rh-positive man, is carrying a baby whose blood is Rh-positive, like his father's. Should some of the baby's red blood cells mix with the mother's blood—an infrequent happening—the mother's body produces antibodies which destroy these foreign substances. This is the same type of reaction that takes place when the body manufactures antibodies against other nonself substances, such as bacteria and viruses. The antibodies don't harm the mother, because they are only directed at invading Rh-positive blood cells, not her own Rh-negative ones.

But the antibodies can seep back into the bloodstream of the growing baby, and because they were manufactured especially to attack his red, Rh-positive blood cells, they do exactly this. If there are enough antibodies, and if they are strong enough, they can destroy so many red blood cells that the developing baby becomes anemic. A by-poduct of the destruction of the red blood cells is a pigment which causes jaundice. This substance can stain and kill brain cells and cause irreparable damage to the baby's central nervous system.

In cases where the antibodies are numerous, the damage may be so great that the growing baby dies in the fifth or sixth month of pregnancy. Or, death may occur any time from then until birth. (Rh type of damage doesn't take place until about the fifth month of pregnancy. An early miscarriage isn't a result of Rh problems.) In other cases, the baby may appear normal at birth, but jaundice—with its danger of brain damage—may develop rapidly in the first days after birth.

Even if all the dangerous Rh factors are present, it almost always takes more than one pregnancy for a mother to produce enough antibodies to injure her infant. The reason is that few of a baby's blood cells ever enter the mother's bloodstream during pregnancy. Most of the mixing takes place at the time of birth, when Rh-positive fetal blood cells from the placenta are pushed into the mother's body through the uterine vein as birth occurs. Within a few days, the mother's body begins producing antibodies to fight these Rh-positive cells. One exception is the woman who has previously received a transfusion or injection of Rh-positive blood and may already have antibodies before she becomes pregnant for the first time.

That's why it's good medical practice that no woman or girl receive a blood transfusion without careful matching for the Rh factor.

Once a mother begins producing antibodies, they generally remain in her body all of her life, ready to injure any other Rh-positive baby she may be carrying. If her infant has been born with this type of anemia or jaundice, or if he has died before birth from this cause, chances are great that future infants will be affected with about the same degree of severity—or worse. There is one exception. Although her husband may be Rh-positive, he may also carry a recessive Rh-negative gene, along with the dominant Rh-positive gene. If so, there is a fifty-fifty chance of passing the negative, instead of the positive gene on to the baby. The child will then be Rh-negative, possessing a negative gene from each parent. And when the infant is Rh-negative, there is no problem of injury, even though the mother may have a high level of antibodies from a previous Rh-positive pregnancy.

Equipment for blood transfusion is readied when the birth of a baby with possible Rh damage is expected. Immediately after birth, blood samples are taken, and if necessary, a massive "exchange transfusion" completely replaces the infant's blood and its perilous substances. Careful watch is kept on the baby's condition and repeated exchange transfusions are performed, if required. As many as half a dozen complete blood replacements have been done on a single infant in the first few days of life—with a normal and healthy baby resulting.

But exchange transfusion can't solve the problem of babies who die before birth. Premature delivery isn't always the answer. Checking the antibody level of the mother is only an indirect indication of the baby's condition before birth. Generally, the higher the count, the greater the injury to the unborn child. But there are many exceptions which make physicians reluctant to induce premature labor, with its extra hazards to survival.

In the early 1960s, a new technique was developed to pinpoint the condition of such a baby precisely by testing the amniotic fluid with which the infant is surrounded in the uterus before birth. This test, called amniocentesis, gives doctors a good guide as to exactly when the endangered infant should be delivered for the best chance of saving his life.

Yet some infants are so badly damaged by the Rh condition that they die even before the pregnancy has lasted thirty-two or thirty-four weeks, before they are old enough to survive if delivered prematurely. Until 1963, doctors had no way in which to help these infants. They could only warn their mothers that future pregnancies would probably end in the same tragic way.

In 1963, a new method of giving blood transfusions to unborn infants was developed by Dr. A. W. Liley, University of Auckland, in New Zealand. It is now saving the lives of many babies previously fated to die before birth.

The technique is used when it is determined that an unborn baby is too severely endangered to survive if he remains in the uterus, but too small to live, if born. (About 10 percent of Rh-complicated pregnancies fall into this category.) Then, an opaque liquid is injected into the amniotic fluid in the mother's uterus. The baby, who constantly drinks amniotic fluid, swallows some of the dye, which is concentrated in his lower intestines and makes them visible to doctors by low-intensity X-ray.

The mother is given sedatives and a local anesthetic. The doctor waits until "the baby gets comfortable and quiets down," according to Dr. Liley, and then he injects three to five ounces of packed red blood cells into the baby's abdominal cavity, from which it is absorbed into the baby's circulation. The procedure takes about one and one-half hours and may be repeated once or twice before the baby's birth, depending upon his condition.

"Provided the fetal condition is detected in time, fetal transfusions can save approximately three-quarters of previously hopeless babies," says Dr. Liley. The technique is now being used in many major U.S. hospitals, in cases in which the risk of death to the baby is 100 percent.

Eventually, the new Rh vaccine should make almost all of these special treatments unnecessary. It works like this: immediately after an Rh-negative mother has given birth to a baby, the infant's blood is tested. If it's Rh-positive, the mother receives an injection of Rh vaccine, a gamma globulin substance with a high concentration of anti-Rh antibodies. The vaccine is produced from the blood of Rh-negative individuals who have already produced antibodies against Rh-positive blood; some of these donors are women who have given birth to Rh-positive infants and others are men who have been deliberately sensitized to the Rh factor so they could contribute to the vaccine.

The antibodies in the Rh vaccine quickly go to work in the bloodstream of the Rh-negative mother, seeking out the baby's Rh-positive blood cells, coating them, and destroying them before the mother's immune system can be turned on to produce antibodies against the invading blood cells. The antibodies last only about four months in the mother's body and will be gone before they can do damage to an unborn child in a future pregnancy.

The injection of Rh immune gamma globulin must be repeated within 72 hours after a woman has given birth to an Rh-positive baby in which fetal cells in the mother's blood reach the critical level, if Rh disease is to be prevented in her next infant. It must also be given following every miscarriage and abortion.

"If this is done correctly, eventually no more women will become sensitized by pregnancy and there will be no more afflicted babies," says Dr. Louis K. Diamond, a pioneer in Rh research.[6] Unfortunately, this procedure will not help women who have already produced their own antibodies because of a mismatched blood transfusion or an Rh-positive baby in the past.

Field trials of this new immunization procedure indicate that it is highly successful in preventing Rh disease. It is expected that the special gamma globulin will be available to mothers of the general public some time in 1968.

The danger of brain damage caused by antibodies is not limited to those triggered by the Rh factor. Other blood groups have been discovered which are involved in similar incompatibilities between husband and wife, resulting in the same type of antibody injury to unborn infants. These are quite rare, except for ABO incompatibility, which occur occasionally when a mother has blood type O and her unborn baby has blood type A or B. The condition can cause brain damage, but it can be treated successfully by exchange transfusion shortly after birth.

A good physician who keeps up with new medical discoveries, plus a modern, well-equipped hospital, are your best protection against a baby with Rh or ABO type of brain damage. One further warning from doctors: A woman should never be given a blood transfusion with her husband's blood. It may contain undetected factors which could stimulate her body to produce antibodies, which could hurt a baby later on.

12. *Let your doctor manage the birth of your baby without your insisting on pain-relieving drugs or medications that let you sleep through the event. His first concern must be for the safety of your baby's brain.*

Sit in at a clinic where parents bring retarded children for evaluation and listen as doctors read each case history. Again and again you hear phrases like these:

"Baby had poor color at birth. Respiration uneven."

"Apgar score at one minute—only 2."

"Prolonged labor. Difficult birth."

"Active resuscitation necessary to start independent breathing."

Check through the case histories of children who have learning problems in school, who can't read at grade level, and who have behavior difficulties. Often you'll find a record of difficult birth, of birth injury, or of delay in breathing.

The period of birth and the weeks just before and after represent the peak incidence of death in this country, according to Dr. Allan C. Barnes, who formerly was chairman of the Department of Gynecology and Obstetrics at the Johns Hopkins School of Medicine. During the eight-week span extending from four weeks before birth to four weeks after, 3.5 percent of babies die, and about the same percentage are discovered to have defects, he says.[7]

The hazards of being born are real, despite the exhilaration and sentiment that surround the entrance of new life into the world, and despite this country's comparatively low infant mortality rate. This is one major reason why you should pick your doctor and your hospital with great care. You don't need to know all of the complications that can endanger your baby at birth. But you do want a doctor who knows. And you must cooperate with him in every way to make the process of birth safe for your infant.

Asphyxia is the major cause of infant death, either during birth itself or shortly after, as a result of brain damage or lung malfunction. It can also result in permanent damage to the brain, which may not be noticeable for several days or even years after birth. Early findings in the Collaborative Perinatal Research Project show that 44 percent of babies whose development was abnormal at the age of eight months suffered from asphyxia at or immediately after birth.

The normal process of labor and birth, even without anesthetics, cuts down markedly on a baby's supply of oxygen. Anesthetics, given in too large a quantity or at the wrong time during labor, can slice this slim margin of safety too thin, resulting in brain damage or even in death.

Drugs, such as muscle relaxants and depressants given to a mother in labor, can be a problem for a baby after birth. These medications don't wear off as quickly in a newborn as they do in the mother. When the infant is suddenly forced to survive on his own, the lingering effects of these drugs may prove more than he can handle, particularly if he has other problems.

Decisions about drugs, of course, belong to your doctor. This is why you have a skilled and knowledgeable physician in charge. You owe it to your baby to cooperate with the medical decisions he makes for your baby's benefit— and yours.

Birth injuries cause about 10 percent of the infant

deaths that occur during labor and the first few days of life. But there has been a marked reduction in such deaths in recent years. Birth injury can also result in brain damage, sometimes so subtle that its effects are not discovered until the child is a year old or until he starts school. Regular prenatal care, coupled with the skill of a trained physician, can usually minimize the chances of birth injury.

13. *Make sure that your baby is checked for PKU shortly after his birth.*

Stan and June Baker couldn't understand what was wrong with their third baby, a cute, blue-eyed, little towhead named Charlie. Charlie seemed to be developing as normally as his older sisters. But he was slow to learn to crawl, even slower learning to walk. The older he got, the more his behavior changed—for the worse. He was a head-banger, a screamer, a hitter, impulsive, compulsive, and impossible to control.

At first, the Bakers' doctor was reassuring. June was just tired, he suggested. She wasn't used to an active boy after two "easy" girls. He could find nothing wrong, medically.

By the time he was two, Charlie was almost impossible to live with. The Bakers began to have serious doubts about his intelligence and about their ability to cope with him, no matter how much they loved him and no matter how much they tried.

When Charlie was two and one-half, the Bakers had a fourth baby, a blue-eyed, fair-haired daughter, Julie. Julie, too, seemed to develop normally at first. But then she began to show the same distressing behavior as Charlie. In desperation, the Bakers took Julie to a well-known children's hospital. There, alert doctors diagnosed her case as phenylketonuria, or PKU.

An inherited disorder, PKU afflicts about one baby in every ten thousand and is responsible for the plight of one to two percent of the mentally retarded in all United States institutions. Doctors call it "an inborn error of metabolism."

Because PKU is carried by a recessive gene, its victims must inherit one from each parent, neither of whom has any obvious symptoms of the disease. New research, however, shows that it is possible to detect such carriers by complicated chemical tests. About one person in seventy carries such a recessive gene; in marriages where both husband and wife have this recessive gene, chances are one in four in each pregnancy that the baby will have PKU.

A baby born with PKU appears normal at birth and for several months afterwards. But his body lacks a liver enzyme necessary for the proper utilization of phenylalanine, a substance in protein. As the infant begins to drink milk and later, as he eats meat, phenylalanine starts piling up in his body and injuring his vulnerable, developing brain.

"Probably 90 percent of these children are committed to institutions with a one-way ticket," comments Dr. Robert Guthrie, of the State University of New York at Buffalo Medical School. They are usually hyperactive, with speech difficulties and convulsive disorders. One-third of PKU victims never learn to walk. Two-thirds never learn to talk. Most of them are blond and blue-eyed. Their life expectancy is normal. It costs society an estimated $200,000 to care for a typical victim of PKU during his lifetime in a state institution.

If a PKU baby can be discovered during the first few weeks of life and placed on a diet low in phenylalanine for several years, he will grow up normally, most research now indicates. The problem has been to diagnose the disorder before the irreversible brain damage is evident. Undetected and untreated PKU can cause a loss of 2 I.Q. points a week in very young children, one researcher has estimated.

The first clue for detecting children with PKU was furnished by a Scandinavian mother who pestered doctors for years about why two of her three children were severely retarded. Their diapers, she pointed out, had a peculiar odor, which she described as something like "old tennis shoes."

From this beginning, researchers worked out a test for PKU which uses a baby's wet diaper, or a few drops of urine. But this "diaper test" is not effective until several weeks after birth, when brain damage is already beginning. Because PKU was thought to be more rare than it is now known to be, most doctors didn't bother to use the diaper test. Few parents were aware of its importance. And many PKU victims still went undetected until brain damage was irreversible.

At the children's hospital where the Bakers took Julie, doctors did make a diaper test and discovered that she had PKU. Although she was already a year old, she was immediately placed on the diet, which the state furnished free of charge to her parents. Alert physicians then checked the other children in the Baker family and found that Charlie, too, had PKU. Even though he was considered too old to benefit from the diet, his parents insisted that a trial be made.

Charles has improved somewhat on the diet, to the doctors' surprise. He is now seven and able to attend a class for the educable mentally handicapped—an achievement most untreated PKU victims cannot attain. His behavior is better, and he is easier to manage at home, without the extreme hyperactivity that disrupted the household before. Although it is too soon to tell, the Bakers hope that Julie will be able to keep up with normal children when she starts school.

The genetic cards seemed to be stacked against the Bakers, for they have had a third baby with PKU. But this time, doctors were alert to the problem at the time of the infant's birth. And this time, a test was available to detect PKU before the baby was ready to leave the hospital.

This means of diagnosing PKU is a blood test, developed by Dr. Guthrie, which requires only a prick on a baby's heel. It is simple, quick, and inexpensive. And it can be given after an infant has had milk feedings for a twenty-four-hour period—usually on the third or fourth day of life, while most babies are still under medical care in the hospital where they were born.

After a year-long, nationwide screening of newborn babies using th Guthrie test, the U.S. Children's Bureau began urging state legislatures to make the PKU testing compulsory, and most states have passed such laws. Many states now furnish the low-phenylalanine diets free to patients young enough to benefit from them.

A few doctors have argued that passing legislation is not the best way to solve the problem of PKU. They point out that the Guthrie test does pick up a substantial number of false-positive cases and that prolonged use of the low-phenylalanine diet could be harmful to a normal infant mistakenly diagnosed as having PKU. The American Academy of Pediatrics has taken the stand that no more legislation requiring compulsory testing for PKU is necessary, but recommends that all newborn infants be tested for the disease before they leave the hospital.

PKU is a complicated medical problem on which much research is still being done. A baby who is picked out by a screening test as probably having the disorder should have further diagnostic tests and be treated by specialists at a medical center. The change in diet which constitutes most of the treatment is a major one and must be carefully regulated.

PKU is not the only inborn error of metabolism that can cause severe mental retardation. More than forty others have been recognized, and there are probably more. The American Academy of Pediatrics now recommends that the urine of all newborn infants be tested for two of these—galactosemia and fructosemia. But these are technical procedures for your physician, and you needn't worry about them. Hospitals in the state of Massachusetts now screen all newborn babies for ten of these metabolic disorders.

Your best protection against such inborn errors of metabolism is to choose a doctor whom you know is up-to-date medically. Arrange with him before the birth of your child to examine and care for the baby in the hospital. And if you should know of any inherited metabolic disorders in your family, be sure that your doctor is informed.

Learning about the known hazards to an unborn infant can be uncomfortable and depressing, especially when they are all lumped together in a chapter like this. But it should be encouraging and hopeful, instead of frightening. When you understand some of the reasons why birth defects and mental retardation occur, then it's possible for you to take steps to prevent them from happening to your baby. With this knowledge, you can increase the odds—already tremendously in your favor—that the doctor will say of your newborn infant, "He's just perfect!"

12. The Joys of Having a Bright Child

If you surround your youngster with the sort of mentally stimulating, encouraging home environment described in this book, will he become a "bright" child? Will he be classed as "highly intelligent" or "mentally superior" on I.Q. tests when he goes to school, and will he be placed in top reading groups and in fast-track programs?

That's too sweeping a promise to make about a specific child at this point in the research about the development of intelligence in children and the effects of early learning. But it's a likelihood that many behavioral scientists and educators are studying seriously.

You can raise the intelligence level of almost every youngster a substantial degree by a stimulating, warm, early home environment. That much seems certain. Whether your child was born with a poor, average, or superior brain, an enriched environment will raise his eventual level of intellectual functioning, regardless of the genes he has inherited. If your youngster has been lucky enough to inherit an average or above-average brain to start with, chances are great that a warm, loving, mentally stimulating environment from infancy on will help him develop into a bright or gifted youngster.

("Bright" and "gifted" are terms often used interchangeably to describe the kind of boys and girls who have superior ability, and who consistently do better, develop sooner, or learn more and faster than children generally in any area of significance. Dr. Paul Witty, who spent most of his career at Northwestern University studying bright youngsters, defines giftedness as "consistently remarkable performance in any worthwhile line of endeavor." Sometimes schools identify bright and gifted children by I.Q. test alone. Most prefer to add teacher evaluation, grades, and other criteria.)

A stimulating home environment in early childhood has played a part in the lives of an impressive number of highly intelligent and highly gifted individuals of great achievement. And when researchers probe into the background of school-age children rated as gifted or mentally superior by I.Q. tests, they typically find a stimulating home life and often deliberate planning by parents to help their children learn to use their brain.

For example, in collecting information about twenty-five youngsters with superior I.Q.s, all of whom could read by the time they were three years old, Dr. Fowler discovered that 72 percent had "definitely enjoyed a great deal of unusually early and intensive" mental stimulation. Information wasn't available on the early childhood of the others.[1]

"The association between cognitive precocity and the application of intensive stimulation from infancy has always been impressively high," emphasizes Dr. Fowler.

Dr. Robert J. Havighurst, of the University of Chicago, puts it this way: "Boys and girls who are mentally superior have become so because of (1) a home and school environment which stimulated them to learn and to enjoy learning; (2) parents and other significant persons who set examples of interest and attainment in education which the children unconsciously imitated; and (3) early family training which produced a desire for achievement in the child. When these influences act upon a child with average or better biological equipment for learning, the child will become mentally superior." [2]

On the other hand, if a youngster who is born with superior biological endowment does not receive adequate early stimulation, he will not develop into a bright or gifted individual, researchers point out. It has been estimated that at least half of our potentially gifted children are wasted for lack of early opportunity to learn at a sufficiently fast and enriched rate.

But even if it's possible that you can help your youngster become mentally superior, is it desirable? Do you want a bright child in your family?

"I couldn't care less about a high I.Q.; I just hope my kids turn out to be nice, average, normal youngsters," you occasionally hear a parent say. Some fathers and mothers —and even a few teachers—still picture a highly intelligent child as being a pale, puny prig who wears glasses and is just as inferior socially, emotionally, and physically as he is superior mentally. But they're just as mistaken as those who used to argue that genius is only a thin line away from insanity.

Another widely held—and mistaken—idea about gifted children is that they are pouring energy and effort into their intellectual life to cover up a painful inadequacy in another area of their life. No evidence exists in dozens of excellent studies about the gifted. For much research has been done about what bright youngsters are really like— if not about precisely how and why they develop.

Researchers have learned that, as a group, bright youngsters are better adjusted emotionally than average children. They have fewer emotional problems and are better able to cope with the ones they do have. They are more emotionally stable and more emotionally mature than classmates of the same age.

Gifted boys and girls are usually well-liked and popular with other young people of all ability levels. They are elected to school offices more frequently and hold more leadership posts in extracurricular activities than their classmates. In the special tests that psychologists some-times use to measure popularity among children, most gifted youngsters rank high, and they are usually chosen by many others as friends.

Studies of the very few children who have I.Q.s above 180 suggest that it's more difficult for these genius-level youngsters to find common interests and make friends with classmates of the same age who have average abilities. But they do get along easily and happily, gen-erally, with high-ability classmates whose I.Q. may be 40 or 50 points lower.

Bright boys and girls aren't grinds who do nothing but study. They participate in extracurricular activities, in-cluding sports, as much or more than average-ability class-mates. They have more hobbies and wider interests. They make more collections—larger and more scientific—than other children. They belong to more clubs. They know more games at a younger age. They are better able to amuse themselves when friends aren't available.

Neither are gifted youngsters stodgy and dull. They have a more active sense of humor than other youngsters, re-search shows. They know, tell, and appreciate more jokes. And they are rated by researchers as happier and more enthusiastic about life in general than other youngsters.

In height, weight, coordination, and physical endurance, bright children as a group also tend to be above average. They have fewer illnesses and better-than-average health.

(These findings seem to point up the inherited aspects of high ability in children. But recent experiments with laboratory animals show clearly that early stimulation and learning experiences not only make the animals more intelligent than others born in the same litter, but also result in larger, stronger animals which are more re-sistant to diseases.)

Many educators have worried that gifted children, par-ticularly if grouped in special high-ability classes, would become conceited, feel superior, and develop into an intellectual elite. Not so, research points up. Bright young people tend to underestimate their abilities and accom-plishments, research makes clear. They boast less than other youngsters. They are more self-critical. And they usually rate the achievements and abilities of average classmates higher than they really are.

Bright children usually score high on measures of creativity and originality, although these are considered different factors in over-all intelligence from those measured by the I.Q. test alone. Groups of high-I.Q. children, as a whole, do better in music and art than average youngsters.

Research shows that bright youngsters cause fewer problems for their parents than average youngsters. They are more self-sufficient and self-directing than others of the same age. They are less likely to have undesirable personality traits. They are dependable and self-starting; they have superior ability to adjust to problems and stress. They are responsible, conscientious, truthful, and trustworthy. They cheat less in school and cause fewer discipline problems than other children.

Contrary to some fears that gifted young people would exploit others, especially if identified openly and grouped together in classes, they tend to be altruistic and have an active social conscience. Their sense of personal responsibility is keen, and they typically feel more disturbed about injustices than classmates. It's apt to be the bright boy or girl who tries to play competitive games according to the rules, who stands up for the underdog, who is aware of the feelings and emotions of others.

Because gifted children are better than most youngsters at applying what they know to new situations and in seeing relationships, they rate high in traits like common sense. They are also adept at finding good, but unusual ways in which to solve problems or to reach goals.

Most gifted youngsters like school—unless it pressures them too much to conform to limited levels of work. They learn quickly, without much repetition, make good grades, and often list difficult subjects as their favorites. They read widely—twice as many books as average students, according to one study.

Gifted young people are more likely than other youngsters to go to college, and they make better grades than classmates when they are in college. They're also more apt to take postgraduate work.

As adults, the gifted typically fulfill the promise of their early youth and become productive, happy, contributing, gifted men and women. There is no indication in any scientific research that the old adage of "early ripe, early rot" applies to bright youngsters.

Individuals who were identified as gifted in childhood and who have been followed well into middle age have done well in high-level occupations, with earnings and achievements well above not only the general population, but above the average college graduate as well. Most are highly satisfied with their occupations. They read widely, particularly biography, history, and current drama. They are active in community affairs and organizations; they enjoy sports and have the same superior physical status and health records as they did in childhood. They report their marriages, generally, to be stable and their own lives to be happy in a greater degree than do average individuals.

Research like this sometimes makes gifted children sound almost too good to be true. Of course, not every bright child has all of these characteristics. Some with superior abilities who aren't challenged enough in school turn into mischievous troublemakers or unhappy introverts. A few are exploited by parents who don't understand that their social and emotional needs are still those of children generally.

But on the whole, bright children are happy, productive, well-liked, and they have fewer problems than other youngsters. They are a joy to know and to rear. You will be glad if your offspring turns out to be gifted. You will undoubtedly feel that it has been worth the effort to give him a mentally stimulating first six years of life.

References

CHAPTER 1

1. Personal interview. More about Debbie can be found in Marilyn Segal, *Run Away, Little Girl*, New York, Random House, 1966.
2. George W. Beadle "What's in the Mind," convocation address, University of Chicago, June 12 and 13, 1964.
3. J. McV. Hunt, *Intelligence and Experience*, New York, The Ronald Press Company, 1961.
4. Dolores Durkin, "Children Who Learned to Read at Home," *Elementary School Journal*, Vol. 62 (October, 1961); and Dolores Durkin, "An Earlier Start in Reading?" *Elementary School Journal*, Vol. 63 (December, 1962); and Dolores Durkin, "Children Who Read Before Grade 1: A Second Study," *Elementary School Journal*, Vol. 64 (December, 1963); and Dolores Durkin, *Children Who Read Early*, New York, Teachers College Press, 1966.
5. Benjamin S. Bloom, Allison Davis, and Robert Hess,

Compensatory Education for Cultural Deprivation, New York, Holt, Rinehart and Winston, Inc., 1965.

6. Urie Bronfenbrenner, "Is Early Intervention Effective? Some Studies of Early Education in Familial and Extra-Familial Settings," in *Race and I.Q.,* Ashley Montagu, ed., New York, Oxford University Press, 1975.

7. William Fowler, "Longitudinal Study of Early Stimulation in the Emergence of Cognitive Processes," a paper delivered at the Conference of Preschool Education, sponsored by the Social Science Research Council, University of Chicago, February 7, 1966.

CHAPTER 2

1. Hunt, *op. cit.*

2. Marjorie P. Honzik, Jean W. MacFarlene, and Lucile Allen, "The Stability of Mental Test Performance Between Two and Eighteen Years," *The Journal of Experimental Psychology,* Vol. 17 (1948).

3. Sonya Oppenheimer and Jane W. Kessler, "Mental Testing of Children Under Three Years," *Pediatrics,* Vol. 31 (May, 1963).

4. Celia Burns Stendler, *Readings in Child Behavior and Development,* 2nd ed., New York, Harcourt, Brace & World, Inc., 1964.

5. Wayne Dennis, "Causes of Retardation Among Institutional Children: Iran," *The Journal of Genetic Psychology,* Vol. 96 (1960).

6. Wayne Dennis and Yvonne Sayegh, "The Effect of Supplementary Experience Upon the Behavioral Development of Infants in Institutions," *Child Development,* Vol. 36 (March, 1965).

7. Hunt, *op. cit.*

8. Mark R. Rosenzweig, David Krech, Edward L. Bennett, and Marian C. Diamond, "Heredity, Environment, Learning and the Brain," a paper presented at the American Association for the Advancement of Science meeting, Berkeley, Calif., December, 1965.

9. Hunt, *op. cit.*

10. Benjamin S. Bloom, *Stability and Change in Human Characteristics,* New York, John Wiley & Sons, Inc., 1964.

11. *Ibid.*

12. Wilder Penfield, "The Uncommitted Cortex," *The Atlantic Monthly,* Vol. 214 (July, 1964).

13. Eckhard H. Hess, "Imprinting," *Science,* Vol. 130 (July 17, 1959).

14. Beadle, *op. cit.*

15. Ronald Illingworth and James Lister, "The Critical Period of Development of Feeding Problems," *The Journal of Pediatrics,* Vol. 65 (December, 1964).

16. Maria Montessori, *The Montessori Method,* new ed., Cambridge, Mass., Robert Bentley, Inc., 1964.

17. Maria Montessori, *The Absorbent Mind,* new ed., New York, Holt, Rinehart and Winston, Inc., 1967; and Maria Montessori, *The Discovery of the Child,* new ed., New York, Ballantine Books, 1972; and Maria Montessori, *The Secret of Childhood,* new ed., New York, Ballantine Books, 1972.

18. George Stevens, "Reading for Young Children," in *Building the Foundations for Creative Learning,* Urban K. Fleege, ed., New York, American Montessori Society, 1964.

19. Wilder Penfield and Lamar Roberts, *Speech and Brain-Mechanisms,* Princeton, N.J., Princeton University Press, 1959.

20. Wilder Penfield, *The Second Career,* Boston, Little, Brown & Company, 1963.

21. Charles D. Smock and Bess Gene Holt, "Children's Reactions to Novelty: An Experimental Study of Curiosity Motivation," *Child Development,* Vol. 33 (September, 1962).

22. Robert W. White, "Motivation Reconsidered: The Concept of Competence," *The Psychological Review,* Vol. 66 (1959).

23. Jean Piaget, *The Origin of Intelligence in Children,* New York, International Universities Press, 1952.

24. White, *op. cit.*

25. Hunt, *op. cit.*

CHAPTER 3

1. Kenneth D. Wann, Miriam Selchen Dorn, and Elizabeth Ann Liddle, *Fostering Intellectual Development in Young Children,* New York, Teachers College Press, 1962.
2. Robert D. Hess, "Social Class Influences Upon Preschool Early Cognitive Development," address to the American Montessori Society Seminar, New York, June, 1965; and Robert D. Hess, and Virginia Shipman, "Early Blocks to Children's Learning," *Children,* Vol. 12 (September–October, 1965).
3. Wann, *op. cit.*
4. Victor Goertzel, and Mildred G. Goertzel, *Cradles of Eminence,* Boston, Little, Brown & Company, 1962.

CHAPTER 4

1. Leon Eisenberg, "Reading Retardation: Psychiatric and Sociologic Aspects," *Pediatrics,* Vol. 37 (February, 1966).
2. Paul Dunn, "Freedom of Movement and Sensory Stimulation as an Aid to Mental Development," presented at the American Montessori Society Seminar, June, 1965.
3. T. Berry Brazelton, Mary Louise Scholl, and John S. Robey, "Visual Responses in the Newborn," presented at the American Academy of Pediatrics annual meeting, October, 1964.
4. Robert L. Fantz, "The Origin of Form Perception," *Scientific American,* Vol. 204 (May, 1961).
5. "Tests Show Day-Old Infants Can Learn, Early Handling Can Influence Behavior," *Modern Medicine,* Vol. 34 (January 17, 1966).
6. Joseph Church, ed. *Three Babies: Biographies of Cognitive Development,* New York, Random House, Inc., 1966.
7. Anneliese F. Korner and Rose Grobstein, "Visual Alertness As Related to Soothing in Neonates: Implications for Maternal Stimulation and Early Deprivation," *Child Development,* Vol. 37 (December, 1966).
8. Fowler, *op. cit.*

9. Hunt, *op. cit.*
10. Newell C. Kephart, "Teaching the Child with Learning Disabilities," address presented to the West Suburban Association for the Other Child, Glen Ellyn, Ill., January 19, 1966.
11. J. McV. Hunt, "How Children Develop Intellectually," *Children,* Vol. 11 (May–June, 1964).

CHAPTER 5

1. Committee on Accident Prevention, "Responsibility Means Safety for Your Child," American Academy of Pediatrics, Inc. (1964).
2. Dorothy Aldis, *All Together,* New York, G. P. Putnam's Sons, New York, 1952.
3. Fisher, Aileen, *Up the Windy Hill,* New York, Abelard-Schuman Limited, 1953.

CHAPTER 6

1. Educational Policies Commission, *op. cit.*
2. Delacato, *op. cit.*
3. Jack E. Forbes, "Mathematical Skills Development for Pre-school Children," Chicago, Systems for Education, Inc., 1965.
4. Jerome Study Group, "Montessori in the Home," Bethesda, Md., Elad Enterprises, 1963.
5. Jerome S. Bruner, *The Process of Education,* New York, Vintage Books, 1960.
6. Wann, *op. cit.*

CHAPTER 7

1. Mabel Morphett and Carleton Washburne, "When Should Children Begin to Read?" *Elementary School Journal,* Vol. 31 (March, 1931).
2. Arthur I. Gates, "Unsolved Problems in Reading: A Symposium," *Elementary English,* Vol. 31 (October, 1954).
3. Montessori, *op. cit.*

4. Durkin, *op. cit.,* 1966.

5. Louise Gurren and Ann Hughes, "Intensive Phonics vs. Gradual Phonics in Beginning Reading: A Review," *The Journal of Educational Research,* Vol. 58 (April, 1965).

6. *Chicago Tribune,* "Short Cuts to Reading You Can Teach Your Child," adapted by Joan Beck, and Becky, from "Listen and Learn with Phonics," by Dorothy Taft Watson, *Chicago Tribune,* August–November, 1964.

7. Gates, *op. cit.*

8. Arthur W. Staats and Carolyn K. Staats, *Complex Human Behavior,* New York, Holt, Rinehart and Winston, Inc., 1964.

9. Joseph E. Brzeinski and John L. Hayman, Jr., Denver Public Schools, "The Effectiveness of Parents in Helping Their Preschool Children to Begin to Read," Denver, Denver Public Schools, September, 1962.

10. Dolores Durkin, "Children Who Read Before First Grade," *Teaching Young Children to Read,* proceedings of a conference, November 14–16, Washington, D.C., U.S. Department of Health, Education and Welfare, Office of Education, Bulletin No. 9, 1964; and Durkin, *op. cit.,* 1966.

11. Dolores Durkin, "A Fifth Year Report on the Achievement of Early Readers," *Elementary School Journal,* Vol. 65 (November, 1964).

12. Paul McKee and Joseph E. Brzeinski, "The Effectiveness of Teaching Reading in Kindergarten," Denver, Denver Public Schools, 1966.

13. Jules H. Shaw, "Vision and Seeing Skills of Preschool Children," *The Reading Teacher,* Vol. 18 (October, 1964).

14. William Fowler, "A Study of Process and Method in Three-Year-Old Twins and Triplets Learning to Read," *Genetic Psychology Monographs,* Vol. 72 (1965); and William Fowler, "Longitudinal Study of Early Stimulation in the Emergence of Cognitive Processes," paper delivered at the Conference on Preschool Education, sponsored by the Social Science Research Council, University of Chicago, February 7, 1966.

CHAPTER 8

1. E. Paul Torrance, "Education and Creativity," in *Creativity: Progress and Potential*, Calvin W. Taylor, ed., New York, McGraw-Hill Book Company, Inc., 1964.
2. E. Paul Torrance, *Guiding Creative Talent*, Englewood Cliffs, N.J., Prentice-Hall, Inc., 1962.
3. Torrance, *op. cit.*, 1964.

CHAPTER 9

1. Montessori, *op. cit.*

CHAPTER 10

1. Richard L. Masland, "Mental Retardation," in *Birth Defects*, Morris Fishbein, ed., Philadelphia, J. B. Lippincott Company, 1963.
2. American Medical Association, "Mental Retardation: A Handbook for the Primary Physician," the report of the American Medical Association Conference on Mental Retardation, April 9–11, 1964, in *The Journal of the American Medical Association*, Vol. 191 (January 18, 1965).
3. Sam D. Clements, *Minimal Brain Dysfunction in Children*, National Institute of Neurological Diseases and Blindness Monograph No. 3. U.S. Department of Health, Educaiton and Welfare, 1966.
4. "Mental Retardation," an editorial in *The Journal of the American Medical Association*, Vol. 191 (January 18, 1965).

CHAPTER 11

1. American Medical Association, *op. cit.*
2. Virginia Apgar and Joan Beck, "Is My Baby All Right?," New York, Trident Press, 1972.
3. John F. Modlin, A. David Brandling-Bennett, John J. Witte, Carlos C. Campbell, and Joel D. Meyers, "A

Review of Five Years' Experience with Rubella Vaccine in the United States," *Pediatrics,* Vol. 55 (January, 1975).

4. Gerald Weiner, "Perinatal, Neurologic and Psychologic Correlates (At 9–10 Years) of Low Birth Weight," paper presented at the annual meeting of the American Academy of Pediatrics, October 24, 1965.

5. American Medical Association, *op. cit.*

6. Louis K. Diamond, "Erythroblastosis," in *Birth Defects,* Morris Fishbein, ed., Philadelphia, J. B. Lippincott Company, 1963.

7. Allan C. Barnes, "Prevention of Congenital Anomalies from the Point of View of the Obstetrician," *Papers and Discussions of the Second International Conference on Congenital Malformations,* July 14–19, 1963, published by the International Medical Congress, Ltd.

CHAPTER 12

1. William Fowler, "Cognitive Learning in Infancy and Early Childhood," *The Psychological Bulletin,* Vol. 59 (March, 1962).

2. Robert J. Havighurst, "Conditions Productive of Superior Children," *Teachers College Record,* Vol. 62 (April, 1961).

Bibliography

ABRUZZI, WILLIAM, "Measles—A Serious Pediatric Disease," *The Journal of Pediatrics,* Vol. 64 (May, 1964).

ALMAY, MILLIE, *The Early Childhood Educator at Work,* New York, McGraw-Hill Book Company, Inc., 1975.

ALMAY, MILLIE, CHITTENDEN, EDWARD, and MILLER, PAULA, *Young Children's Thinking,* New York, Teachers College Press, 1966.

ANASTASI, ANNE, "Heredity, Environment and the Question How?", *The Psychological Review,* Vol. 65 (1958).

APGAR, VIRGINIA, and BECK, JOAN, *Is My Baby All Right?,* New York, Trident Press, 1972.

BAIRD, SIR DUGALD, "The Epidemiology of Prematurity," *The Journal of Pediatrics,* Vol. 65 (December, 1964).

BARTON, K., DIELMAN, T. E., and CATTRELL, R. B., "Child Rearing Practices and Achievement in School," *The Journal of Genetic Psychology,* Vol. 124 (March, 1974).

BEADLE, MURIEL, *A Child's Mind,* Garden City, N.Y., Doubleday & Company, Inc., 1970.

BECKWITH, LEILA, "Relationships between Attributes of

Mothers and Their Infants' I.Q. Scores," *Child Development*, Vol. 42 (October, 1971).

————, "Relationships between Infants' Social Behavior and Their Mothers' Behavior," *Child Development*, Vol. 43 (June, 1972).

BEREITER, CARL, and ENGELMAN, SIEGFRIED, *Teaching Disadvantaged Children in the Preschool*, Englewood Cliffs, N.J., Prentice-Hall, Inc., 1966.

BERMAN, ELEANOR, "The Biochemistry of Lead: Review of the Body Distribution and Methods of Lead Determination," *Clinical Pediatrics*, Vol. 5 (May, 1966).

BERMAN, PHYLLIS W., WAISMAN, HARRY A. and GRAHAM, FRANCES K., "Intelligence in Treated Phenylketonuric Children: A Developmental Study," *Child Development*, Vol. 37 (December, 1966).

BERRY, HELEN K., and WRIGHT, STANLEY, "Conference on Treatment of Phenylketonuria," *The Journal of Pediatrics*, Vol. 70 (January, 1967).

BING, ELIZABETH, "Effect of Childrearing Practices on Development of Differential Cognitive Abilities. *Child Development*, Vol. 34 (September, 1963).

BLOOM, BENJAMIN S., *Stability and Change in Human Characteristics*, New York, John Wiley & Sons, Inc., 1964.

————, Davis, Allison, and Hess, Robert, *Compensatory Education for Cultural Deprivation*, New York, Holt, Rinehart and Winston, Inc., 1965.

BOSTON CHILDREN'S MEDICAL CENTER, *Pregnancy, Birth and the Newborn Baby*, New York, Delacorte Press/Seymour Lawrence, 1972.

BOWMAN, JOHN M., and POLLOCK, JANET M., "Amniotic Fluid Spectrophotometry and Early Delivery in the Management of Erythroblastosis Fetalis," *Pediatrics*, Vol. 35 (May, 1965).

BRITTAIN, CLAY B., "Preschool Programs for Culturally-Deprived Children," *Children*, Vol. 13 (July–August, 1966).

BRONFENBRENNER, URIE, *Is Early Intervention Effective?* Washington, D.C., Department of Health, Education and Welfare, Office of Child Development, 1974.

BRONSON, GORDON, "The Postnatal Growth of Visual Capacity," *Child Development,* Vol. 45 (December, 1974).

BRONSON, WANDA C., "Mother-Toddler Interaction: A Perspective on Studying the Development of Competence," *Merrill-Palmer Quarterly,* Vol. 20 (October, 1974).

BROPHY, JERE EDWARD, "Mothers As Teachers of Their Own Preschool Children: The Influence of Socioeconomic Status and Task Srtucture on Teaching Specificity," *Child Development,* Vol. 41 (March, 1970).

BROWN, GORDON C., and EVANS, TOMMY N., "Serologic Evidence of Coxsackievirus Etiology of Congenital Heart Disease," *The Journal of the American Medical Association,* Vol. 199 (January 16, 1967).

BRUNER, JEROME S., *On Knowing, Essays for the Left Hand,* Cambridge, Mass., Harvard University Press, 1963.

———, "Organization of Early Skilled Action," *Child Development,* Vol. 44 (March, 1973).

———, *The Process of Education,* New York, Vintage Books, 1960.

———, *Toward a Theory of Instruction,* Cambridge, Mass., Harvard University Press, 1966.

———, Olver, Rose R., and Greenfield, Patricia M., *Studies in Cognitive Growth,* New York, John Wiley & Sons, Inc., 1966.

BRZEINSKI, JOSEPH E., and HAYMAN, JOHN L., JR., "The Effectiveness of Parents in Helping Their Preschool Children to Begin to Read," Denver, Denver Public Schools, September, 1962.

BURTON, GRACE MAE, "A Parent's Guide to Teaching Preschoolers New Math," *Children's House,* Vol. 4 (Summer, 1970).

CALDWELL, B. M., "Decade of Early Intervention Programs: What Have We Learned?" *American Journal of Orthopsychiatry,* Vol. 44 (July, 1974).

CARLSON, PATRICIA, and ANISFELD, MOSHE, "Some Observations on the Linguistic Competence of a Two-Year-Old Child," *Child Development,* Vol. 40 (June, 1969).

CARPENTER, GENEVIEVE, C., "Visual Regard of Moving and Stationary Faces in Early Infancy," *Merrill-Palmer Quarterly,* Vol. 20 (July, 1974).

CARTER, CHARLES H., ed. *Medical Aspects of Mental Retardation,* Springfield, Ill., Charles C. Thomas, 1965.

CHALL, JEANNE, *Learning to Read: The Great Debate,* New York, McGraw-Hill Book Company, Inc., 1967.

CHUKOVSKY, KORNEI, *From Two to Five,* trans. by Miriam Morton, Berkeley, Calif., University of California Press, 1963.

CHURCH, JOSEPH, ed., *Three Babies: Biographies of Cognitive Development,* New York, Random House, Inc., 1966.

CLEMENTS, SAM D., *Minimal Brain Dysfunction in Children,* National Institute of Neurological Diseases and Blindness Monograph No. 3, Washington, D.C., U.S. Department of Health, Education and Welfare, 1966.

DAEHLER, MARVIN W., and BUKATKO, DANUTA, "Discrimination Learning in Two-Year-Olds," *Child Development,* Vol. 45 (June, 1974).

DOUGLAS, J. W. B., "Ability and Adjustment of Children Who Have Had Measles," *The British Medical Journal,* Vol. 2 (November 21, 1964).

DUBKIN, LEONARD, *The Natural History of a Yard,* Chicago, Henry Regnery Co., 1955.

DURKIN, DOLORES, *Children Who Read Early,* New York, Teachers College Press, 1966.

———, "A Six-Year Study of Children Who Learned to Read in School at the Age of Four," *Reading Research Quarterly,* International Reading Association, Vol. 10 (1974–75).

ELARDO, RICHARD, BRADLEY, ROBERT, and CALDWELL, BETTYE M., "The Relation of Infants' Home Environments to Mental Test Performance from Six to Thirty-Six Months: A Longitudinal Analysis," *Child Development,* Vol. 46 (March, 1975).

ELKIND, DAVID, "Misunderstandings about How Children Learn," *Today's Education,* Vol. 61 (March, 1972).

ENGELMANN, SIEGFRIED and ENGELMANN, THERESE, *Give Your Child a Superior Mind,* New York, Simon and Schuster, Inc., 1966.

ESCALONA, SIBYLLE K., "Basic Modes of Social Interaction: Their Emergence and Patterning during the First Two

Years of Life," *Merrill-Palmer Quarterly*, Vol. 19 (July, 1973).

EVANS, THOMAS W., *The School in the Home*, New York, Harper & Row, 1973.

EVELOFF, HERBERT H., "Some Cognitive and Affective Aspects of Early Language Development," *Child Development*, Vol. 42 (December, 1971).

FANTZ, ROBERT L. and FAGAN, JOSEPH F., III, "Visual Attention to Size and Number of Pattern Details by Term and Preterm Infants during the First Six Months," *Child Development*, Vol. 46 (March, 1975).

FANTZ, ROBERT L., and MIRANDA, SIMON B., "Newborn Infant Attention to Form of Contour," *Child Development*, Vol. 46 (March, 1975).

FISH, STUART A., "Viral Diseases Complicating Pregnancy: Practical Management," *The Southern Medical Journal*, Vol. 58 (September, 1965).

FISHBEIN, MORRIS, ed., *Birth Defects*, Philadelphia, J. B. Lippincott Company, 1963.

FISHER, DOROTHY CANFIELD, *Montessori for Parents*, new ed., Cambridge, Mass., Robert Bentley, Inc., 1965.

———, *The Montessori Manual for Teachers and Parents*, new ed., Cambridge, Mass., Robert Bentley, Inc., 1964.

FLAVELL, JOHN H., *The Developmental Psychology of Jean Piaget*, Princeton, N.J., D. Van Nostrand Company, Inc., 1963.

FLEEGE, URBAN K., ed., *Building the Foundation for Creative Learning*, New York, American Montessori Society, 1964.

FLEEGE, VIRGINIA, MITCHENER, VIRGINIA, and ORTMAN, SR. M. EDNA, *Montessori Index*, Chicago, Midwest Montessori Teacher Training Center, 1965.

FOWLER, WILLIAM, "Cognitive Learning in Infancy and Early Childhood," *Psychological Bulletin*, Vol. 59 (March, 1962).

———, "Concept Learning in Early Childhood," paper presented at the annual meeting of the American Educational Research Association, February 12, 1965.

———, "Longitudinal Study of Early Stimulation in the Emergence of Cognitive Processes," paper delivered at the Conference on Preschool Education, sponsored by the Social Science Research Council, University of Chicago, February 7, 1966.

———, "Structural Dimensions of the Learning Process in Early Reading," *Child Development,* Vol. 35 (December, 1964).

———, "A Study of Process and Method in Three-Year-Old Twins and Triplets Learning to Read," *Genetic Psychology Monographs,* Vol. 72 (1965).

———, "Teaching a Two-Year-Old to Read: An Experiment in Early Childhood Learning," *Genetic Psychology Monographs,* Vol. 66 (1962).

FREDA, VINCENT J., "The Rh Problem in Obstetrics and a New Concept of Its Management Using Amniocentesis and Spectrophotometric Scanning of Amniotic Fluid," *The American Journal of Obstetrics and Gynecology,* Vol. 92 (June, 1965).

FREDA, VINCENT J., and others, "Prevention Rh Isoimmunization," *The Journal of the American Medical Association,* Vol. 199 (February 6, 1967).

FREEHILL, MAURICE F., *Gifted Children: Their Psychology and Education,* New York, The Macmillan Company, 1961.

FRENCH, JOSEPH L., ed., *Educating the Gifted,* rev. ed., New York, Holt, Rinehart and Winston, Inc., 1964.

FRIEDRICH, LYNETTE K., and STEIN, ALETHA H., "Prosocial Television and Young Children: The Effects of Verbal Labeling and Role Playing on Learning and Behavior," *Child Development,* Vol. 46 (March, 1975).

GARDNER, RILEY W., "A Psychologist Looks at Montessori," *Elementary School Journal,* Vol. 67 (November, 1966).

GETZELS, JACOB W., and JACKSON, PHILIP W., *Creativity and Intelligence,* New York, John Wiley & Sons, Inc., 1962.

GIBBS, FREDERIC A., and others, "Electroencephalographic Abnormality in 'Uncomplicated' Childhood Diseases," *The Journal of the American Medical Association,* Vol. 171 (October 24, 1959).

———, "Common Types of Childhood Encephalitis," *Archives of Neurology,* Vol. 10 (January, 1964).

GLASER, KURT, and CLEMMENS, RAYMOND L., "School Failure," *Pediatrics,* Vol. 35 (January, 1965).

GOLDBERG, MIRIAM L., *Research on the Talented,* New York, Teachers College Press, 1965.

GORDON, IRA J., ed., *Human Development: Readings in Research,* Chicago, Scott, Foresman and Company, 1965.

GOWAN, JOHN CURTIS, and DEMOS, GEORGE D., *The Education and Guidance of the Ablest,* Springfield, Ill., Charles C. Thomas, 1964.

GRAY, SUSAN W., and KLAUS, RUPERT A., "The Early Training Project: A Seventh-Year Report," *Child Development,* Vol. 41 (December, 1970).

GREENBERG, DAVID J., and O'DONNELL, WILLIAM J., "Infancy and the Optimal Level of Stimulation," *Child Development,* Vol. 43 (June, 1972).

GREENSTEIN, BETTY LESSER, GARMAN, MAC K., and SANFORD, JOAN STEVENSON, "Summer Mobile Preschool: A Home-Centered Approach," *Young Children,* Vol. 29 (March, 1974).

GURREN, LOUISE, and HUGHES, ANN, "Intensive Phonics vs. Gradual Phonics in Beginning Reading: A Review," *The Journal of Educational Research,* Vol. 58 (April, 1965).

HAIMOWITZ, MORRIS L., and HAIMOWITZ, NATALIE READER, *Human Development: Selected Readings,* 3rd edition, New York, Thomas Y. Crowell, 1973.

HECHINGER, FRED M., ed., *Pre-School Education Today,* New York, Doubleday & Company, Inc., 1966.

HESS, ROBERT D., and BEAR, ROBERTA MEYER, *Early Education: Current Theory, Research and Action,* Chicago, Aldine Publishing Company, 1968.

HOFFMAN, MARTIN, and HOFFMAN, LOIS WLADIS, *Review of Child Development Research,* Vol. 1, New York, Russell Sage Foundation, 1964.

HOLZMAN, MATHILDA, "The Verbal Environment Provided by Mothers for Their Very Young Children," *Merrill-Palmer Quarterly,* Vol. 20 (January, 1974).

HOWREN, HARRY H., JR., "A Review of the Literature Concerning Smoking During Pregnancy," *The Virginia Medical Monthly,* Vol. 92 (June, 1965).

HSIA, DAVID YI-YUNG, "Phenylketonuria: A Study of Human

Biochemical Genetics," *Pediatrics,* Vol. 38 (August, 1966).

HUDSON, WALTER W., *Project Breakthrough: A Responsive Environment Field Experiment with Pre-School Children from Public Assistance Families,* Chicago, Cook County Department of Public Aid, 1969.

HUNT, J. MCV., "How Children Develop Intellectually," *Children,* Vol. 11 (May–June, 1964).

———, *Intelligence and Experience,* New York, The Ronald Press Company, 1961.

———, Introduction to *The Montessori Method,* new ed., New York, Schocken Books, Inc., 1964.

JACOBZINER, HAROLD, "Lead Poisoning in Childhood: Epidemiology, Manifestations and Prevention," *Clinical Pediatrics,* Vol. 5 (May, 1966).

JORDAN, THOMAS E., ed., *Perspectives in Mental Retardation,* Carbondale, Ill., Southern Illinois University Press, 1966.

KAGAN, JEROME, "Do Infants Think?" *Scientific American,* Vol. 226 (March, 1972).

———, "On the Meaning of Behavior: Illustrations from the Infant," *Child Development,* Vol. 40 (December, 1969).

KAPLAN, LOUIS, *Foundations of Human Behavior,* New York, Harper & Row, 1965.

KILMER, SALLY, and WEINBERG, RICHARD, "The Nature of Young Children and the State of Early Education," *Young Children,* Vol. 30 (November, 1974).

KORNER, ANNELIESE F., and GROBSTEIN, ROSE, "Visual Alertness As Related to Soothing in Neonates: Implications for Maternal Stimulation and Early Deprivation," *Child Development,* Vol. 37 (December, 1966).

LAVATELLI, CELIA STENDLER, and STENDLER, FAITH, *Readings in Child Behavior and Development,* 3rd edition, New York, Harcourt, Brace, Jovanovich, 1972.

LENZ, W., "Malformations Caused by Drugs in Pregnancy," *American Journal of Diseases of Children,* Vol. 112 (August, 1966).

LEVINE, SEYMOUR, "Stimulation in Infancy," *Scientific American,* Vol. 202 (May, 1960).

LEWIS, M., and MCGURK, H., "Evaluation of Infant Intelligence," *Science,* Vol. 182 (November 16, 1973).

LICHTENBERG, PHILIP, and NORTON, DOLORES G., *Cognitive and Mental Development in the First Five Years of Life,* Chevy Chase, Maryland, National Institutes of Mental Health, 1970.

LILEY, A. W., "The Use of Amniocentesis and Fetal Transfusion in Erythroblastosis Fetalis," *Pediatrics,* Vol. 35 (May, 1965).

LITTLE, WILLIAM A., "Drugs in Pregnancy," *The American Journal of Nursing,* Vol. 66 (June, 1966).

MCCRORY, WALLACE W., "Psychometabolism," *The Journal of Pediatrics,* Vol. 67 (November, 1965).

MCKAY, R. JAMES, JR., and LUCEY, JEROLD F., "Neonatalogy," *The New England Journal of Medicine,* Vol. 270 (June 4 and 11, 1964).

MCKEE, PAUL, and BRZEINSKI, JOSEPH E., "The Effectiveness of Teaching Reading in Kindergarten," Denver, Denver Public Schools, 1966.

MENDEL, GISELA, "Children's Preferences for Differing Degrees of Novelty," *Child Development,* Vol. 36 (June, 1965).

"Mental Retardation," *The Journal of the American Medical Association,* Vol. 191 (January 18, 1965).

MILLER, JAMES R., and DILL, FRED J., "The Cytogenetics of Mongolism," *International Psychiatry Clinics,* Vol. 2 (January, 1965).

MONTAGU, ASHLEY, ed., *Race and I.Q.,* New York, Oxford University Press, 1975.

MONTESSORI, MARIA, *The Absorbent Mind,* new ed., New York, Holt, Rinehart and Winston, Inc., 1967.

———, *The Discovery of the Child,* new ed., New York, Ballantine Books, 1972.

———, *Dr. Montessori's Own Handbook,* new ed., Cambridge, Mass., Robert Bentley, Inc., 1964.

———, *The Montessori Elementary Material,* new ed., Cambridge, Mass., Robert Bentley, Inc., 1964.

———, *The Secret of Childhood,* new ed., New York, Ballantine Books, 1972.

————, *Spontaneous Activity in Education*, new ed., Cambridge, Mass., Robert Bentley, Inc. 1964.

————, *What You Should Know About Your Child*, Madras, India, Kalakshetra, Printed in India by the Vasanta Press, Adyar, Madras, 20, 1948.

————, *A Montessori Handbook*, R. C. Orem, ed., New York, G. P. Putnam's Sons, 1965.

MOORE, OMAR KHAYYAM, "Autotelic Responsive Environments and Exceptional Children," Responsive Environments Foundation, Inc., Hamden, Conn., 1963.

OPPENHEIMER, SONYA, and KESSLER, JANE W., "Mental Testing of Children Under Three Years," *Pediatrics*, Vol. 31 (May, 1963).

OREM, R. C., *Montessori for the Disadvantaged*, New York, G. P. Putnam's Sons, 1967.

PASSOW, A. HARRY, ed., *Education in Depressed Areas*, New York, Teachers College Press, 1963.

PASSOW, A. HARRY, and LEEPER, ROBERT R., eds., *Intellectual Development: Another Look*, Washington, D.C., Association for Supervision and Curriculum Development, 1964.

PARNES, SIDNEY J., and HARDING, HAROLD F., *A Source Book for Creative Thinking*, New York, Charles Scribner's Sons, 1962.

PENFIELD, WILDER, *The Second Career*, Boston, Little, Brown & Company, 1963.

————, and Roberts, Lamar, *Speech and Brain-Mechanisms*, Princeton, N.J., Princeton University Press, 1959.

PERLSTEIN, MEYER A., and ATTALA, RAMZY, "Neurologic Sequelae of Plumbism in Children," *Clinical Pediatrics*, Vol. 5 (May, 1966).

PETERSON, C. DAVID, and LUZZATTI, LUIGI, "The Role of Chromosome Translocations in the Recurrence Risk of Down's Syndrome," *Pediatrics*, Vol. 35 (March, 1965).

PHILIPS, JOHN L., JR., *The Origins of Intellect: Piaget's Theory*, San Francisco, W. H. Freeman, 1969.

PIAGET, JEAN, *The Language and Thought of the Child*, Cleveland, World Book Company, 1955.

————, *Psychology of Intelligence*, new ed., Paterson, N.J., Littlefield, Adams & Company, 1963.

PLOTKIN, STANLEY A., "Congenital Rubella Syndrome in Late Infancy," *The Journal of the American Medical Association,* Vol. 200 (May 8, 1967).

PLOTZ, E. JURGEN, "Virus Disease in Pregnancy," *The New York State Journal of Medicine,* Vol. 65 (May 15, 1965).

RABINOWITZ, F. MICHAEL, MOELY, BARBARA E., FINKEL, NANCY, and MCCLINTON, SANDRA, "The Effects of Toy Novelty and Social Interaction on the Exploratory Behavior of Preschool Children," *Child Development,* Vol. 46 (March, 1975).

RAMBUSCH, NANCY MCCORMICK, *Learning How to Learn,* Baltimore, Helicon Press, Inc., 1962.

RAVENTOS, ANTOLIN, "X-Rays in Pregnancy," *The American Journal of Nursing,* Vol. 66 (June, 1966).

READ, CHARLES, "Pre-School Children's Knowledge of English Phonology," *Harvard Educational Review,* Vol. 41 (February, 1971).

RICHARDSON, FREDERICK, ed., *Brain and Intelligence: The Ecology of Child Development,* Hyattsville, Maryland, National Educational Press, 1973.

RICHARDSON, SYLVIA, O., "A Pediatrician Looks at Montessori," paper presented at the annual convention of the National Society for Crippled Children and Adults, November, 1965.

RICHMOND, JULIUS B., "A Report on Project Head Start," *Pediatrics,* Vol. 37 (June, 1966).

RIESSMAN, FRANK, *The Culturally Deprived Child,* New York, Harper & Row, 1962.

RILEY, H. D., "The Rubella Syndrome," *Clinical Pediatrics,* Vol. 5 (November, 1966).

RIPPLE, RICHARD E., *Readings in Learning and Human Abilities: Educational Psychology,* New York, Harper & Row, 1964.

ROBISON, HELEN F., and SPODEK, BERNARD, *New Directions in the Kindergarten,* New York, Teachers College Press, 1965.

ROEPER, ANNEMARIE, "Gifted Preschoolers and the Montessori Method," *The Gifted Child Quarterly,* Vol. 10 (Summer, 1966).

ROSENBLITH, JUDY F., and ALLINSMITH, WESLEY, *The Causes of Behavior: Readings in Child Development and Educational Psychology*, Boston, Allyn & Bacon, 1964.

ROSSIE, JOSEPH P., "High Risk Babies: Determining the Problem," *Connecticut Health Bulletin*, Vol. 78 (November, 1964).

SCARR-SALAPATEK, SANDRA, and WILLIAMS, MARGARET L., "The Effects of Early Stimulation on Low-Birth-Weight Infants," *Child Development*, Vol. 44 March, 1973).

SCHREIBER, DANIEL, ed., *Guidance and the School Dropout*, Washington, D.C., National Education Association and American Personnel and Guidance Association, 1964.

SELTZER, ROBERT J., "The Disadvantaged Child and Cognitive Development in the Early Years," *Merrill-Palmer Quarterly*, Vol. 19 (October, 1973).

STAATS, ARTHUR W., and STAATS, CAROLYN K., *Complex Human Behavior*, New York, Holt, Rinehart and Winston, Inc., 1964.

STERN, CAROLYN, "Language Competencies of Young Children," *Young Children*, Vol. 22 (October, 1966).

SUTHERLAND, BETTY S., UMBARGER, BARBARA, and BERRY, HELEN K., "The Treatment of Phenylketonuria," *American Journal of Diseases of Children*, Vol. 111 (May, 1966).

TAYLOR, CALVIN W., ed., *Creativity: Progress and Potential*, New York, McGraw-Hill Book Company, Inc., 1964.

TORRANCE, E. PAUL, *Guiding Creative Talent*, Englewood Cliffs, N.J., Prentice-Hall, Inc., 1962.

———, *Rewarding Creative Behavior*, Englewood Cliffs, N.J., Prentice-Hall, Inc., 1965.

———, "Stress-Seeking as a Factor in High Achievement," *The Gifted Child Quarterly*, Vol. 10 (Winter, 1966).

TULKIN, STEVEN R., and COHLER, BERTRAM J., "Childrearing Attitudes and Mother-Child Interaction in the First Year of Life," *Merrill-Palmer Quarterly*, Vol. 19 (April, 1973).

TULKIN, STEVEN R., and KAGAN, JEROME, "Mother-Child Interaction in the First Year of Life," *Child Development*, Vol. 43 (March, 1972).

UZGIRIS, INA C., "Patterns of Cognitive Development in Infancy," *Merrill-Palmer Quarterly,* Vol. 19 (July, 1973).

VORE, DAVID A., "Prenatal Nutrition and Postnatal Intellectual Development," *Merrill-Palmer Quarterly,* Vol. 19 (October, 1973).

VYGOTSKY, L. S., Thought and Language, ed. and trans. by Eugenia Hanfman and Gertrude Vakar, Cambridge, Mass., The M.I.T. Press, 1962.

WACHS, THEODORE D., UZGIRIS, INA C., and HUNT, J. MCV., "Cognitive Development in Infants of Different Age Levels and from Different Environmental Backgrounds: An Explanatory Investigation," *Merrill-Palmer Quarterly,* Vol. 17 (October, 1971).

WALLACH, MICHAEL A., and KOGAN, NATHAN, *Modes of Thinking in Young Children,* New York, Holt, Rinehart and Winston, Inc., 1965.

WANN, KENNETH D., DORN, MIRIAM SELCHEN, and LIDDLE, ELIZABETH ANN, *Fostering Intellectual Development in Young Children,* New York, Teachers College Press, 1962.

WEISER, MARGARET G., "Parental Responsibility in the Teaching of Reading," *Young Children,* Vol. 29 (May, 1974).

WELLER, THOMAS H., ALFRED, CHARLES A., JR., and NEVA, FRANKLIN, "Changing Epidemiologic Concepts of Rubella, with Particular References to Unique Characteristics of the Congenital Infection," *The Yale Journal of Biology and Medicine,* Vol. 37 (June, 1965).

WHIMBEY, ARTHUR, with WHIMBEY, LINDA SHAW, *Intelligence Can Be Taught,* New York, E. P. Dutton & Co., 1975.

WHITE, B. L., *Human Infants: Experience and Psychological Development,* Englewood Cliffs, N. J., Prentice-Hall, Inc., 1971.

WHITE, BURTON L., and CASTLE, PETER, "Visual Exploratory Behavior Following Postnatal Handling of Human Infants," *Perceptual and Motor Skills,* Vol. 18 (1964).

WOLFF, PETER H., and WHITE, BURTON L., "Visual Pursuit and Attention in Young Infants," *The Journal of the*

American Academy of Child Psychiatry, Vol. 4 (July, 1965).

WOOLF, CHARLES M., "Stillbirths and Parental Age," *Obstetrics and Gynecology,* Vol. 26 (July, 1965).

Problem," *Consecticut Health Bulletin,* Vol. 78 (Novem-